IMMANUEL
KANT

SUNY Series in Ethical Theory
Robert B. Louden, editor

IMMANUEL KANT

by

Otfried Höffe

Translated by Marshall Farrier

C. H. Beck'sche Verlagsbuchhandlung (Oscar Beck), 1992

State University of New York Press

Originally published in German by
© C.H. Beck'sche Verlagsbuchhandlung (Oscar Beck), 1992

Published by
State University of New York Press, Albany

© 1994 State University of New York

For information, address State University of New York
Press, State University Plaza, Albany, N.Y., 12246

Production by Marilyn P. Semerad
Marketing by Nancy Farrell

Library of Congress Cataloging-in-Publication Data

Höffe, Otfried.
    [Immanuel Kant. English]
    Immanuel Kant / Otfried Höffe : translated by Marshall Farrier.
      p. cm—(SUNY series in ethical theory)
    Includes bibliographical references (p. xxx-xxx) and indexes.
    ISBN 0-7914-2093-0 (alk. paper).—ISBN 0-7914-2094-9 (alk. paper
    : pbk.)
      1. Kant, Immanuel, 1724–1804. I. Title. II. Series.
    B2798.H6313 1994
    193—dc20   93-45476
                                                          CIP

10 9 8 7 6 5 4 3 2 1

CONTENTS

PART V. THE PHILOSOPHICAL AESTHETICS AND THE
PHILOSOPHY OF THE ORGANIC

PART VI. KANT'S INFLUENCE

TRANSLATOR'S PREFACE

In translating Otfried Höffe's insightful and informative study of Kant, I have strived for both readability and preservation of the author's meaning. I apologize to the readers for my shortcomings in fulfilling either task but do hope that they will be patient enough to work their way through the difficulties inherent in any account of Kant's complex but rewarding philosophy.

In citing the *Critique of Pure Reason*, *The Groundwork of the Metaphysic of Morals*, and the *Critique of Practical Reason*, I have made extensive use of the translations of Norman Kemp Smith, H. J. Paton, and Lewis White Beck respectively. I have given my own translation for other quotations and for foreign titles of such books and articles as are not to my knowledge available in an adequate English translation. The original title appears in a footnote. The titles of secondary literature and of all journals appear in the original language.

I owe special thanks to Otfried Höffe and to Robert Louden for their many helpful suggestions. Any errors in translation remain entirely my own responsibility.

REFERENCES AND QUOTATIONS

References to Kant are from the Academy edition—for example, VII 216 = vol. VII, p. 216.

For the *Critique of Pure Reason* the page numbers of the first (=A) or the second edition (=B) are given—for example, A413 = 1st edition, p. 413.

In the case of the letters (e.g. *Letters*, 744) the number designates the letter number in the Academy edition (vols. X–XIII).

ABBREVIATIONS

"Beginning"	"Conjectural Beginning of Human History" ("Mutmaßlicher Anfang der Menschengeschichte," VIII 107–23)
CJ	*Critique of Judgment* (*Kritik der urteilskraft*, V 165–485)
"Commonplace"	"On the Commonplace: That may be right in theory but is not valid in practice" ("Über den Gemeinspruch: Das mag in der Theorie richtig sein, taugt aber nicht für die Praxis," VIII 273–313)
Conf.	*The Conflict of the Faculties* (*Der Streit der Fakultäten*, VII 1–116)
CPR	*Critique of Pure Reason* (A:IV 1–252, B: III 1–552)
CPrR	*Critique of Practical Reason* (V 1–163)
GMM	*Groundwork of the Metaphysic of Morals* (IV 385–463)
"Idea"	"Idea for a Universal History with Cosmopolitan Intent" ("Idee zu einer allgemeinen Geschichte in weltbürgerlicher Absicht," VIII 15–31)
Log.	*Logic. A Handbook for Lectures* (*Logik, Ein Handbuch zu Vorlesungen*, ed. G. B. Jäsche, IX 1–150)
LT	*Metaphysical Origins of Legal Theory* (*Metaphysische Anfangsgründe der Rechtslehre*, 1st part of *MM*, VI 203–372)
MM	*Metaphysic of Morals* (VI 203–493)
MOS	*Metaphysical Origins of Science* (*Metaphysische Anfangsgründe der Naturwissenschaft*, IV 465–565)
Peace	*On Eternal Peace* (*Zum ewigen Frieden*, VIII 341–386)
Prol.	*Prolegomena to Any Future Metaphysics* (IV 253–383)
Refl.	*Reflections* (*Reflexionen*, XIV et seq.)
Rel.	*Religion within the Bounds of Reason Alone* (*Die Religion innerhalb der Grenzen der bloßen Vernunft*, VI 1–202)
TV	*Metaphysical Origins of the Theory of Virtue* (*Metaphysische Anfangsgründe der Tugendlehre*, 2nd part of *MM*, VI 373–493)

INTRODUCTION

Is Kant merely a figure in the history of philosophy, or does he still merit our interest for substantive reasons? Kant ranks among the greatest thinkers of Western civilization and has shaped modern philosophy more than almost any one else. But Galileo and Newton are also acclaimed as outstanding scientists, although today they stand for an antiquated physics which the theory of relativity and quantum theory have rendered obsolete. Does this also hold for philosophers? Does Kant represent an outstanding yet obsolete form of human thought?

Historically, Kant belongs to the age of the European Enlightenment, the fundamental idea of which has in many respects begun to lose its appeal: the notion that everything is controllable, faith in the steady progress of mankind, optimism with respect to rationality in general. As an historical movement, the Enlightenment is over. Have all of its main ideas thus become worthless? Or do reason and freedom, critique and responsibility rather designate basic human attributes and tasks, which, correctly understood, remain valid beyond the seventeenth and eighteenth centuries?

Kant developed an understanding of the ideas of the Enlightenment which is as far away from naïve faith in reason as it is from the anti-Enlightenment attitude that whatever exists is good and beautiful. The philosophy of Immanuel Kant represents not only the intellectual climax but also the transformation of the European Enlightenment. "Sapere aude! Have the courage to use your *own* understanding!"—this slogan of the age is taken up by Kant ("What is Enlightenment?" VIII 35) and applied universally. Enlightenment as a process—the elimination of errors and prejudices prompted by the decision to think independently, the gradual transcendence of particular interests, and the progressive liberation of "universal human reason"—is a leading idea of the period. For Kant it leads to the critique of all dogmatic philosophy and to the discovery of the ultimate foundation of reason. The principle of reason lies in autonomy: freedom as self-legislation. At the same time, Kant rejects untainted optimism, which had already been shaken by Rousseau's *First Discourse* (1750) as well as the "senseless" earthquake in Lisbon (1755), as a matter of principle. Proceeding from specifically philosophical problems, Kant advances not only to the origins but also to the limits of pure reason, theoretical as well as practical.

Kant is profoundly impressed by the progress of modern science (Galileo, Newton) as well as the previous development of logic and mathematics. It thus seems to him all the more unbearable that in the area of "First Philosophy," traditionally called metaphysics, a fight over questions about God, freedom and immortality rages endlessly. Kant considers this fight about fundamentals a scandal which philosophy must remedy if it seriously wishes to claim its place among the sciences.

In order to place metaphysics on the sure path of a science, Kant postpones the investigation of God, freedom and immortality. He begins on a more basic level and asks whether there can be First Philosophy, metaphysics, as a science at all. Prior to the task of studying the principles of our natural and social world, philosophy has the task of investigating its own possibility. Philosophy no longer begins as metaphysics; it begins as the theory of philosophy, as the theory of a scientific metaphysics.

The question of metaphysics as a science radicalizes philosophical discussion in a manner previously unknown. This complete radicalization is only rendered possible by a new, more fundamental way of thinking. Kant finds this new way of thinking in the transcendental critique of reason. With the help of this critique, he discusses the capabilities of reason and vindicates an autonomous scientific philosophy while recognizing its inherent limits. Whoever sees in Kant only the origin of a new metaphysics thus has as one-sided an understanding as one who, following Moses Mendelssohn, views Kant merely as a "pulverizer of metaphysics."

The question of whether an autonomous scientific philosophy is possible cannot be answered in the abstract but only in connection with the investigation of central substantive problems. An autonomous philosophy, philosophy as a rational science, presupposes that there are in human cognition and action, in law, history and religion, in aesthetic and teleological judgments elements which are valid independently of any empirical evidence; only then can they be known not by the empirical sciences but only by philosophy. Kant's fundamental question concerning the possibility of an autonomous scientific philosophy thus is not a prefatory question; it leads straight to the discussion of substantive problems. In investigations characterized by exemplary originality and conceptual clarity, Kant seeks to show how various fields are constituted by elements independent of experience. He thus explains how the universal validity and necessity of true knowledge, of moral action, etc. are possible despite the finite nature (receptivity of the senses) of man.

On the other hand, a scientific philosophy can only exist if the elements independent of experience can be methodically found and systematically described. For Kant this occurs in the transcendental critique of reason. The discovery of elements independent of experience and of the critique of reason illuminating them was truly epoch-making. This discovery revolutionized the previous way of thinking and, on Kant's view, finally provided philosophy with a truly secure foundation. Even those who remain skeptical about the foundational claim cannot deny that Kant fundamentally changed the philosophical scene: epistemology and ontology, ethics, the philosophy of history and of religion, as well as the philosophy of art. Whether we consider *a priori* and *a posteriori* knowledge, synthetic and analytic judgments, transcendental arguments, regulative and constitutive ideas, the categorical imperative, or the autonomy of the will—the number of concepts and problems traceable to Kant in present discussions is surprisingly large. Highly diverse schools of thought have chosen Kant as a point of reference with respect to which they critically or affirmatively orient their own thought.

The key concepts of Kantian philosophy—critique, reason and freedom—are the decisive catchwords of the "age of the French Revolution" (roughly 1770 to 1815). Kant is thus not just one of the outstanding classics of philosophy and an important voice in contemporary discussions. He is at the same time one of the most significant representatives of the era which Karl Jaspers has rightly called the "axis age" and which even today fundamentally influences our thought and our sociopolitical environment.

Nonetheless, we cannot extol Kant as herald of the present. For one thing, many contemporary philosophers criticize Kant quite severely. For another, Kant is neither a father of modern natural science, social science and humanities nor a founder of contemporary philosophy of science. Nor does Kant serve as chief witness for the development of constitutional democracies into social states. Logical positivism and analytical philosophy dispute the existence of elements of cognition completely free of experience, and demand, as does structuralism, the renunciation of ultimate justification. In ethics Kant is challenged by ultilitarianism, then by discourse ethics, in his philosophy of freedom by determinism and behaviorism, in the philosophy of law by legal positivism. In short: Kant stands in contradiction to important tendencies in philosophy, science and politics.

To the extent to which Kant does not agree with our present modes of thought, the study of his writings can easily meet with inner resistance. The following introduction into his life, his philosophical development and his influence, but above all into his work seeks to diminish this resistance to Kant and, if not to win the reader over to Kant's thought, at least to interest him in it and to make the unbroken influence of this philosophy from its inception up to the present day understandable.

An introduction to Kant's thought can be guided either by the history of its development or by the history of its influence. There are good reasons for both approaches. Hence, its development (chap. 1–2) is sketched first and in conclusion its influence (chap. 3); the account of Kant's works is also occasionally interspersed with some historical references. But the focus here is upon Kant's main writings, for in them Kant's thought, after years and decades of preparatory work, attains that form which the philosopher himself took as decisive. Without doubt Kant's posthumously published works reveal historical and material roots, without which many a theory remains unclear or seems unrealistic; the lectures certainly disclose important assumptions and additions, and the unpublished writings from his late period, the so-called Opus Postumum, indicate elaborations and changes which a more extensive portrayal of Kant cannot neglect. But the main critical writings—their lines of questioning and fundamental concepts, their proposed solutions and their argumentational structure— should receive material priority.

An introduction cannot provide a detailed commentary highlighting the whole range of substantive problems. It should, however, draw the reader's attention to the high level of reflection, the refined system of concepts and the general consistency which one can find in Kant's philosophical project, despite certain obscurities and contradictions. On the other hand, critical transcendental philosophy is occasionally interspersed with scientific and political biases—for example, the opinion that all geometry is Euclidean or the conviction that self-sufficient professions have political priority over economically dependent workers. It is the task of a thorough account to point out such elements in Kant's thought as well as the fact that they do not belong to the plane of a transcendental reflection on principles. That does not of course rule out that a fundamental criticism of Kant may elsewhere be appropriate. On the whole this introduction to Kant's life, works and influence feels bound by the following maxim: since Kant in any case can no longer speak, it is sensible to interpret him dynamically and to his advantage.

Serious philosophy is directed toward the basic problems of man—according to Kant: insofar as an interest of reason finds expression in them. This interest is united in the three famous questions: (1) What can I know? (2) What should I do? (3) For what may I hope? (*CPR*, B 833). The present introduction accepts this division and presents the *Critique of Pure Reason*, then the moral and legal philosophy, and thirdly the philosophy of history and religion. Any one who took this division as absolute, however, would overlook the important intermediary task of the *Critique of Judgment*; because of its great systematic and substantive significance, it is treated in a separate section.

I owe particular thanks to my colleagues Rüdiger Bittner, Norbert Hinske and Karl Schuhmann for their amicable critique and to Marshall Farrier for his great care in translating the text into English.

PART I
Life and Philosophical Development

An exciting biography of Kant would be difficult to write; his life was regular and uniform. We find no affairs which created a sensation among his contemporaries and no adventures which could capture the curiosity of future generations. Kant did not lead the life of a rover, as Rousseau did, nor did he correspond with all of the great men of his age, as Leibniz did; in contrast to Plato and Hobbes he was not involved in political enterprises nor, in contrast to Schelling, in romances. Nothing extravagant taints his life-style: no unusual clothing or hair style, no moving gesture such as the "Sturm und Drang" period loved. Kant was unusually reserved. Although his critical works may, similar to Augustine's, Descartes' or Pascal's philosophy, have arisen from a sudden inspiration (cf. *Refl.* 5037), nowhere in his writings does Kant speak of a philosophical experience which immediately transformed his previous thought. We thus find nothing corresponding to our conception of a genius. Are, then, the personality and biography of Kant disappointing? Was Kant perhaps not a genius, as Heine (*Beiträge zur deutschen Ideologie*, 240) claimed?

Kant can be understood only through his work, in which he immerses himself with unwavering discipline and an almost superhuman exclusiveness. This work is science,[1] above all the science of reason: knowledge of nature and morals, of law, religion, history and art from *a priori* principles. For Kant even more than for other philosophers, the real events occur in thought; Kant has no other biography than the story of his philosophizing.

Of the great modern philosophers Kant is (perhaps after Christian Wolff) the first to earn his living as a professional teacher of his field. In contrast to most representatives of the British and French Enlightenment, Kant led the assiduous but uneventful life of a bourgeois scholar. And that means that with Kant university philosophy becomes capable of epoch-making originality. This tradition continues with Fichte, Schelling and Hegel and then comes to a halt; Schopenhauer, Kierkegaard and Marx are no less estranged from academic thinkers than Comte, Mill and Nietzsche.

Kant never ventured beyond the outposts of his birthplace Königsberg. Nonetheless, in addition to creativity and a good sense of humor, an extraordinary knowledge of the world manifests itself in Kant's numerous non-speculative writings. Kant derives this knowledge from reading, conversation and an unusually productive imagination.

We gain our knowledge of the philosopher's life, personality and philosophical development for the most part from Kant's correspondence. The letters form an important supplement and continuation of Kant's treatises. They document his academic development and Kant's relationship to friends, relatives, colleagues and students. They provide information on his relationship to famous contemporaries, to cultural trends and events and acquaint us with the immediate impact of Kantian philosophy. But they accommodate "only occasionally and reluctantly a personal mood and a personal interest."[2] No less important than the correspondence are the early biographies of Kant's contemporaries Borowski, Jachmann, Wasianski, Hasse and Rink who without exception themselves lived in Königsberg and knew the philosopher from long personal association.

Because most letters to and from Kant date back no further than 1770, when Kant was already forty-six years old; since, moreover, the biographies of contemporaries regard Kant mainly in his later years; and because, finally, the anecdotes about Kant's charming idiosyncracies stem from this period, there is a danger of describing Kant's personality too much from the standpoint of late adulthood and his rigid, pedantic leanings. In reality, Kant was social, indeed genteel in manner. But his life work, the critical transcendental philosophy which Kant himself perceived as a conceptual revolution and which would in fact radically transform the history of European philosophy, developed more and more until it finally dominated everything else.

1.

The Pre-Critical Period

ভঙ্গভঙ্গভঙ্গভঙ্গভঙ্গ

1.1 FAMILY, SCHOOL, UNIVERSITY

Immanuel Kant was born on 22 April 1724 in the outskirts of Königsberg as the fourth of nine children of a simple harnessmaker. On the
following day he was baptized under the name "Emanuel" ("God with
us"). Like other scholars of the German Enlightenment, Kant stems
from a modest, indeed poor background. His hometown is the flour-
ishing capital of East Prussia with a harbor for international trade, in
which particularly English merchants exchanged wine and spices from
the colonies for Russian grain and livestock. The city, which lay on the
northeastern border of the German-speaking world, is founded in the
year of Kant's birth out of three cities (Altstadt, Löbenicht, Kneiphof)
merged into one: Kant and Königsberg are equally old.

Archival data do not confirm Kant's opinion that his grandfather
immigrated from Scotland (*Letters*, 744). His great-grandfather,
Richard Kant, presumably still stems from the Courland (two daugh-
ters, however, were married to Scotsmen); the family of Kant's mother
Anna Regina comes from Nurenberg and Tübingen.

Young Immanuel attends the Vorstädter Hospitalschule
(1730–32) and from the age of eight on, the Friedrichskollegium
(1732–40). Due to the poverty of his parents, Kant depends upon the
support of friends, specifically Albert Schultz (1692–1763), principal
of the school and a professor of theology. Schultz is an important student of the great philosopher of the German Enlightenment Christian
Wolff and soon discovers Kant's talent.

The Friedrichs-Gymnasium, pejoratively called the "Pietists' Inn" by the local population, has a strict religious regimen. Religious instruction (learning the catechism) and church services make up a significant portion of the curriculum; Hebrew and Greek are taught with the aid of the Old and New Testaments; mathematics and natural sciences play a minor role. Only Latin, which attracts Kant's sustained interest, appears to have been taught well. In the fall of 1740 Kant graduates from the Friedrichs-Gymnasium as second in his class. In later years he still remembers its "enslavement of youth" with "fear and trembling."

Kant's family is likewise influenced by pietism, a movement in German Protestantism which arose in the seventeenth century and which wanted to renew a pious life-style and to reform the church accordingly. Despite his disapproval of pietistic cult forms, Kant always esteemed the basic pietistic stance, which recalls the imperturbable equanimity of the Stoic sage. Kant's mother, whom he admires during her lifetime for her common sense and her genuine godliness, dies in 1737 and is buried by the thirteen-year-old Kant on the evening before Christmas Eve.

After passing the entrance examination, Kant enrolls at sixteen years of age at the Albertina, the University of Königsberg. With the help of friends and with earnings from private lessons—according to his college friend Heilsberg also by winnings in billiards—he is able to study mathematics and natural sciences, theology, philosophy and classical Latin literature from 1740 to 1746. Martin Knutzen (1713–51), a professor of logic and metaphysics who—also a student of Wolff— might have become an important philosopher if not for his early death, gains particular influence. This diverse scholar draws Kant's attention to the natural sciences; after this time the physics of Isaac Newton (1643–1725) exemplifies for Kant strict scientific knowledge.

1.2 PRIVATE TUTOR, FIRST WRITINGS

After the death of his father (1746), Kant leaves the university and earns his living—as was usual for unmoneyed scholars—as a private tutor ("Master of the Household"), first for the preacher Andersch, then for the landowner Major von Hülsen (until about 1753), and finally for Count Keyserling. During this period Kant not only acquires social skills but also increases his philosophical and scientific knowledge. But with his first work *Thoughts on the True Estimation of Living*

Forces[3] (1746, published in 1749) Kant attempts too much. Calling upon "the freedom of human understanding" (I 8), he tries to resolve "one of the greatest schisms . . . among the geometers of Europe" (I 16) by means of a compromise. In the conflict on the calculation of force (F) from mass (m) and velocity (v)—this force is now known as kinetic energy—he supports the Leibnizians (F = m•v^2) with regard to "living forces," that is, free movements, and Descartes and his followers (F = m•v) with regard to "dead forces," that is, unfree movements. The correct solution (F = $\frac{1}{2}$ m•v^2), which d'Alembert had published in 1743, is ignored. The self-confidence of the twenty-two year-old young man is remarkable: "I have already marked the course that I want to hold. I will begin my journey, and nothing will keep me from continuing it" (I 10).

Kant does not write in Latin, the international academic language, but rather—as Leibniz, Thomasius and Wolff have to some extent already done—in clear German. Although he produces no significant result, the constructively critical endeavor toward compromise which motivates Kant's transcendental critique of reason already comes to light here. Kant's interest in natural science, which will dominate his work for the next ten years, also becomes manifest. At the same time, Kant makes his appearance as a philosopher, since he places the controversy about the calculation of force in the context of a more far-reaching issue. Kant is disturbed by the experience that the most prominent scientists of the age can find no agreement on a well-defined problem. He sees the Enlightenment idea of a universal human reason thus called into question. Simultaneous doubt and faith in human reason will accompany Kant all the way to the elaboration of his critical transcendental philosophy.

After his return to Königsberg the philosopher becomes remarkably productive. In March of 1755 his *Universal Natural History and Theory of the Heavens*,[4] "treated according to Newtonian principles," appears anonymously. Kant here sketches a theory of the origin of the solar system and of the entire cosmos. He dispenses with theological considerations and rests his argumentation exclusively upon "natural causes." Important parts, in particular Kant's theory of the rings around Saturn and of nebula, are later confirmed by observations of the astronomer Herschel (1738–1822). Kant's purely mechanical explanation of the formation of the universe remains, however, practically unknown, and its significance for natural science is discovered only in the mid-nineteenth century. With some modifications due to *Laplace*'s independent hypothesis on the origin of the universe (1796), the Kant-Laplace theory forms an important basis of astronomical discussion for quite some time.

In 1755 Kant completes his doctoral work in Königsberg with a dissertation about fire: *Meditationum quarundam de igne succincta delineatio.*[5] His public lecture on 12 June, "On Easier and on More Thorough Philosophical Speech," is attended by particularly many respected and scholarly men of the city. In the same year, he completes his "habilitation"[6] with the treatise *Principiorum primorum cognitionis metaphysicae nova dilucidatio.*[7] Kant becomes "magister legens," a private teacher with no university salary, who must earn his living from lecture attendance fees and private instruction.

In the *Nova dilucidatio* Kant criticizes Wolff's academic metaphysics, a systematic elaboration of Leibniz' philosophy. He discusses the relationship of Leibniz' "real principle" of sufficient reason to the logical principle of contradiction. Along with the philosopher Christian August Crusius (1715–75), a student of Leibniz and critic of Wolff, Kant considers the attempt to subordinate the real principle to the logical to have failed. He thus contests the basic assumption of Wolff's rationalism: that all principles of knowledge can ultimately be traced to a single common principle. Kant is, however, still far from his later assertion of the synthetic nature of any knowledge of reality.

Kant continues to study questions of natural science. A strict division between empirical and philosophical knowledge of nature does not exist during this period in any case. The philosopher writes about the "shakings of the earth perceived for some time," particularly about the earthquake which destroyed two-thirds of the city of Lisbon on 1 November 1755 and which led to a keen interest in the question of theodicy, the justification of God with regard to the suffering in the world, throughout Europe. The priority of practical over theoretical reason, of great importance later, comes into view here (I 460).

Kant's definition of the smallest particles as "spacefilling force" in his *Monadologia physica*[8] (1756) makes a quite modern impression. The public disputation of this third treatise after *De igne* and the *Nova dilucidatio* was required for a position as associate professor. Scientifically important is Kant's explanation of the cause of trade-winds and monsoons (*New Notes Explaining the Theory of Winds,*[9] 1756).

1.3 THE SUCCESSFUL TEACHER AND ELEGANT SCHOLAR

In the fall of 1755 Kant begins his activity as a lecturer, which demands on the average sixteen hours a week of hard work (cf. Letters, vol. XIII: 13). Short finances sometimes require him to lecture for twenty hours a week and more. Kant's first years as an academic teacher hence mark a period lacking in publications; no piece of importance appears in the years 1757–61.

In 1756 and again in 1758 the philosopher applies for an associate professorship in logic and metaphysics. The position, vacant during the five years since Knutzen's death, remains unoccupied due to the outbreak of the Seven Years' War. He also unsuccessfully applies for a full professorship in logic and metaphysics which falls to his older colleague F. J. Buck. In the summer of 1764 Kant turns down a professorship in literature which would have required him to write certain greeting messages to the king. In the year 1766 he finally receives his first remunerative post, the modestly paid position of assistant librarian in the palace library. Despite his great success in research and teaching, Kant must wait until 1770, that is, until the age of forty-six, to achieve the desired professorship in logic and metaphysics. However, in the autumn of the previous year, invoking his ties to Königsberg, his broad circle of friends and acquaintances as well as his poor health, he has rejected both an appointment at the University of Erlangen and overtures by the University of Jena.

In accordance with the customs of the time, Kant does not teach his own philosophy. Not only during his pre-Critical period does he give lectures on the basis of manuals (*compendia*)— logic according to the *Science of Reason*[10] by G. F. Meier (1718–77), Wolff's successor in Halle; ethics and metaphysics usually according to *A. G. Baumgarten* (1714–62), a student of Wolff and an important philosopher in his own right; natural law according to the *Jus naturale* of Achenwall, a law professor in Göttingen, and so on. But his lecture does not pedantically paraphrase prefabricated ideas; it is a "free discourse, spiced with wit and emotion. Often quotes and references to works which he had just read, occasionally anecdotes, which were nonetheless always pertinent."[11] Kant understands better than any of his colleagues how to teach not philosophy but philosophizing: unbiased critical thought. Kant has a vivid and at the same time very accurate imagination; he once surprised an Englishman with a precise description of Westminster Bridge. The philosopher has a highly inquiring mind and thus feels at home in remarkably many areas of study; he is not only an exact analytic thinker but also likes to study the "book of the world."

The lectures, which demand from the students independent thought, attract lively interest right from the start. The audience, a mixture of Prussians and foreigners, mainly Baltics, Russians and Poles, "virtually deified" Kant for decades.[12] In personal contact the young teacher exhibits a warmth and cordiality which we would not expect of Kant. We find among his students the poet and philosopher Johann Gottfried Herder (1744–1803), to whom Kant immediately devotes attention. (In his *Treatise on the Origin of Language*,[13] 1772, Herder anticipates important results of modern science and philosophy: the adaptability and the organic and instinctual weaknesses of man, the dependence of man's linguistic capability on his frailty, and the connection between language and thought. But he also lays the cornerstone for his subsequent critique of Kant (cf. below, sect. 13.1.)

In his classes, Kant demonstrates the unusual breadth of his horizon. He teaches not only logic and metaphysics but also mathematical physics and physical geography (an academic discipline which he proudly introduces for the first time), anthropology (as of the winter semester of 1772–73) and education (as of the winter semester of 1776–77), philosophy of religion (natural theology), moral philosophy, natural law (as of the winter semester 1776–77) and philosophical encyclopedia (as of 1767–68), even fortress-building and fireworks. Frequently, Kant is dean of his department and in the summer terms of 1786 and 1788, president[14] of the university.

As much as Kant devotes himself to teaching and research, this activity fills only the first half of his day. The other half belongs to social life. Within his circle of friends and acquaintances Kant spends his time with a long noon dinner, with billiards and cards, in the theater and in the most respected salons of the city. As a witty conversationalist, Kant becomes a coveted guest. Maria Charlotta Jakobi, the wife of a banker and Privy Counselor for Commerce with whom Kant is on friendly terms, makes a sword-belt for the "great philosopher" and sends him "a kiss, in favorable regard."[15] In the salon of the Countess von Keyserling, a place of honor is always available for Kant. The philosopher Johann Georg Hamann (1730–88), also living in Königsberg, even fears that Kant will be torn from his scholarly plans by a whirlwind of social diversions. "Really, Herr Magister Kant was then the most genteel man of the world, wore bordered clothes, a postillon d'amour and visited all coteries."[16]

The first Russian occupation of Königsberg in 1758–1762 was presumably partially responsible for Kant's-cheerful attitude. The liberal occupation of the city brought "the entire breadth and open-mindedness of the eastern life-style into the old, musty city."[17] The class hierarchy loosens up; pietistic seriousness gives way to a freer attitude, and Prussian austerity to an almost luxurious life-style. Kant, too, participates "in the gay bustle of the officers in private homes and officers' casinos."[18]

The style of the publications with which Kant first gains fame in Germany as a writer corresponds to the cosmopolitan's social adeptness. To the same extent to which Heine[19] mocks the "dry, grey packing-paper style" of the *Critique of Pure Reason*, with which Kant wants to "distinguish himself politely from the popular philosophers of the time, who strive for the most bourgeois clarity," he praises the elegant style of the early publications: "full of good humor in the manner of French essays."

2.

The Critical Transcendental Philosophy

2.1 ON THE WAY TO THE CRITIQUE OF PURE REASON

After 1761 Kant again develops an astonishing productivity. In theoretical philosophy David Hume (1711–76) and in practical philosophy Jean-Jacques Rousseau (1712–78), whose picture forms the sole decoration in Kant's study, exert the greatest influence. Kant delves into the classical problems of metaphysics, the proofs of the existence of God and the foundations of morals. He recognizes, however, with increasing clarity the difficulty of solving these by the traditional means. In the end he sees himself forced to set metaphysics aside and to develop a "propaedeutic science" (II 395), which first surveys the field open to metaphysics. In the beginning Kant belongs completely to the movement of the German Enlightenment at its zenith. Like the Enlightenment and in contrast to Wolff's synthetic method, he understands philosophy as analysis. Kant enters into amicable correspondence with leading representatives of the Enlightenment: from 1765, for example, with the philosopher and mathematician Johann Heinrich Lambert (1728–77) and from 1766 with Moses Mendelssohn (1729–86). Mendelssohn, a friend of Gotthold Ephraim Lessing and the publisher Nicolai, paves the way for the emancipation of the Jews in Germany. But Kant's "Metaphysical Propaedeutics" in the end takes the form of a revolutionary new philosophy quite distinct from that of the German Enlightenment; the *Critique of Pure Reason* is understood, in intentional contrast to analysis, as a philosophy of synthesis.

In the treatise *The Only Possible Basis for a Proof Demonstrating the Existence of God*[20] (late 1762, although the publisher gives 1763), the examination of the speculative proofs for the existence of God does not come to such an unqualified negative conclusion as in the *Critique of Pure Reason*. But Kant does here make the claim that "existence is not a predicate at all" (II 72), a claim which later acquires central importance. He rejects three of the traditional proofs for the existence of God and also dismisses Descartes' version of the fourth, the ontological argument, but concedes to another version all of the clarity "required in a demonstration" (II 161). Kant does not, however, provide the full demonstration but develops only the basis for a proof.

The Enquiry Concerning the Clarity of the Principles of Natural Theology and Morals[21] (completed in 1762 but not published until 1764) is awarded the second prize by the Academy of Sciences in Berlin; the first prize goes to Mendelssohn. This piece, written for the competition, is still based on analysis. Like modern analytical philosophers, Kant is convinced that in philosophy, and particularly "in metaphysics one must proceed entirely by analysis. For its job is indeed to disentangle confused knowledge" (II 289). Kant requires not only for the principles of natural theology but also for those of ethics the highest degree of philosophical manifestness. It must of course "first of all be determined" whether in ethics rationalism or empiricism is right, that is, whether "the cognitive faculty alone or the emotions (the first, inner cause of the appetitive faculty) determine its [ethics] first principles" (II 300). With this piece and that on the existence of God, Kant becomes known throughout Germany—and to some extent an object of criticism.

The *Attempt to Introduce the Concept of Negative Quantities into the Wisdom of the World*[22] (1763) brings the first self-criticism against an analytical conception of philosophy. Kant emphasizes the dissimilarity of metaphysical and mathematical knowledge and places importance in the difference between a real contrast and a logical contradiction because a real contrast, like a real cause (the cause of an effect), is inaccessible to analytic knowledge.

In the treatise *Dreams of a Sorcerer, Explained by Dreams of Metaphysics*[23] (1766), Kant uses the example of the Swedish clairvoyant ("arch-dreamer") Emanuel Swedenborg (1689–1772) to show how one—as soon as one leaves the solid ground of experience—can arrive in a strictly logical manner at the strangest theorems and systems. Kant here departs irrevocably from Leibniz's and Wolff's rational metaphysical doctrine, as well as that of their independent "successors" A. G. Baumgarten and C. A. Crusius. Kant no longer defines metaphysics as a system of reason but as "a science dealing with the *limits of human reason*" (II 368); however, he is not yet able to specify these limits exactly. Their specification is from now on his main task. In this context Kant stumbles across recent British epistemology, above all the skeptic and empiricist David Hume, of whom he later says that he "first interrupted my dogmatic slumber and gave a new direction to my investigations in the field of speculative philosophy" (*Prol.*, IV 260). Kant finds Hume's criticism of dogmatic metaphysics convincing (*An Enquiry concerning Human Understanding*, 1748), but he does not accept the skeptical and empiricist conclusions. According to Hume, the principle of causality arises from habit; according to Kant, from pure understanding.

Kant's Inaugural Dissertation, *De mundi sensibilis atque intelligibilis forma et principiis*,[24] plays a particularly important role on the way to his critical philosophy. Here, Kant gives us a taste of an "introductory exercise" (propaedeutic) for metaphysics. Since the latter, as pure philosophy, contains no empirical principles (§§ 8 and 23), it is necessary to distinguish clearly between two kinds of knowledge: the sensible knowledge of things as they appear (phenomena) and the intellectual knowledge of things as they are (noumena). Here, Kant still considers the knowledge radically denied in the *Critique of Pure Reason*—knowledge of things in themselves extending beyond mathematics and experience, free of all sensibility—to be possible on the basis of the pure concepts of the understanding, the later categories.

Kant does, however, already have at his disposal several important prerequisites for his transcendental critique of reason. Knowledge of appearances, he says, is completely true (§ 11). Intuition is not confused knowledge (§ 7) but an independent source of knowledge. The representations of space and time do not stem from the senses; they are rather pure intuitions presupposed by the senses and constitute the universal, albeit subjective conditions for the ordering of sense data (§§ 13–15). It is mathematics which discusses the form of all our sensible knowledge (§ 12). With regard to ethics, Kant claims that moral concepts are recognized by pure understanding and thus belong to pure philosophy (§§ 7 and 9, cf. *Letters*, 54). But he refers to perfection as the criterion (§ 9), a principle which he later rejects.

In order that pure philosophy, metaphysics, should be possible as a science and not "eternally roll its stone of Sisyphus," its method must come first (§ 23). According to the most important methodological regulation, one must "anxiously prevent *the indigenous principles of sensible knowledge from overstepping their limits and affecting the intellectual sphere*" (§ 24). The dissertation closes in the spirit of the later transcendental dialectic with an attempt to explain on the basis of principles the delusions to which metaphysics succumbs. Here, they are still explained from the mixture of pure intellectual knowledge with sensible elements (§§ 24–30).

At first Kant intends only to revise the dissertation and add "a few pages." But during this attempt he becomes entangled in a process of reflection which unexpectedly and despite the tense, often reproachful impatience of his friends and philosophical admirers (cf. *Letters*, 101) lasts ten years. His correspondence with his favorite student and later friend *Marcus Herz* (1747–1803) best documents the way in which Kant repeatedly drafts various plans and projects, which then become obsolete or turn out to conflict with one another. The road to his critical philosophy is by no means a straight, linear development. To his set of projects belongs a *Phaenomenologia generalis*,[25] which is not, however—in anticipation of Hegel's *Phenomenology of the Mind*—intended as a "science of the appearances of consciousness" but rather—closer to Lambert—as a "science of the consciousness of appearances." An extended project, which is again rejected, aims toward *The Limits of Sensibility and Reason*.[26] Kant is here concerned with the question, "how my understanding is to form concepts entirely *a priori* of things with which matters are necessarily to harmonize" (*Letters*, 65). The answer to this question, the "transcendental deduction of the pure concepts of the understanding" in the *Critique of Pure Reason*, corrects once and for all the basic position of the dissertation of 1770. Of the understanding it is now said that it is not able to know things in themselves: the categories do not allow any real knowledge of the intelligible world but do nothing more than anticipate all possible experience. The problem of the antinomies, too, the beginnings of which date back to the 1750s (cf. *Monadologia physica*, 1756), receives a new formulation. It is no longer the transposition of sensibility and understanding but instead the confusion of appearance and thing in itself which forms the root of those contradictions in which reason necessarily becomes entangled. The individual antinomies can be understood but not resolved; dialectics becomes a constitutive characteristic of human reason, a sign of its finitude.

During the "quiet decade" (Dilthey), a far-reaching reorganization of concepts occurs hand in hand with the revision of the problems considered (cf. *Letters*, 101). Kant, who does not like to introduce new words, adopts expressions such as "perception," "intuition" and "pure" from Locke's *Essay* and Leibniz' *New Essays*. "Category," transcendental," "analytic" and "dialectic" stem from the Aristotelian tradition in Germany. We find "antinomy," "paralogism" and "amphiboly" in seventeenth-century textbooks. In the end the vocabulary of the first *Critique* has changed considerably in comparison to the pre-Critical period.[27]

2.2 WORKING OUT THE CRITICAL TRANSCENDENTAL PHILOSOPHY

After more than ten years of thinking out, drafting and rejecting attempts at solutions, Kant writes down the *Critique of Pure Reason* "within about four or five months, as if in flight" (*Letters*, 188; cf. 187). That a work of such magnitude, even in a purely quantitative sense, is composed so quickly compels one to suppose that Kant drew upon extensive preparatory studies. This fact and the lack of enough time "to give, file in hand, each part a rounded smoothness-and light mobility" (ibid.) explain why "in some places carelessness and a hurried style, in others even obscurity" remain (*Letters*, 155).

After an eleven-year interruption in publication, contrasting grossly with the expressive force of the contemporaneous "Sturm und Drang" movement, in May of 1781, Kant's first magnum opus, anxiously awaited by friends and colleagues, appears. It is according to Schopenhauer "the most important book ever written in Europe."[28] The hard-working teacher, researcher and author, revered by many and considered a dilettante by others (such as the Göttingen group), proves himself now, at the age of fifty-seven, to be a philosophical genius.

But first Kant must note with consternation that his book finds almost no echo. Moses Mendelssohn, whose opinion he awaits with particular eagerness, lays the book, which "consumes the fluid of the nerves" (*Letters*, 174), disgustedly aside (153). On 19 January 1782 an anonymous condemnation full of nasty irony—composed by the "popular philosopher" Christian Garve (1742–98) and shortened considerably by J. G. H. Feder, the publisher—appears in the highly reputable *Göttingische Anzeigen von Gelehrten Sachen*. Johann Schultz, professor of mathematics in Königsberg and one of Kant's closest colleagues, gives expression to the prevailing mood when he regretfully declares in his *Explications concerning the Critique of Pure Reason of Professor Kant*[29] (1784) that even professional philosophers complain about insurmountable obscurity and incomprehensibility of this work; moreover that it "is even for the greatest part of the academic community just as much as if it were composed exclusively of hieroglyphics."[30]

Kant is nonetheless convinced that the "first daze, which a multitude of quite unfamiliar concepts and of even less familiar ... new language had to bring forth, will pass" (*Letters*, 187). After a few years the mood actually does shift. The *Critique of Pure Reason* unfolds its secular significance continuing up to the present day. Despite the works of Hegel, Marx, Mill and Nietzsche, despite Frege, Husserl, Heidegger, Russell or Wittgenstein, surely no one could propose a more significant watershed in the history of modern philosophy than the *Critique of Pure Reason*.

First the German readership, then that of neighboring countries venture onto "the thorny path of the Critique" (B XLIII) and discover its philosophical explosiveness. Kant is discussed everywhere and soon becomes famous far beyond the borders of Germany. The philosopher receives numerous honors. In 1786 he becomes a member of the Berlin Academy of Sciences, in 1794 of the Petersburg Academy, and in 1798 of the Siena Academy.

After the First *Critique*, a number of further works appear in rapid succession. In the *Prolegomena* ("preliminary remarks") *to any Future Metaphysics that Will Be Able to Come Forward as Science* (1783), Kant, provoked by reluctant reception and fundamental misunderstandings, gives a summarizing introduction to his transcendental critique of reason. He here uses the "analytic method" in contrast to the "synthetic manner of teaching." The basic work on the philosophy of history, the "Idea for a Universal History with Cosmopolitan Intent,"[31] the treatise "Answer to the Question: What is Enlightenment?"[32] (both 1784), and the first main work on moral philosophy *Groundwork of the Metaphysic of Morals* (1785) follow.

Exactly a hundred years after Newton's epoch-making work *Philosophiae Naturalis Principia Mathematica* and in visible allusion to this famous title, the *Metaphysical Principles of Natural Science*[33] appears in 1786 with the attempt to more precisely determine the scope of the *a priori* principles of physics. After the greatly changed second edition of the *Critique of Pure Reason* (1787), the *Critique of Practical Reason* (1788), the *Critique of Judgment* (1790) and *Religion within the Bounds of Reason Alone*[34] (1793) are published. With the essay on religion Kant comes into conflict with the Prussian censor.

2.3 THE CONFLICT WITH THE CENSOR

Kant's life first falls within the reign of the Prussian kings Frederick William I, the Soldier King (1713–40), and Frederick II, the Great (1740–86), two exemplary representatives of enlightened absolutism. Constitutionally, all governmental power converges in the crown of Prussia, which with the acquisition of Silesia and West Prussia rises to the status of a major European power. In reality, however, the powers of the intermediate classes play a significant role. On the initiative of the government, an authoritarian welfare state with a disproportionately strong army is formed, mainly during the reign of the Soldier King. This state adheres to mercantilistic economic policies, which serve the military as much as the development of a sparse country; it has a modern bureaucracy, a strict system of taxation and an organized legal system. Both kings abstain from giving judiciary powers to their cabinets and recognize in principle the independence of the courts; judicial sentences become less severe, and torture is abolished; lawyers are tested and paid by the state; a unified system of appeals and regulations governing trials, sentences and prisons are introduced. These improvements transform Prussia from a police state to a constitutional government with separation of powers. Prussia thus becomes one of the most advanced commonwealths of the period.

Above all, religious tolerance is exemplary in Prussia. Frederick William I cultivated it, and Frederick II, the admirer of French literature and philosophy, finally makes it one of the basic values of the Prussian state. Religious refugees are always welcome in Prussia: Huguenots from France or Catholics from Bohemia, Moravia or the Salzburgerland; nor are the Jews excluded from the reforms. According to the *Universal Law of the Land for the Prussian States*, prepared by Frederick II and instituted by his successor, no one is to be harassed, called to account, ridiculed or persecuted because of his religious beliefs. With such constitutional measures, Prussia reaches a level of religious freedom which is not far from that of the newly founded United States and is reached in Great Britain only in the course of the nineteenth century. The privileges of the nobility and the servitude of the peasants, however—criticized by Kant—remain. For even the originally free peasants of the east have become bondsmen who have no secure right of inheritance and are treated as serfs because the nobility cannot manage its sizeable lands without socage.

Frederick the Great's successor, Frederick William II (1786–97), only partially continues the development toward an enlightened constitutional government. He does implement the *Universal Law of the Land* in the year 1794, but he puts an end to the enlightened tolerance of his predecessors with the religious edict (1788) of his Minister for Culture, J. C. von Wöllner. Kant comes into conflict with this edict when he presents his essay on religion to the infamous Immediate-Examination-Commission in Berlin, although he is not obligated to do so. For it is to appear in the Berlin Monthly, which is printed in Jena, that is, abroad. The first part nonetheless passes the censor without complaint. Only for the second part is permission to publish refused. Kant resolves to publish the four parts of the work together as a book. To obtain permission to publish Kant turns to the theology department in Königsberg in order that it settle the question of whether or not the work falls under the scope of theology at all (*Letters*, 494). After this department has answered his question in the negative, Kant turns to the dean of the philosophy department in the place of publication, Jena, and receives permission to publish. But his case is still being arbitrated in Berlin; the king himself takes up opposition against Kant. While rumors of an inquisition against Kant, of dismissal, exile and emigration spread in Germany, the philosopher in June publishes his second treatise on religious philosophy, *The End of all Things*.[35] It is a masterpiece of philosophical irony with shades of melancholy. With clear reference to Prussian religious policy, Kant describes Christianity which arms itself with "imperious authority" instead of "moral kindness" as the rule of the "*Antichrist*," who thus would "begin his short regime (presumably based on fear and expediency)" (VIII 339). Kant is obviously aware of the risk involved in such utterances, for he is prepared for the worst: "convinced of having acted conscientiously and legally, I look calmly toward the end of these odd events" (*Letters*, 590).

On 1 October 1794 Frederick William II issues a cabinet order signed by Wöllner himself. Kant has "misused philosophy to deface and devaluate several main and basic teachings of the gospel and of Christianity" and has violated his "duty as teacher of the young." Kant, who has at seventy reached the height of his renown, is asked, "in avoidance of Our utmost disgrace," in the future not to do such wrong. "On the most gracious special order of His Majesty the King," Wöllner concludes with the threat: "otherwise you will in case of continued disobedience have to experience infallibly unpleasant decrees" (*Conf.*, VII 6).

In his detailed response Kant dismisses the charges raised against him. As a "*teacher of the people*" he could not have cast aspersions on "the *national religion*" because his religious work is "an esoteric book incomprehensible to the public and merely presents an argument between scholars. Moreover, the work contains "no *evaluation* of Christianity at all," so it "is also not guilty of *devaluating* the same. For it actually contains only the evaluation of natural religion" (*Conf.*, VII 8; cf. *Letters*, 607). Kant nonetheless to the surprise of his friends and foes closes with a renunciation of any further utterance in the area of philosophy of religion (*Conf.*, VII 10)—as long as the king lives.

2.4 THE LATER WORKS

During the long preparation for the *Critique of Pure Reason* Kant's life-style has changed. The genteel scholar has become a reclusive academic who leads a disciplined and even pedantic life depicted kindly by the early biographers and with vicious ridicule by Heine. Without his exact daily routine with fixed allotments of scholarly and social activity, without his lifelong endeavor to escape all notice and to elude the spotlight (cf. *Letters*, 70, 121), Kant, who had a weak constitution from birth and was in addition a bit stunted, would hardly have mastered his large teaching program and above all his massive amount of research. The style of his letters, which are completely lacking in personal feelings for the recipient, also belong to the personality of the elder Kant. For "banalities" of daily life, for remarks about the weather, nature or his present mood, there is—except for repeated remarks about ailments—no room. One gets the impression that Kant became shy of people in his old age. But one can more aptly say that only the strict subservience of his person to his work allows Kant laboriously to piece together the critical transcendental philosophy and with it to set new norms for European thought.

As his first work following the conflict with the censor, Kant publishes the treatise *On Eternal Peace* (1795), on the philosophy of law and history. But a systematic treatment of legal philosophy first appears in the *Metaphysic of Morals* (1797), the first part of which is entitled *Metaphysical Origins of Legal Theory*; the second part, *Metaphysical Origins of the Theory of Virtue*, contains Kant's systematic moral philosophy.

Having reduced his teaching duties in the previous years, Kant delivers his last lecture in July 1796 at the age of seventy-three. Two years later he publishes, in addition to his *Anthropology from a Pragmatic Point of View*[36] (1798) *The Conflict of the Faculties*, in which he again takes up the question of religion after the death of Frederick William II. In 1799 the first signs of deterioration start to become noticeable. In 1801 Kant must entrust the biographer and preacher Wasianski with the management of all his business. The last work begun by Kant, now known as the *Opus postumum*, thus does not reach fruition. The significant changes, which Kant intends to make here, show, as does his entire philosophical development, that he never understands his thought as a fixed doctrine but rather as a continuous process of new insights and new questions.

In the *Opus postumum* Kant wants to lead *a priori* thought step by step to the empirical sphere in order to bridge the gap between the transcendental critique of reason and actual experience. His plans for a "transition" from the *Metaphysical Origins of Science* to physics (*Letters*, 781) date back to the beginning of the 1790s. The earliest coherent draft stems from the time around 1796. The idea of an *a priori* theory of corporeality plays a decisive role. For the body as a system of forces aware of themselves plays not only the role of an object of experience; it is also the subjective system in which the movement of reason proceeds (cf. XXII 357).

Because Kant places extraordinary importance in the new work, he feels all the more distressed that he is not making any progress (ibid.). In his last year Kant registers with frightening clarity that his body and mind are rapidly deteriorating. On 8 October 1803 he has a serious illness for the first time in his life, and four months later, on 12 February 1804, Sunday morning at 11 o'clock, death ends his aged, weakened life. On 28 February Immanuel Kant is transported "with all the bells of the city ringing" in a funeral procession "joined by thousands" to the Dome and university chapel of his native town and buried there in the professors' crypt.[37] The citizens later put a plaque over the grave with the famous quote from the *Critique of Practical Reason* (V 161): "Two things fill the mind with ever new and increasing admiration and awe, the more often and more steadily we reflect on them: *the starry heavens above me and the moral law within me.*"

Some of the lectures were already printed during Kant's lifetime: the *Logic* (1800), *Physical Geography* (1802) and *On Education*[38] (1803). The lectures *On the Philosophy of Religion*[39] (1817), *The Metaphysics* (1821), the *Study of Man or Philosophical Anthropology*[40] (1831) and *Ethics* (not until 1924) are published later. On Kant's request, his early biographies appear only after his death.

PART II

What Can I Know?—The *Critique of Pure Reason*

3.

The Project of a Transcendental Critique of Reason

3.1 THE BATTLEFIELD OF METAPHYSICS ("PREFACE" TO THE FIRST EDITION)

Kant calls his fundamental philosophical science transcendental philosophy. In order to distinguish it from medeival transcendental philosophy, one can speak of critical transcendental philosophy. Kant develops it first with regard to reason as a cognitive faculty. He calls such reason theoretical or speculative in contrast to practical reason, the ability to will. The first *Critique* could thus be named more exactly "Critique of Pure Speculative Reason" (B xxii). The fact that Kant refrains from the addition shows that when writing this work, he contemplated only one critique of reason.

Although in matters of detail the argumentation occasionally adopts circuitous routes, the *Critique of Pure Reason* is on the whole a well-composed work. With a sense for dramatic tension, the "preface" to the first edition describes the tragic situation of human reason, which necessitates its critique, guides the subsequent investigations, and finds its resolution in the second part, the "Dialectic," only after an extensive detour.

Without elaborate explanations Kant jumps immediately into the scene, the muddled situation of metaphysics, which appears necessary and at the same time impossible. Certain questions which can be neither dismissed nor answered force themselves upon human reason (A vii). They cannot be dismissed because reason, faced with the variety of observations and experiences, looks for general principles through which this manifold appears not as chaos but rather as a structured whole, as interconnected and unified. Even the natural sciences seek such principles, which they put together in general theories. Metaphysics desires only that we carry the search to its final completion instead of quitting midway. The search ends only with principles which are not conditioned by others. The ultimate principles are unconditioned. As long as reason holds to experience, it finds only further and further conditions but nothing unconditional. In order to complete the search, it thus resorts "to principles which overstep all possible empirical employment, and which yet seem so unobjectionable that even ordinary consciousness readily accepts them" (A viii). The ultimate foundation for experience seems to lie beyond all experience. Its examination is thus called metaphysics, literally: beyond (meta) physics, the experience of nature.

The attempt to acquire knowledge independent of experience flings reason "into darkness and contradictions" (ibid.). On the one hand, as Kant later shows, there are good reasons to think that the world has a beginning, that God exists, the will is free and the soul immortal; on the other hand one can find equally good reasons for the opposite claims, and we cannot say which view is correct. Since the proposed principles are supposed to constitute the foundation for experience, one is tempted to test them on experience. But experience is excluded as a standard because metaphysical principles by definition lie beyond all experience. That which defines metaphysics, the transcendence of experience, at the same time keeps it from being a science. It is not external hurdles which impede metaphysics. Its own essence, knowledge from pure reason independent of experience, stands in its way. Metaphysics thus becomes the battlefield of intrinsically endless controversies (A viii).

One of the contending parties is rationalistic metaphysics, represented in the modern age by Descartes, Spinoza, Malebranche and Leibniz. Kant has primarily Wolff's school of metaphysics in mind, which predominated in scholarly discussions of the time. Wolff sees experience as a genuine source of knowledge but believes that we can discern something about reality by mere thought (pure reason). Kant considers the rationalists to be dogmatic and despotic because they force upon us certain fundamental assumptions—for instance that the soul is of a simple nature and immortal or that the world has a beginning and God exists without a preliminary critique of reason.

Due to controversies of the dogmatics among themselves, metaphysics degenerates into anarchy, and the skeptics, who in "technical . . . ignorance" undermine "the foundations of all knowledge" (B 451) and make "short work with all metaphysics" (B xxxvi), emerge as the second major party. But they cannot keep the dogmatics from repeatedly taking the floor. In more recent times, Kant sees in *John Locke* (1632–1704) an attempt to end all controversies by means of a "*physiology*" (literally: science of nature) "of the human understanding" (A ix). Locke, who in *An Essay Concerning Human Understanding* (1690) rejects Descartes' doctrine of innate ideas and principles, stands for empiricism, which ultimately traces all knowledge to internal or external experience. Empiricism thus denies that knowledge has foundations completely free from experience. Since the philosopher whose skepticism first woke Kant from his "dogmatic slumber" (sect. 2), David Hume, also belongs to the empiricists (cf. B 127f.), Kant in the "Transcendental Dialectic" depicts the battle for metaphysics as the controversy between rationalism and empiricism.

The controversies among dogmatics, skeptics and empiricists lead to the sort of indifference which no longer even poses the questions of metaphysics and bans them in any case from the field of investigation of any scientific philosophy. This is the attitude of a trivialized enlightenment philosophy which punishes metaphysics, previously "*queen* of all sciences," with contempt (A viii–ix). But indifference toward metaphysics, says Kant, cannot be maintained because "these pretended *indifferentists* . . . inevitably fall back, in so far as they think at all, into . . . metaphysical assertions" (A x). For they make statements about ultimate principles, about the empirical or supra-empirical base of knowledge; contradicting themselves, they take sides in the controversy and renew the battlefield of metaphysics.

Kant neither sidesteps the questions of metaphysics nor joins one of the parties in the controversy. He adopts the sole, but previously undiscovered way to liberate metaphysics from its muddled situation: the institution of a tribunal. The battle yields to a trial, which examines the possibility of knowledge from pure reason in an unpartisan manner, enforces legitimate claims and dismisses unfounded presumptions. Such an examination, differentiation and justification is critique (in Greek *krinein*: distinguish, judge, take to court) in the original sense of the word. Kant's titular concept "critique" does not mean a condemnation of pure reason but rather a "determination of its sources, its extent, and its-limits—all in accordance with principles" (A ii). (We find first steps toward a critique in the question of Locke and Hume: What are the capabilities of the human cognitive faculty?)

Since knowledge independent of experience by definition cannot have its foundation in experience, the possibility of knowledge from pure reason can be investigated only by pure reason itself. In the tribunal to which Kant delegates the case "dogmatism vs. empiricism and skepticism," pure reason presides over its own case. *The Critique of Pure Reason* is the self-examination and self-justification of reason independent of experience.

In the self-critique reason manifests its power; however, its power is self-limiting. In the first part of the *Critique*, the Aesthetic and Analytic, the legal code which contains a preliminary judgment of the controversy regarding metaphysics is found: in contrast to empiricist views, there are foundations free of experience and hence also strictly universal and necessary knowledge; this is, however, in contradiction to rationalism, restricted to the sphere of possible experience. In the second part of the *Critique*, the Dialectic, the trial is carried out formally and arrives at a verdict. With reference to objects beyond all experience, reason proves to have no foothold. As soon as it becomes occupied solely with its own notions, it runs into contradictions. Kant rejects both empiricism and rationalism. There are pure ideas of reason—but only as regulative principles in the service of experience .

In the course of its self-examination, reason dismisses rationalism because reality cannot be known by mere thought. But reason also rejects empiricism. Kant admits that all knowledge begins with experience, but it does not follow, as empiricism assumes, that knowledge originates solely in experience. On the contrary, even empirical knowledge proves impossible without sources independent of experience.

A basic kind of empirical knowledge lies in the connection of two events as cause and effect. Locke derived the concepts of cause and effect from experience and still ventured forth with knowledge above and beyond experience. Kant views this as "enthusiasm" ("Schwärmerei," B 128): fundamental presuppositions of experience such as the principle of causality ("All changes occur according to the principle of cause and effect") are neither due to experience nor make knowledge above and beyond experience possible. The basic presuppositions do not stem, though, as Hume believes, from (psychological) habit (ibid.). They are universally valid, so that Kant ultimately in contrast to skepticism deems objective knowledge possible. With the demonstration of conditions of experience themselves free of experience and hence universally valid, Kant shows that metaphysics is possible—but in contrast to rationalism only as a theory of experience, not as a science transcending the sphere of experience, and in distinction to empiricism not as an empirical but rather as a transcendental theory of experience (sect. 3.5).

In proud awareness of the historic importance of his critique of reason, Kant speaks of "putting an end to all errors" (A xii). He believes that he has specified the "questions exhaustively, according to principles" (ibid.) and claims boldly "that there is not a single metaphysical problem which has not been solved, or for the solution of which the key at least has not been supplied" (A xiii). With this claim Kant goes too far. Not only the history of philosophy after Kant but also Kant's own further development up to the *Opus postumum* speak against the idea that "no task will remain for our successors save that of adapting it all in a didactic manner" (A xx). One could, however, agree with Kant that through his project of a critique of reason and its main elements—the Copernican turn to the transcendental subject, the connection of the theory of knowledge and of objects, the demonstration of *a priori* elements in all knowledge, and the separation of appearances from things in themselves—he launched a profound reform in first philosophy, traditionally called metaphysics.

3.2 THE COPERNICAN REVOLUTION ("PREFACE" TO THE SECOND EDITION)

Whereas Kant in the first preface is still trying to attract the attention of the reader, he exudes in the preface to the second edition the calmness of an author sure of his earth-shaking insights. Kant works ideas from the *Prolegomena* into the second edition and achieves greater clarity in many places. Because the problems as a rule emerge more clearly in the second edition, the following presentation of the *Critique* is based on this edition. The main thought of the new preface lies in the Copernican revolution in the manner of thinking.

Kant wants to guide metaphysics onto "the secure path of a science" (B vii). Hence metaphysics cannot just keep starting up again and again but must make progress. Progress is possible only if one proceeds in accord with plans and goals and if representatives of the field are agreed regarding their procedures. In metaphysics, however, a universally recognized method is lacking; despite the work of two thousand years, metaphysics hence still cannot expect progress. In the *Critique of Pure Reason*, Kant wants to provide the missing method. This work does not yet contain metaphysics as a science but does contain its prerequisite; the *Critique* is a "treatise on the method" (B xxii).

Taking as examples three disciplines—logic, mathematics and the science of nature—which today are without doubt viewed as sciences, Kant shows how the secure path of science is found. Logic has the least difficulties. Because it investigates "nothing but the formal rules of all thought" (B ix), it has "from the earliest times" (B viii), namely since Aristotle, taken the secure path of science. But because here the understanding has "nothing to deal with save itself and its form," logic is merely the "vestibule of the sciences" (B ix) and plays in the course of the critique of reason essentially only the role of a negative counterpart to the real sciences.

The real sciences deal also with objects. Following a phase of blind "groping," they have consistently found the secure path of science through the "happy idea of a single man." The idea establishing science consists in a "revolution in its mode of thought" (B xi). In the case of mathematics this revolution occurred in antiquity and lies in an insight carried out in every proof of geometrical theorems: for science, one cannot merely look at a geometrical figure or merely inspect its concept. One must construct it *a priori* in accordance with one's own concepts (B xi–xii). This insight has profound significance: about an object one can know with certainty only what one himself sets into its concept; only by creative thought and construction does scientific knowledge become possible. That which one sets into the object cannot stem, though, from personal preconceptions; for otherwise one would have random notions but no objective knowledge. Mathematics hence owes its scientific character to a seemingly impossible condition: subjective presuppositions which have objective validity.

In the case of the science of nature, Kant discovers the same pattern. In order to become a science, physics, too, requires a "revolution in its mode of thought" (B xiii). This revolution consists in the insight proposed by the British philosopher Bacon (1561-1626) and realized in Galileo's and Torricelli's experiments, that reason recognizes in nature only "that which it produces after a plan of its own." As modern scientists confirm in practice and theory, they do not find themselves with regard to nature in the role "of a pupil who listens to everything that the teacher chooses to say, but of an appointed judge who compels the witnesses to answer questions which he has himself formulated" (ibid.).

In order for metaphysics finally to achieve the status of a science, Kant proposes here, too, a revolution in the mode of thought which, as in the case of mathematics and the science of nature, brings the subject of knowledge into a creative relationship to its object. Kant understands his proposal as a hypothesis, as an experiment of reason to be tested by its success. His transcendental philosophy in no way claims, as is frequently contended, to infallibility, which would contradict refutability as the minimal requirement accepted by present-day theory of science. But the refutation of transcendental theories does not occur with the means of the empirical sciences. Since we are dealing with experiments of reason, they can work or not work only with regard to reason.

The experiment of reason vindicates itself in two steps. For one thing, Kant believes that his proposal allows a justification of the objectivity of mathematics and the (mathematical) science of nature; this occurs in the "Transcendental Aesthetic" and the "Transcendental Analytic." The *Critique of Pure Reason* contains in its first two parts a philosophical theory of mathematics and of the mathematical science of nature. Although Neo-Kantianism has tended to reduce the first critique of reason to a "theory of experience" (Cohen 1924), the writing has another part, too, the "Transcendental Dialectic." Kant shows here that in the traditional way of thinking, the object of metaphysics, the unconditioned, "*cannot be thought without contradiction*" (B xx). The new way of thinking resolves the contradictions (antinomies), and therein lies the test for the proposed revolution in the mode of thought: reason is reconciled with itself, so that the experiment can be considered successful, and Kant's proposal can be regarded as true and justified; it acquires the status of a valid theory.

Kant compares his proposal with the achievement of the astronomer Copernicus; the experiment of reason has thus become famous as the "Copernican revolution." Kant sees the historical significance of Copernicus not in the refutation of received astronomic theory. Far more fundamentally, Copernicus overcomes the standpoint of common sense, unmasks the notion that the sun revolves around the earth as appearance, and discerns the truth in a new, counter-intuitive relationship of the subject to its object, the movements of the sun and the planets. Similarly, Kant claims to achieve in the *Critique of Pure*

Reason more than a refutation of metaphysical theories. He overcomes not merely rationalism, empiricism and skepticism; above all, he establishes a new relationship of the subject toward objectivity. Knowledge is no longer supposed to conform to the object, but the object to our knowledge (B xvi).

This demand seems absurd to common sense. For one only speaks of objective in contrast to subjective knowledge when one sees things as they are in themselves, independently of the subject. Kant's revolution in the mode of thought requires, however, that human reason liberate itself from the biases of the natural perspective, epistemological realism. The necessity and universality belonging to objective knowledge, he claims, do not stem, as we usually assume, from the objects. They are due to the thinking subject. Kant does not say that objective knowledge depends upon the empirical constitution of the subject, the structure of the brain, the evolution of man, and social experience. Such an assertion would seem to Kant rather nonsensical. The conditions of objective knowledge independent of experience, which lie in the pre-empirical constitution of the subject, are the object of investigation.

Kant's Copernican revolution maintains that the objects of knowledge do not appear of their own accord but must be brought to appearance by the (transcendental) subject. They are thus no longer to be referred to as things which exist in themselves but instead as appearances. Because the foundations of objectivity change and the theory of objects, ontology, depends upon a theory of the subject, there can no longer be an autonomous ontology. The same holds for epistemology. The idea of the *Critique of Pure Reason* is to dovetail both sides. A philosophical theory of being, a theory of the nature of objects, can be achieved according to Kant only as a theory of the knowledge of being; and a theory of knowledge only as the clarification of the notion of an object.

3.3 METAPHYSICS AS A SCIENCE OR: CONCERNING THE POSSIBILITY OF SYNTHETIC JUDGMENTS *A PRIORI* ("INTRODUCTION")

Kant explains the specifically metaphysical type of knowledge (knowledge from pure reason) as well as the character of knowledge in mathematics and the pure physical sciences in terms of a twofold disjunctive division: (1) knowledge is valid either *a priori* or a *posteriori*; (2) judgments are either synthetic or analytic. The significance of both distinctions for epistemology and the theory of science has not decreased since Kant's time. Kant's definitions no longer appear to be sufficiently exact, though, and the search for precise concepts gets lost in difficulties which make pragmatists like Morton G. White and Quine doubt the usefulness of the concepts.

A Priori–A Posteriori

Kant first places himself on empiricist grounds as if this were the most natural thing in the world. He follows Locke's criticism of Descartes' introduction of innate ideas and asserts that at least temporally, "all our knowledge begins with experience" (B 1). Of course, even rationalists such as Leibniz or Wolff would have had few qualms about saying, with Kant, that no knowledge is possible without "objects affecting our senses and partly of themselves producing representations, partly arousing the activity of our understanding" (ibid.). But the temporal beginning—Locke overlooks this fact (cf. XVIII 14)—is not necessarily the substantive origin; it does not follow from the temporal priority of experience that there is no source of knowledge other than experience. Empiricism, which asserts exclusiveness, thus makes an inadmissible generalization. According to Kant, the conjecture (hypothesis) "that even our empirical knowledge is made up of what we receive through impressions and of what our own faculty of knowledge (sensible impressions serving merely as the occasion) supplies from itself" (B 1) is likewise compatible with the temporal priority of experience and thus worthy of closer investigation. With this conjecture Kant chooses a route midway between Locke's empiricism and Descartes' rationalism.

Kant calls knowledge originating in experience *a posteriori* ("from the later," because justified by sensible impressions) and knowledge which is independent of all impressions of the senses *a priori* ("from the earlier," because the justification is free from all experience). In accord with his criticism of empiricism and with his project of presenting knowledge from pure reason, Kant is interested in knowledge which is purely *a priori*, since in it "there is no admixture of anything empirical"; such knowledge is not only "independent of this or that experience, but ... absolutely independent of all experience" (B 3).

In order to distinguish pure *a priori* knowledge from empirical knowledge, Kant cites two characteristics which Plato and Aristotle (e.g., *Prior Analytics*, chap. I 2) introduced to distinguish real knowledge (*episteme*: science) from mere opinion (*doxa*): strict necessity, according to which something cannot be other than it is, and unrestricted universality, on which "no exception is allowed as possible" (B 4). Since experience demonstrates only facts but neither the impossibility of their being otherwise nor the impossibility of an exception, unrestricted universality and strict necessity are indeed the hallmarks of the pure *a priori*.

Analytic–Synthetic

The first pair of concepts "*a priori—a posteriori*" divides knowledge according to its origin in reason or in experience. The second pair of concepts "analytic—synthetic" has to do with the criteria for the truth of a judgment: "Does the justification for the connection of the subject with the predicate lie in the subject or outside of it?" Although many of Kant's explanatory remarks can lead to a psychological misunderstanding, Kant conceives "judgment" not (psychologically) as the making of judgments but rather (logically) as a proposition or assertion, as the sort of connection (synthesis) of representations which can claim to objective validity. Kant sees judgments as being expressed in sentences composed of subject and predicate; the definition of analytic and synthetic judgments presupposes such a sentence structure. Since there are judgments which do not have a subject-predicate structure, Kant's definition certainly needs to be expanded.

Kant designates all judgments as *analytic* whose predicates are already included in the concept of the subject (B 10). He thus considers the claim that all bodies are extended to be analytically true because one can ascertain that the subject "body" contains within itself the predicate "extended" independently of all experience by mere analysis of the subject. The concepts of the subject and the predicate alone, along with the law of contradiction (B 12), which Kant views as the principle of all formal logic (cf. B 189ff.), decide the truth of analytic propositions. According to Leibniz analytic propositions are true in all possible worlds; according to Kant their negation contains a contradiction. Both explanations, say M. G. White and W. V. O. Quine, give no further help since the concepts of a possible world and of a self-contradiction themselves require explanation. This criticism, however, has not remained uncontested.

"Analytically true" is for Kant not identical in meaning to "true by definition" since Kant considers exact and complete definition to be a more restrictive condition; analytic judgments may be composed of concepts with whose exact and complete definitions we are not (yet) familiar. Analytic judgments can definitely deal with objects belonging to the empirical world and can assert, for example, that every palomino is tan, that no bachelor is married, or—with Kant (B 192)—that an unlearned person is not learned. But the truth of the asserted state of affairs is determined not by experience but solely with the help of elementary logical laws under the assumption of the semantic rules of the language in which the assertion is formulated. Although semantic rules describe empirical facts and can change, analytic judgments are according to Kant necessarily true. For analyticity relates not to the semantic rules but—given the semantic rules—only to the relationship between the concepts of the subject and the predicate. If the semantic rules change and, say, "palomino" no longer means "tan horse," then we would have a different judgment, which is despite the identical wording no longer analytic.

All non-analytic judgments are *synthetic*: thus all assertions are synthetic whose truth (presupposing the semantic rules of the language) cannot be determined only with the help of the law of contradiction or more generally with the aid of the rules of logic. In analytic judgments the subject is only explicated by the predicate. Synthetic judgments, by contrast, expand our knowledge about the subject.

The twofold distinction "analytic–synthetic" and "*a priori–a posteriori*" yields four possibilities of combination: (1) analytic *a priori* judgments, (2) analytic *a posteriori* judgments, (3) synthetic *a priori* judgments and (4) synthetic *a posteriori* judgments. Of these, two, namely (1) and (4), are unproblematic, while a third possibility, (2), does not apply. The very notion of analytic judgments makes them valid *a priori* (1). There thus cannot be analytic *a posteriori* judgments (2). That the expansion ("synthetic") of human knowledge occurs through experience, is familiar to us and presents no difficulties. Empirical judgments (4) are as a whole synthetic (B 11): experience provides their legitimation.

In contrast to analytic *a posteriori* judgments, synthetic *a priori* judgments (3) are conceptually possible. Whether or not the conceptual possibility can also be realized and there actually are synthetic judgments *a priori*, that is, an expansion of knowledge prior to experience—this question decides the possibility of metaphysics as a science. For in constrast to logic, metaphysics is supposed to expand human knowledge; its assertions are synthetic. Since metaphysics consists in knowledge from pure reason, it lacks experience for its legitimation; its judgments are valid *a priori*. The basic question of the *Critique of Pure Reason* is thus: "How are synthetic *a priori* judgments possible?" This is also the "fateful question" of philosophy. Whether or not philosophy has its own object of investigation and there can be genuine philosophical knowledge different from the analytic and empirical sciences depends on the answer to this question.

At first glance synthetic knowledge free of experience seems unusual, and thus the chances of an autonomous philosophy poor. But the chances improve significantly if not only in metaphysics but in all theoretical sciences, as Kant says, synthetic *a priori* judgments occur. For then metaphysical knowledge does not depart from the "continuum of the sciences." In its early stages, logical empiricism (Schlick, Carnap, Reichenbach) will claim that the very concept of synthetic knowledge *a priori* is nonsense, since logic and experience are the only sources of knowledge. But this school later admits that the empirical sciences contain propositions, namely those expressing laws, which can at most be confirmed or refuted by experience but not justified.

According to Kant the synthetic *a priori* character of geometry and of mathematics in general derives primarily from their basic principles—for example, that a straight line is the shortest distance between two points (B 16). Even if mathematical theorems can be derived in a purely logical manner from the basic principles and thus appear analytic, they are still only valid under the assumptionof synthetic principles. Kant thus says, *"All mathematical judgments are synthetic"* (B 14). In the case of the science of nature (physics), only its basic principles have synthetic *a priori* character. As examples, Kant cites from classical physics: the principle of the conservation of matter and the principle of the equality of action and reaction, the third Newtonian axiom (B 17f.).

Since mathematics and the science of nature owe their objective validity to elements free of experience, the basic question of the *Critique* as to the possibility of synthetic judgments *a priori* branches off into two constituents: (1) How is pure mathematics possible, and (2) how is a pure science of nature possible? In addition the central question remains: (3) How is metaphysics possible as a science? Kant answers the first two questions in the Transcendental Aesthetic and the Transcendental Analytic. The first part of the *Critique* thus provides a theory of science for mathematics and for the science of nature, albeit not an empirical-analytical theory but one based on a critique of reason. Moreover, the *Critique* develops a theory of the non-philosophical sciences exclusively for mathematics and the mathematical science of nature. For according to Kant they are the sole indisputable examples of objective knowledge. The historical, literary and social sciences are ignored. This is due not only to the fact that they were not very developed in Kant's lifetime. Kant has a very strict notion of science, which does not include everything designated as science today. For a "genuine science," certainty is apodeictic (necessary); "Knowledge which can contain only empirical certainty is only erroneously called *knowledge*" (*MOS*, IV 468). In the *Critique*, Kant claims that the real world, which we, distinguishing it from all apparent or subjective worlds, call objective, coincides with the world of mathematics and of the mathematical science of nature.

One of the decisive reasons for the victorious emergence and continued success of the *Critique of Pure Reason* doubtless lies in this twofold circumstance: First, Kant not only recognizes the epistemological primacy of mathematics and the mathematical science of nature but also explains it philosophically. Second, he discovers in the course of explanation even for mathematics and physics elements and assumptions which do not stem from scientific research within the limits of the relevant discipline but which research instead always presupposes. Thus the secular task posed to philosophy by the emergence of the mathematical science of nature finds a solution fair to both sides: to the obsession for research in the autonomous specialized sciences, which reject all philosophical fixation, and to the metaphysical legacy of philosophy, due to which Western intellectual history from the Greeks on has been shaped by the claim to "eternal truths."

The philosophical justification of autonomous scientific research is not, however, for Kant an end in itself. Mathematicians, natural scientists and exponents of the theory of science who study the *Critique of Pure Reason* often overlook the fact that Kant really wants to know how metaphysics—hence the third and central question—is possible as a science. The investigation of the synthetic *a priori* elements of mathematics and of the pure science of nature provides the basis for an answer to this question. The conditions allowing the sole indisputable objectivity—that of mathematics and the science of nature—determine whether or not there can also be objective knowledge outside of all experience, whether or not metaphysics can exist as a science. In the second part of the *Critique*, the Transcendental Dialectic, Kant takes up this question. Here, too, he attends to a "reality"—"metaphysics as a natural capacity"—which, however, tends toward self-deception as to the range of knowledge. Human reason believes that it can know objects beyond all experience objectively. But all attempts to answer the "natural questions" as to the beginning of the world, the existence of God, and so on entangle reason in contradictions. These can only be resolved if one accepts as a result of the Copernican revolution the separation of appearance and thing in itself, and if one restricts objective knowledge to the range of possible experience.

3.4 DOES MATHEMATICS CONTAIN SYNTHETIC JUDGMENTS *A PRIORI*?

Leibniz already believed that mathematics could be founded solely on definitions and on the principle of contradiction (*Nouveaux essais sur l'entendement humain* [New Essays on Human Understanding], book 4 chap. 7), thus that it is analytic. In more recent work, criticism of the synthetic *a priori* character of mathematics has become commonplace. Most prominently, the mathematician and philosopher Gottlob Frege (1848–1925) and the mathematician David Hilbert (1862–1943) have advocated the analytic character of mathematics— Frege with the demonstration that the notion of number and with it the basic concepts of arithmetic can be defined by purely logical means (*Foundations of Arithmetic*, 1884), Hilbert by axiomatizing arithmetic and geometry. By way of the *Principia Mathematica* of the philosophers and mathematicians A. N. Whitehead (1861–1947) and B. Russell (1872–1970) as well as the work of the philosopher Rudolf Carnap (1891–1970), the thesis of the analytic character of mathematics found entry into analytical philosophy, and it has since remained essentially uncontested.

On the other hand, in light of the development of non-Euclidean geometries and their application in the general theory of relativity, Albert Einstein (1879–1955) claimed that even the axioms of geometry are empirical propositions, while the physicist Henri Poincaré (1854–1912) considers them conventions. In both cases the axioms lose their *a priori* character. Mathematicians and philosophers thus contest the synthetic character of mathematics, natural scientists its *a priori* character.

Despite all appearances, both positions can be reconciled. One must simply distinguish between mathematical (pure) and physical (applied) geometry. Then mathematical geometry can be valid *a priori*, but only because it is analytic. Physical geometry, however, becomes an empirically testable system of hypotheses concerning the properties of physical space. It is to be considered synthetic, but only because it is based on experience, thus not *a priori*. Both mathematical and physical geometry lose the status of synthetic *a priori* knowledge; so Kant's opposite opinion today seems completely wrong.

Since Kant deals with pure mathematics, the thesis of the empirical nature of applied geometry need not disturb him. But the assertion of the analytic nature of pure mathematics is not so uncontroversially clear as analytic philosophy assumed for a long time. Two influential mathematical schools dispute this assertion: the intuitionist school of the Dutchman L. E. J. Brouwer (1881–1966) and the constructivist (operative) view of Paul Lorenzen (*Einführung in die operative Logik und Mathematik* [Introduction to Operative Logic and Mathematics], 1955) or of E. Bishop (*The Foundations of Constructive Mathematics*, 1967). Even among philosophers who identify with analytic thinking such as J. Hintikka, before him E. W. Beth and, subsequent to both, Gordon G. Brittan (1978, chap. 2–3), the analytic character of mathematics is viewed skeptically. Hintikka's main argument runs as follows: Intuitive figures and individual representations belong to mathematics. Neither belongs to logic, so mathematics is not entirely analytic. According to K. Lambert and C. Parsons (cf. Brittan 1978, 56ff.) assertions of existence are to be found among the axioms of geometry (e.g., "There are at least two points"); no assertions of existence count among the logical truths, which are according to Leibniz true in all possible worlds; the assertions of existence in mathematics are not valid in "all possible" but only in all "really possible" worlds.

According to Brittan 1978, 69ff.), the analyticity of pure geometry can be understood in three ways, but in none of these senses is it convincing. In one sense one can consider pure geometry analytic because the opposite of geometric propositions would be self-contradictory. This is not, however, the case since for example the parallel postulate can be disputed, thus invalidating the propositions of Euclidean geometry; a new, non-Euclidean geometry is established. (There are also two distinct set theories, each of which is internally consistent.) In a second sense pure geometry is analytic because its propositions can be derived with the help of definitions and logic alone. Geometry thus becomes a body of purely logical truths and must hold in all possible worlds. This is not in fact the case for Euclidean geometry. In other words: If the theorems of geometry were true on the basis of logic alone, they would be true under all interpretations. In reality geometrical theorems appear true under some interpretations and false under others. Finally, one can view pure geometry as a set of uninterpreted sentences, and thus not speak of points, lines and planes but of Ps, Ss, Bs, and so forth—that is, of elementary concepts of an axiomatic theory (in Hilbert's sense). A proposition holds analytically because it is uninterpreted, thus "empty" and "without content," and mathematical geometry becomes an analytical science since it makes no assertions of fact. Brittan counters that here a distinction, namely that between uninterpreted and interpreted sentences, is erroneously taken for an argument. More forceful is the objection that uninterpreted sentences do not yet constitute a geometry since they have nothing to do with spatial concepts and relations. Only the spatial interpretation (first-level interpretation) of the axioms makes a geometry out of the set of uninterpreted sentences, while the interpretation (second level) of mathematical geometry leads to physical geometry.

Considering these arguments, there are thus even after Frege, Hilbert and Russell good reasons to view mathematics as a non-analytic science and pure mathematics as synthetic *a priori* knowledge. (Kant's own arguments follow in chapter 4.)

If one nonetheless holds pure mathematics to be analytic, what implications does this have for the *Critique of Pure Reason*? For Kant, the thesis of the synthetic *a priori* character of mathematics has a twofold significance. *For one thing*, by associating a problematic science with recognized sciences, it is supposed to support the critique of reason as a theory of metaphysics. In order to allay doubts about metaphysics Kant shows that at least the propositional form of this science is beyond all doubt. This propositional form is also found in mathematics, the scientific status of which practically no one since antiquity has called into question. This allusion can allay doubts as to the possibility of a scientific metaphysics but cannot guarantee its scientific status. Vice versa, scientific metaphysics could be possible even if elsewhere no synthetic *a priori* knowledge should be found. The answer to the central question of the first *Critique*, whether or not a scientific metaphysics is possible, therefore does not depend upon the synthetic *a priori* character of mathematics.

Secondly, the thesis of the synthetic *a priori* character of mathematics supports the critique of reason as a theory of objective knowledge since it provides a reason to look for *a priori* presuppositions of all knowledge. If objective knowledge is synthetic and *a priori*, its presuppositions must be all the more so. But since the presuppositions lie deeper than the knowledge, Kant could be right in claiming synthetic presuppositions even if on the level of the *theory of science*, his assumption as to the nature of mathematical knowledge does not hold.

3.5 THE CONCEPT OF THE TRANSCENDENTAL

Kant calls the investigation with which he answers the threefold question as to the possibility of synthetic judgments *a priori* "transcendental." This central concept for the critique of reason has been subjected to "in part horrible misinterpretations" (Vaihinger 1976, I 467). Just like "transcendent" and "transcendence," "transcendental" comes from the Latin verb *transcendere*, which means literally "to go beyond a limit." While "transcendent/transcendence" can point to a world beyond our realm of experience, Kant rejects the notion that the "next world," the supra-sensible world, is an objective entity about which we could in theory have valid knowledge. Kant's transcendental investigation, of course, also goes beyond experience. But in the opposite direction. Kant—at least at first—turns backward, not forward. In the theoretical sphere he does not look "in the far distance" or "airy heights" for a "hereafter" beyond experience, ridiculed by Nietzsche as the object of traditional philosophy. Kant wants to illuminate the conditions of experience which lie *before* it. The origin of our objective knowledge of our world takes the place of knowledge of another world. Kant examines the pre-empirical deep structure of all experience, which he—in accord with the experiment of the Copernican revolution—conjectures to be in the subject. In its reflective "descent," the critique of reason seeks the *a priori* elements constituting theoretical subjectivity.

Due to Kant the notion "transcendental" has become such a commonplace that one no longer asks about its origins. As early as the end of the eighteenth century, it is claimed that the notion was introduced by Kant. In fact, even medieval philosophy makes use of it. Medieval philosophy takes as transcendentals, or *transcendentia*, those ultimate determinations of being which transcend its division into species and genera and are valid for everything existing. That which we presuppose when we conceive being has transcendental character: *ens*, the being of being; *res*, what-ness or objectivity; *unum*, unity and inner inseparability; *verum*, knowability and relatedness to the mind; *bonum*, value and desirability.

Before Kant, there existed not only the "transcendental philosophy of the ancients" (B 113), with which Kant was not well acquainted. The metaphysicians of the seventeenth and eighteenth centuries, particularly Wolff and Baumgarten, likewise use the term "transcendental." Wolff utilizes the expression both in its traditional, primarily ontological sense and, in connection with his "cosmologia transcendentalis," in a new, more epistemological meaning. For Baumgarten, whose metaphysics Kant constantly discusses in his lectures, "transcendental" means roughly the same thing as "necessary" or "essential"; in his case one can hardly speak of a *transcendere* in any sense at all (Hinske 1968, 107). It is not one of Kant's least achievements that after a long clarification process, he restores the dimension of going beyond to the eroded concept and at the same time gives it a new aspect on the basis of his own theoretical concerns. Despite certain fluctuations, which are not surprising for a concept with such a long tradition, the eroded notion of the transcendental regains with Kant the clarity of a philosophical concept. In accord with the Copernican turn, the Kantian concept combines the ontological with the epistemological meaning.

In the introduction to the *Critique* Kant calls "*transcendental* all knowledge which is occupied not so much with objects (as with our *a priori* concepts of objects in general— A 11f.) as with the mode of our knowledge of objects in so far as this mode of knowledge is to be possible *a priori*" (B 25). Transcendental knowledge is a theory of the possibility of *a priori* knowledge, in short: a "*theory of the a priori*" (Vaihinger 1976, I 467). That does not mean, as Kant later explains, that all *a priori* knowledge is transcendental. Mathematics and the science of nature are according to Kant bodies of *a priori* knowledge or contain such elements. "Transcendental" refers in the *Critique* only to that knowledge "by which we know that—and how—certain representations (intuitions or concepts) can be employed or are possible purely *a priori*" (B 80).

"That and how" refers to the twofold task of transcendental knowledge. Such knowledge demonstrates first that certain representations "are not of empirical origin" (B 81) and shows secondly "the possibility that they can yet relate *a priori* to objects of experience" (ibid.). Due to the first requirement, no empirical prerequisite of human knowledge, however important it may be, belongs to the domain of transcendental philosophy; only non-empirical knowledge of experience is transcendental. Due to the second requirement, the propositions of mathematics and the science of nature are an object but not a part of transcendental theory. "Transcendental" are those presuppositions which are neither mathematical nor physical in character but are nonetheless always "at work" when we do mathematics or physics.

An interpretation which ignores the twofold task of transcendental investigation misses the central thought of the *Critique*. A system of thought which does not recognize this task cannot be described as transcendental in Kant's sense. Because of the double specification, the Transcendental Aesthetic (in the second edition) and the Transcendental Analytic of Concepts are divided into two main parts. In connection with a "metaphysical" discussion or deduction, *a priori* representations are sought in the subject; then the "transcendental" discussion or deduction in the stricter sense shows why *a priori* representations are indispensable for objective knowledge.

Insight into the presuppositions of all knowledge of objects which are independent of experience does not increase our knowledge of objects. The Transcendental Critique hence does not compete with the specialized sciences nor with the proto-sciences and theories of science. The specialized sciences seek to know their specific object; the proto-sciences introduce the requisite concepts; theories of science illuminate methods and conceptual development. By way of contrast, the Transcendental Critique asks whether or not the endeavor of the specialized sciences to seek knowledge of specific objects and to subject hypotheses to constant attempts at refutation can be seen as meaningful because it is in principle possible to carry out such an endeavor. The *Critique* turns away from the usual line of questioning, which asks which (systems of) propositions are true and which are false, and asks whether or not and how there can be an objective, true reference to objects. It investigates how true knowledge of objects, understood as universal and necessary commitment, can be conceived without contradictions and paradoxes.

In a transcendental sense, Kant's *Critique* contains a "logic of truth" (B 87). It looks neither (semantically) for the meaning of "truth" nor (pragmatically) for the criterion by which to decide which (systems of) propositions are true. The first part of the *Critique* deals more radically with the basic possibility of truth and with the question what genuine objects, about which true statements can be made, actually are. In dealing with this question, Kant takes up the traditional definition of truth as the correspondence of thought with its object; however, in accord with the Copernican revolution, he shows that the object is nothing in itself independent of the subject but that it is constituted only through the *a priori* conditions of the subject of knowledge.

This insight into the pre-empirical conditions of objective knowledge entails an insight into the bounds of knowledge. To this extent the utility of the critique of reason is "in speculation . . . properly . . . only negative." The *Critique* serves "not to extend, but only to clarify our reason" (B 25).

Although Kant in his pre-Critical period made several notable contributions to natural science (sect. 1.2), the *Critique* no longer seeks to expand the knowledge of natural science. This does not mean, though, as is repeatedly argued, that the *Critique* is "in the end of no consequence." It indeed does not directly promote our knowledge of objects but rather our knowledge concerning the knowledge of objects. Nonetheless, it can, in connection with discussions about foundations, acquire indirect significance for the specialized sciences. Moreover, second-order knowledge is gained through transcendental reflection; science becomes transparent for itself and understands itself as rational.

The claim of objective knowledge belongs to the idea of science. This claim is dismissed as unjustified by skeptics from antiquity up to David Hume; they maintain that there is no objective (universally valid and necessary) knowledge. In this situation the Transcendental Critique views the claim to objectivity as something conditioned, as a consequence for whose condition or legitimation the *Critique* is looking. If the search is successful, the claim to objective knowledge can be considered justified in two respects. The legitimating foundation of knowledge (according to Kant the pure forms of intuition, the pure concepts and principles) shows first that objective knowledge is possible and second what it consists in. Apart from many obscurities, perhaps even contradictions, Kant does not proceed from mathematics and natural science as irrefutable facts, as has been claimed in Neo-Kantianism. This would indeed be a dogmatic assumption irreconcilable with the idea of a critique of reason. Kant starts instead with the hypothesis that science or objective knowledge is universally valid and necessary. Then, in agreement with the skeptics, he asks whether there can possibly be such a thing. His answer has two aspects: First, because of pure intuitions, concepts and principles, universally valid and necessary knowledge is possible but, second, only in the form of mathematics and physics (natural science). In short, the scientific nature of mathematics and physics is not a premise but a conclusion, not a presupposition but instead that which is to be proved.

In the context of this project, "objectivity" has two interrelated meanings. For one thing, (in the sense of truth) "objectivity" designates the act of knowing the real world, hence of being valid not only for a particular subject but rather intersubjectively, more precisely: universally and necessarily valid. Secondly, (in the referential sense) "objectivity" means the reference of knowledge to real objects, to genuine facts and not to fictions and mere figments of the imagination. The first meaning presupposes the second. Objective knowledge can only make objective assertions because in such knowledge actual facts (objects) are known. Since this meaning is more fundamental, Kant is interested primarily in it.

4.

The Transcendental Aesthetic

⋘⋘⋘⋘⋘⋘

The Transcendental Aesthetic of the first *Critique* is not a theory of the beautiful or of taste (on these matters sect. 12.2) but rather a science dealing with the *a priori* principles of sensibility or intuition (*aisthesis*). As a part of the Transcendental Critique it does not investigate all intuition but only its pure forms, space and time, as sources of knowledge. Hence, Kant should not be blamed for failing to discuss certain problems of a general theory of intuition. We have no reason to expect a discussion of all problems.

In its definitive form, the Transcendental Aesthetic contains two distinct parts. In the metaphysical discussion, Kant shows that space and time are pure forms of intuition; in the transcendental discussion, that they make synthetic *a priori* knowledge possible. The Transcendental Aesthetic thus offers on the one hand a new solution to the dispute of modern philosophy concerning the "essence" of space and time, and it contains on the other hand Kant's first step in laying the foundation for mathematics and natural science.

The possibility of *a priori* knowledge through universal concepts of the understanding has been repeatedly asserted before and after Kant. The thesis, however, that elements free of experience belong to intuition, and thus to sensibility, and that these elements are indispensable for mathematics and physics, is due to Kant alone. Regardless of all the problems it brings up (cf. Vaihinger 1976, II), the Transcendental Aesthetic hence comprises one of the most original parts of the first critique of reason.

4.1 THE TWO STEMS OF KNOWLEDGE:
SENSIBILITY AND UNDERSTANDING

Following Baumgarten, Kant distinguishes the lower from the higher faculty of knowledge, sensibility from understanding (occasionally reason, too) in a broad sense. Parallel to the threefold division of traditional logic, the higher faculty of knowledge is divided into understanding in the strict sense ("concepts"), judgment ("judgments") and reason in the strict sense ("inferences") (cf. B 169). The *Critique of Pure Reason* is divided accordingly. After the "overture" (preface and introduction), it begins with (1) the theory of sensibility in the Transcendental Aesthetic; within the Transcendental Analytic (2) the Analytic of Concepts and (3) the Analytic of Principles follow; the *Critique* closes with (4) the theory of inferences (on the part of reason) in the Transcendental Dialectic and (5) a Transcendental Doctrine of Method.

The Transcendental Aesthetic assumes that knowledge—viewed logically, not psychologically—is due to the interaction of two stems of knowledge, sensibility and understanding. Both faculties have equal standing and are reciprocally dependent upon one another.

(1) The direct reference of knowledge to objects and the point of orientation for all thought is intuition, which directly grasps a particular. Intuition entails that an object is given. The only possibility for objects to be given to man lies in receptive sensibility, the capacity of the mind to be affected by objects. Hence we can see, hear, smell, taste and feel. (Kant discusses sensibility and the five senses more extensively in the first book of his *Anthropology from a Pragmatic Point of View*.) Only receptive sensibility enables man to have intuitions. Man is barred from active, spontaneous and intellectual intuition, from creative observation. The effect of an object on the mind is called sensation; it comprises the material for sensibility. Without the formative understanding, the object of sensibility is indeterminate but determinable; it comprises the material for knowledge. Sensibility as the requisite basis for knowledge indicates the finitude of all human knowledge. Man cannot on his own produce the objects of knowledge and place them before him as God's infinite reason does. He relies upon objects given to him. In the insight that the pure concepts of our understanding also rely upon sensibility, that one hence can know nothing without the senses, lies the discovery which leads Kant from his pre-Critical position to the *Critique*.

(2) Merely taking in what is given does not yield knowledge, in which sensations are not simply replicated but processed. For knowledge we thus need concepts which originate in the understanding in the strict sense and with the help of which sensations can be "thought": brought together and ordered according to rules.

Kant did not justify the assumption "that there are two stems of human knowledge" (B 29). He only suspects that sensibility and understanding "perhaps spring from a common, but to us unknown, root" (ibid.). The lack of a further derivation corresponds to the intention of Kant's critique of reason, which does not wish to provide an "ultimate" justification of knowledge as do Descartes, German Idealism or Husserl. It also shows that a critique of reason is not the last word in philosophy. Kant's initial thesis does, however, receive indirect justification through its success in solving the most important task: It avoids the difficulties of empiricism and rationalism by taking a new, intermediary position. But the specification of sensation as an "effect" of the object creates internal difficulties in the *Critique*, which in the opinion of F. H. Jacobi, Fichte and Schelling cannot be resolved without going beyond it.

In recognizing sensibility, Kant assents to the basic empiricist idea that human knowledge relies upon something given; he thereby rejects pure rationalism. With his insight as to the necessity of the understanding, Kant assents to the rationalist view that without thought no knowledge is possible; he thereby criticizes pure empiricism. In modern terms: Kant argues against a strict separation of observational and theoretical language since theoretical (conceptual) elements are already contained in all knowledge, even in everyday knowledge: "Without sensibility no object would be given to us, without understanding no object would be thought. Thoughts without content are empty, intuitions without concepts are blind." (B 75; cf. B 33).

In distinguishing two mutually dependent stems of knowledge, Kant rejects Leibniz's notion of a merely gradual distinction between sensibility and understanding. In contrast to Leibniz, he does not take intuition to be imperfect thought, lacking in clarity. In truth, Kant says, intuition has a different origin; it stems from sensibility, a source independent of the understanding and indispensable for all knowledge. According to Kant, the misconstrual of this state of affairs constitutes the foundation for Leibnizian metaphysics, and the illumination of this misconstrual the refutation of the latter.

(3) In the second part of the Transcendental Analytic, Kant investigates an additional faculty of knowledge: judgment, the capacity to subsume things under rules (concepts of the understanding).

For all three faculties, which are indispensable for human knowledge, Kant encounters elements free of experience: for sensibility the pure forms of intuition, space and time; for the understanding the pure concepts of the understanding, the categories; for judgment the transcendental schemata and the principles of pure understanding (table 4.1).

Table 4.1 The Three Faculties of Knowledge

Sensibility	*Understanding*
The object is *given* by means of an *affection* upon the mind.	The object, an indeterminate manifold of intuition, is *thought*, i.e. *determined*.
The capacity of the mind to be affected is called *sensibility* (receptivity). The effect of the object, the material of sensibility, is called *sensation*.	The capacity to determine an object, i.e. to create representations of one's own accord (spontaneously), is called *understanding*, the faculty of concepts (rules).
The pure forms of intuition are *space* and *time*.	The pure concepts of the understanding are the *categories*.
The relation to an object by means of sensation is called *empirical* (*a posteriori*).	The relation to an object by means of the categories of the understanding is called *pure* (*a priori*).

Judgment

Judgment is the faculty of subsuming under rules, i.e. of discerning whether or not something falls under a given rule. The conditions of the possibility of applying pure concepts of the understanding to appearances are transcendental specifications of time: they are both conceptual and sensible: the *transcendental schemata*, a transcendental product of imagination .

A modification of temporal intuition corresponds to each category. For example, the schema of substance is permanence in time; the schema of necessity the permanence of an object at all times.

Synthetic judgments which "flow" *a priori* from the pure concepts of the understanding under the conditions of the schemata and upon which all other *a priori* knowledge rests are *principles of the pure understanding*: for analytic judgments the law of contradiction, for synthetic judgments the axioms of intuition, the anticipations of perception, the analogies of experience (e.g., the principle of causality) and the postulates of empirical thought.

4.2 THE METAPHYSICAL DISCUSSION: SPACE AND TIME AS *A PRIORI* FORMS OF INTUITION

The metaphysical discussion of space and time follows a two-stage process of abstraction (B 36), which, beginning with knowledge as a whole, first isolates intuition from the contribution of the understanding and then sets aside everything in intuition which belongs to sensation—colors, sounds, sensations of warmth, and so on. What is left are those forms of intuition which are independent of experience, the original representations of space and time. The discussion is metaphysical since it establishes the original representations of space and time, spatiality and temporality, as intuitions given *a priori* (cf. B 38). It shows first that we are dealing with *a priori* representations, which, secondly, are not conceptual but rather intuitive in character.

When we think of space, we think not only of intuitive space (the spatial relationships of intuitions), which underlies our experience with objects and plays an important role in natural science. We also think of the space in which various activities and experiences occur. We similarly distinguish intuitive time (the temporal order of intuitions in general) from the duration of particular actions and from the subjective experience of time (as passing by quickly or slowly, for example). The Transcendental Aesthetic deals exclusively with intuitive space—with such relations as being outside of or contiguous to something—and with intuitive time—with such relations as after and at the same time. Kant claims only of these items that they have a component independent of experience.

Space and time belong to two distinct realms. Space is the intuitive form of outer sense, which with the aid of the five senses provides us with aural, visual, olfactory, . . . impressions, whereas time belongs to inner sense with its representations and desires, emotions and moods. Inner sense has priority, for every representation of outer sense is known by the subject, thus likewise a representation of inner sense. Time is therefore the form of all intuition, of inner intuition directly, and of outer indirectly. But the priority of time does not mean that space is a subspecies of time or that time can be substituted for space. For Heidegger, the priority of time is a reason to view the *Critique of Pure Reason* as a predecessor of his own Fundamental Ontology published under the title of *Being and Time*. Time does in fact play a far greater role in the *Critique* than space—in the Transcendental Deduction of the Categories and above all in the Schematism, with which

Heidegger deals extensively (sect. 6.1). The priority of time is perhaps also the reason why time is treated before space in the inaugural dissertation of 1770.

Kant justifies the thesis that space and time are pure forms of intuition with two groups of two arguments. With the first two, he shows, in opposition to empiricism, that space and time are *a priori* representations; with the other two, that they are in contrast to rationalism not conceptual but intuitive in character. (In the case of time, an additional argument, placed in the middle, belongs substantively to the transcendental discussion; cf. B 48.)

According to the first, negative argument, space and time cannot stem from experience since every outer or inner intuition relies upon them. In order for me to be able to perceive a chair as "outside of myself" and "beside the table," I must presuppose—in addition to the representation of myself, the table and the chair—a representation of the external; I thus presuppose a space in which the chair, the table and my empirical self occupy a specific position in relationship to one another, without space being a property of the chair, the table or my empirical self. Among the properties of external perception we do find colors, forms and noises but not space. Mental activities similarly have certain qualities which we sense in temporal sequence without any of these sensations having the quality of time. A positive argument follows upon the negative one: Space and time are necessary representations. For we can indeed imagine space and time without objects or appearances, but we cannot imagine that there is no space or time. Even in the sensible realm there is something which one knows not only because of empirical perception but "in advance." Space and time are due to the *a priori* structure of the knowing subject.

Bennett raises against the *a priori* character of time the objection that one could also assume the contrary, a nontemporal world, without contradicting oneself, since the proposition, "All sense-data are temporal," is not analytic. Consistent with this objection, Bennett (1966, 49) thinks that temporality is not necessary but only that, although contingent, it cannot be thought away. According to Kant, though, whatever cannot be otherwise is to be considered necessary (B 3). This description holds for space and time as the pure forms of intuition for all human knowledge. For sensible intuition grasps individual objects, which in external perception can only be given as beside, behind or above other objects and in inner perception can only be given as before or after other inner states.

In the second pair of arguments, Kant derives first from the singularity and unity of space and time that they are not (discursive) concepts but instead intuitions. For concepts relate to independent instances—the concept of a table, for example, to all particular instances of tables—whereas there is only the whole of one single space and of one unified time, which encompass all subspaces and periods of time as dependent parts. The second argument demonstrates the intuitive nature of space on the basis of its infinite extent and the fact that a concept cannot include an infinite set of representations *within it* but only as falling *under it*.

4.3 THE TRANSCENDENTAL JUSTIFICATION OF GEOMETRY

Kant appends an extremely brief transcendental discussion to the "metaphysical" proof that space and time are pure forms of intuition. The transcendental discussion is supposed to show that space and time are not mere representations ("figments of thought") but that they are constitutive for objects; space and time make objects of synthetic *a priori* knowledge possible. Because space and time are forms of intuition free of experience, there can be a science independent of experience dealing with them: mathematics. The pure intuitive form of space makes geometry possible; time makes the *a priori* part of the general theory of motion (mechanics) possible, and according to the *Prolegomena* (§ 10; cf. *CPR*, B 182), due to counting, time also makes arithmetic possible. The Transcendental Aesthetic thus also contains a portion of the philosophical foundations of mathematics and physics. But aside from internal difficulties in his account, Kant does not develop a complete theory even for mathematics. On the one hand, Kant completes his justification of the objective validity of mathematics only with the Axioms of Intuition (sect. 6.3). On the other hand, the philosophy of mathematics includes far more than just its transcendental justification.

The transcendental discussion of space takes up the interpretation of geometry as a science which "determines the properties of space synthetically, and yet *a priori*" (B 40). The transcendental question is: What kind of representation must we have of space in order for such knowledge of it to be possible. Kant answers this question in three steps. First, space cannot be a concept but must be mere intuition, for synthetic propositions cannot be won from concepts alone. Second, it cannot be an empirical intuition since geometry would then not be *a priori* in character. With his third reason, Kant, to the detriment of argumentative clarity, switches from pure (mathematical) to applied (physical) geometry (similarly in *Prol.*, part 1): An outer intuition which precedes the objects and nonetheless determines them *a priori* is only possible if it stems from the subject and specifies the form of an outer intuition.

It follows from the three arguments that only the result of the metaphysical discussion of space as a subjective yet pure form of intuition makes it comprehensible that geometry is synthetic *a priori* knowledge. Because space is an *a priori* intuition, pure geometry is possible; because space is in addition the form which all empirical objects must, as our intuitions, take, applied geometry is possible.

In the course of the transcendental justification, Kant cites as an example of a necessary proposition of geometry, "Space has only three dimensions" (B 41). For natural intuition and Euclidean geometry, which alone was known in Kant's time, this proposition is correct. Later, however, non-Euclidean geometries were discovered, of which Riemannian geometry is utilized in the general theory of relativity. Euclidean geometry is hence neither in mathematics nor in physics universally valid, and Kant's Transcendental Aesthetic, which asserts their universal validity, appears to be hopelessly antiquated. Are Kant's critics right in seeing his theory of geometry only as an additional example for the way in which all "*a priori* knowledge," heralded by philosophers since Plato, is shattered by the progress of the sciences?

In order to avoid this fatal consequence, Bröcker has proposed a distinction between two kinds of space: (1) the intuitively given three-dimensional space of Euclid, with which even physics must begin and which he calls "transcendental space" and (2) empirical space, to which physicists proceed in the course of their experiences and into which they transcribe that which they have determined in transcendental space. With this distinction Bröcker reduces Kant's thesis of the singularity of Euclidean geometry to an exceptional transcendental status. Strawson (1973 277ff.) makes a similar attempt with the "phenomenal geometry" which he develops in defense of Kant against "positivist views."

The transcendental priority of Euclidean geometry accounts not only for our natural representation of space. It also explains the circumstance that even today three dimensional Euclidean geometry is viewed

THE TRANSCENDENTAL AESTHETIC

as mathematically possible and as empirically valid in the range of experience intermediate between atomic and astrophysics. Nonetheless, weighty reservations against an exceptional transcendental status arise. Neither in the metaphysical nor in the transcendental discussion does Kant justify the three dimensionality of space, and in his first treatise, *Thoughts on the True Estimation of Living Forces* (§§ 9–11), he considers non-Euclidean spaces to be possible. The *a priori* intuitive character, to which the transcendental discussion refers, is treated only for the basic form of all outer intuition in the metaphysical discussion—thus only for being outside of or beside, without any structural properties. This basic form is designated terminologically as "spatiality" or as "space in general." Mere spatiality is not yet the object of geometry. This object comes to be only by means of the objectification of spatiality; through imagination and by declaration the mathematician conceives the mere form of intuition as an object in its own right with certain structural characteristics, which he studies free from experience in the context of pure geometry. An unbridgeable difference exists between space as a transcendental condition and space as an object of geometry. Hence in the transcendental discussion, the three dimensions of space justifiably do not count as an argument in favor of the possibility of geometry. They are only an example for a purportedly apodeictic statement; they are the predicate of a geometrical, not of a transcendental proposition. Mathematical and physical propositions do not have transcendental significance, but only—on a deeper level—their conditions, which according to the Copernican revolution lie in the "constitution" of the knowing subject free of all experience. Due to their more fundamental lines of questioning, neither the metaphysical nor the transcendental discussion of space are bound to a certain geometry. The *Critique* remains neutral with respect to the later alternative "Euclidean or non-Euclidean geometry."

According to the most weighty objection to Kant, geometry is not a synthetic but instead an analytic science. To this objection one can reply, as mentioned above (sect. 3.4), that all geometry is a science of space and thus presupposes spatiality. Spatiality, however, as the metaphysical discussion shows, is the pure form of outer intuition. It stems neither from experience nor from mere concepts (definitions) and thus has synthetic *a priori* character. Therefore geometry, viewed from the perspective of its ultimate presupposition, spatiality, can be considered to be synthetic *a priori* knowledge even if one constructs geometry purely analytically (axiomatically)—which construction is controversial among mathematicians (sect. 3).

Because geometry investigates an object, space, which presupposes the pure form of intuition of outer sense, spatiality, it can have empirical content and provide the basis for theories of natural science concerning external objects. But because the Transcendental Aesthetic only justifies spatiality and not certain representations of space, it can demonstrate no virtue of Euclidean over non-Euclidean geometry nor can it declare a certain mathematical geometry to be the foundation for physical theories. We must thus distinguish three levels: (1) transcendental spatiality, (2) mathematical space, and (3) physical space. Each of the succeeding levels depends upon the preceding without being derivable from it. The propositions of mathematical geometries cannot be justified in transcendental philosophy; the geometrical framework of physical theories depends not only upon mathematical knowledge but in addition upon empirical knowledge; a judgment with regard to the alternative "classical (Newtonian) or relativistic (Einsteinian) view of space and time" is in any case not the job of a transcendental critique of reason.

The critical account of Kant's Transcendental Aesthetic outlined here has four consequences. *First*, it does not follow from the synthetic *a priori* character of the universal intuition of space that the specific spatial axioms of a geometry are synthetic and *a priori*. One could perhaps speak of the theorems of mathematics as synthetic and *a priori* in the weak sense that they are bound to a non-analytic presupposition, transcendental spatiality. The presupposition does not, however, figure as a premise within a certain geometrical argument but is the transcendental basis for any given geometry. It thus does not suffice as an argument for the characterization of a geometrical space and its axioms as synthetic and *a priori* in the strict sense of the theory of science. Second, pure (mathematical) geometry has the nature of knowledge only in a more restricted sense than Kant thought. It does not determine the structure of experienceable reality but offers various mathematically possible geometries, among which physics chooses, subject to the results of experience. Third, the Transcendental Aesthetic is bound to the results of contemporary mathematics and physics neither in the metaphysical nor in the transcendental discussion. Fourth, the transcendental justification of geometry and physics on the basis of the pure forms of intuition has no direct voice in controversies regarding the foundations of science. A critique of reason cannot make a decision with regard to axiomatic or constructivist mathematics nor a decision for or against relativistic physics. A transcendental theory is invariant with respect to many changes in mathematics or physics.

4.4 THE EMPIRICAL REALITY AND TRANSCEN- DENTAL IDEALITY OF SPACE AND TIME

The essence of space and time is highly controversial in modern metaphysics (for space cf. Heimsoeth 1966–71, I 93–124): Are they something objective and real or merely something subjective and ideal (Berkeley)? And if they are real, do they constitute substances (Descartes), or properties of divine substance (Spinoza), or rather a relation between finite substances (Leibniz)? The various theories lead to difficulties which Kant seeks to overcome with his novel solution: Space and time are something quite different from all other familiar entities; they are the *a priori* forms of our (human) outer intuition and inner sensing.

Because empirical knowledge is not possible without outer and inner sensations, and these are not possible without space and time, "empirical reality" is to be accorded to the pure forms of intuition (B 44 with B 52). In contrast to the "dogmatic idealism" of Berkeley (1684–1753), who according to Kant takes space together with all things as merely imaginary (B 274), space and time are for Kant objective: without them objects of outer and inner intuition, hence of objective knowledge, cannot exist. It does not follow, however, that space and time subsist in themselves and in the form of substances, properties or relations. On the contrary, they are the sole conditions under which objects can appear to us; they have, says Kant, "transcendental ideality" (B 44 with B 52). With this theory Kant rejects Newton's notion of space as God's infinite, uniform sensorium and thereby shows that he recognizes Newton's physics as a paradigm of exact science without uncritically accepting its philosophical presuppositions.

5.

The Analytic of Concepts

⸨⸨⸨⸨⸨⸨⸨⸨⸨⸨

5.1 THE IDEA OF A TRANSCENDENTAL LOGIC

The Analytic of Concepts makes up the first part of a new theory of thought (Greek: *logos),* Transcendental Logic. Modern philosophy from Bacon through Descartes to Leibniz and Lambert has consistently demanded a new logic, but the demand has remained essentially unfulfilled. Prior to Kant, only formal logic exists as a full-fledged science. It investigates thought solely on the basis of its form, without regard for content. Its appropriate manner of presentation is a formal language with concept variables (A, B, C, . . .) and logical symbols ($\land$, $\lor$, $\neg$ . . .) of the sort introduced in part by Aristotle. Formal logic, for example, (in syllogistic logic, Aristotle's two-place logic of relations) investigates the conditions under which from two sentences or parts of sentences (the premises) a third part (the conclusion) follows: "*If* mortality (A) attaches to all (a) human beings (B) and ($\land$) humanity to all Athenians (C), *then* necessarily ($\rightarrow$) mortality attaches to all Athenians" (AaB $\land$ BaC $\rightarrow$ AaC). Modern formal logic has extended the range of logical laws far beyond syllogisms. But it, too, investigates the connections between concepts and statements (or judgments, propositions) only in their implicational correctness, in abstraction "from all content of knowledge, that is, from all relation of knowledge to the object" (B 79).

Kant's Transcendental Logic develops a science for the contents of thought, too, and thus adds to formal logic a material logic likewise having *a priori* validity. Transcendental Logic examines in particular the way in which it is possible for the concepts of thought not to be empty but instead to relate to real objects. It thus does not treat the broad variety of specific contents; their study is the task of various specialized sciences. Transcendental Logic asks more basically how it is possible for human thought to relate to objects; it investigates the origin, extent and limits of empirical knowledge.

The division of the new logic follows that of traditional logic; Kant treats Transcendental Logic first analytically, then dialectically. The first division, the "Transcendental Analytic," is a "logic of truth" (B 87). In both of its parts, the "Analytic of Concepts" and the "Analytic of Principles," it discloses by means of analysis the subjective, *a priori* presuppositions which together with space and time, the forms of intuition, make the reference to objects in objective knowledge, and thus its truth, possible. The second division of Transcendental Logic comprises the "Transcendental Dialectic," which is to be dealt with extensively later (chapter 7). As a "*logic of illusion*" it shows how reason inevitably becomes entangled in contradictions as soon as it transcends the realm of possible experience.

5.2 EMPIRICAL AND PURE CONCEPTS (CATEGORIES)

Intuition provides us with a manifold of unstructured sensations: visual, aural and other sensible impressions spread out through space and time. In order for unstructured sensations to become something objective (a chair, for example), which is present in the same manner for everyone and about which one can communicate with others, one needs a rule. This rule is the concept of a chair, according to which sensations are combined into the unity of a bundle of sensation and the unity is then referred to as a certain form and structure. The concept of a chair specifies how something must be configured in order to be a chair and not a table or book. Through concepts, the material of intuition, which is taken in receptively, is formed into the unity and structure of a determinate object. Concepts effect both synthesis (connection) and determinacy.

The rules of synthesis and determinacy do not stem from sensations. Nor are they gained by mere combination. They are due to the spontaneity of the understanding, which "thinks up" rules in order to comprehend what is intuitively given, and checks whether what it thinks works as an interpretation of what is given. Thought is not subsequently directed toward a world which already exists in a structured form. Without thought there is only an unconnected, indeterminate something, a jumble of sensations but not the unity and determinacy of a reality; without thought there is not yet a world at all. On the other hand, thought has no direct contact with reality; it is discursive: transmitted by concepts, not intuitive: looking directly.

Since concepts are rules, they necessarily mean something general. Even the empirical concept of a chair does not pick out an individual, such as the chair in front of my desk, but designates any seat of the chair sort, regardless of how it is formed or of the material of which it is made. Nonetheless, empirical concepts rest in content upon experience and receive through the understanding, by means of comparison, reflection and abstraction, only the form of generality. Pure concepts of the understanding, however, say, the concept of causality, arise from the understanding in content, too (*Log.*, § 3). Only through them, Kant claims, is the unity and determinacy of a given intuition possible. Since the pure concepts of the understanding are no longer derived from more general concepts, Kant, following Aristotle, speaks of "categories."

In his *Categories* (chap. 4) Aristotle presents ten categories: substance, quantity, quality, relation, where, when, position, having, doing and being-affected. Kant praises Aristotle's achievement but reproaches him for picking the categories up "as they came his way"; he thereby takes up pure modes, and even an empirical mode of sensibility as well as derivative concepts, and he overlooks several pure concepts (B 107). This criticism assumes that Aristotle was looking for the same thing that Kant was, namely a table of pure concepts of the understanding. In fact, Aristotle has a more modest interest. Proceeding from an individual object, for instance, Socrates, he asks what forms of meaningful statements can be made: he is a man, so many years old, well-educated, older than Plato, and so forth. The categories designate the broadest classes of statements which can be attributed neither to one another nor to an additional, broader class. Aristotle gains them from an abstraction on observable linguistic behavior.

While Kant is the first to look for pure forms of intuition, the study of the fundamental concepts of the understanding belongs to the tasks of that philosophical discussion in the seventeenth and eighteenth century out of which the *Critique of Pure Reason* arises. Locke and Hume seek simple ideas, ultimate elementary concepts, which, however, due to their empiricist point of view, they do not attribute to pure

understanding. By way of contrast, Descartes and Leibniz believe—
their rationalist leaning—that the system of pure concepts of the
understanding, the simple ideas (Descartes) or the "alphabet of human
thoughts" (Leibniz), allow us to know things in themselves. Kant's discovery in this controversy is a position beyond empiricism and rationalism.

Kant, in presenting not only in intuition but also in thought original forms which are not due to experience but make experience possible, rejects empiricism. Wherever the manifold of sense impressions
given in intuition is brought into an objective, universal and necessary
unity, we are dealing with a unity corresponding to the categories;
without the categories objective knowledge is not possible. But it does
not follow that rationalism is right. For the categories depend upon the
combination of the sense impressions which present themselves in
space and time. Without these impressions there would not be anything to combine; so knowledge beyond the limits of experience is
impossible.

The Analytic of Concepts reaffirms the insight of the Transcendental Aesthetic that objects are constituted only due to advance *a priori* activities of the subject. Because the categories, like the pure forms
of intuition, are rooted in the knowing subject and not in the objects,
the access of man to *things in themselves* is permanently barred. Kant
does not thereby say, as a stubborn prejudice holds, that true reality is
hidden to average mortals behind a "veil of Maya" and that the essence
of things is revealed only to the philosopher. He asserts instead that all
human knowledge has the nature of appearance since it relies upon
subjective, albeit *a priori* elements. What the subject contributes to
knowledge on its own but independent of all experience—the pure
forms of intuition and the pure concepts—does not veil the truth. On
the contrary, it makes truth possible in the first place—the truth, however, of objects and states of affairs as they present themselves to us and
not as they are in themselves. In contrast to materialism, matter cannot
be referred to as a thing in itself. Even the most strict natural sciences
reside immutably in the realm of appearances.

The pure forms of intuition do not simply stand next to mathematical and empirical intuition; they are the conditions for their possibility. The categories likewise are not placed beside empirical
concepts but are always presupposed for the objective use of the latter.
The categories—this is what the Analytic of Concepts wishes to

prove—are the conditions originally seated in the subject without which no conceptual unity of a given intuition is possible. In analogous manner to the Transcendental Aesthetic, Kant reaches his goal through two progressive steps. These steps are likewise preceded by a process of abstraction isolating the thought factor from all other factors of knowledge. The first step, the Metaphysical Deduction, then shows how to find the pure concepts of the understanding and wherein they lie, while the second step, the Transcendental Deduction, explains how the categories—although they originate in the mere spontaneity of the understanding—can be at the same time subjective and still indispensable for the constitution of all objects, hence objectively valid.

5.3 THE METAPHYSICAL DEDUCTION OF THE CATEGORIES

Kant does not want to pick up the categories rhapsodically and "merely at random" *Letters*, 65/42) as Aristotle does; he derives them "systematically from a common principle" (B 106). He finds this principle in the forms of judgment. A category corresponds to each form of judgment. Formal logic provides a complete list of the forms of judgment. The "clue to the discovery of all pure concepts of the understanding" (the title of the metaphysical deduction of the categories) hence lies in the table of judgments supplied by formal logic. As to its specifics, the Deduction, which Kant undertakes in a somewhat roundabout way, can be reconstructed in four steps.

It must *first* be determined how the understanding fulfills its specific task. The particular combination (unity, synthesis) to be performed by the understanding in the face of an unconnected manifold occurs in judging. Subject-predicate sentences, for example, "all bodies are divisible" (B 93), make up the basic linguistic pattern. In such a judgment various representations—here the subject "bodies" and the predicate "divisible"—are bound together to a determinate unity, the divisibility of all bodies. Since the understanding undertakes the connection, it can, having been previously viewed only as the capacity to think, also be thought of as the "capacity to judge," and each concept is the predicate of possible judgments (B 94).

If *pure* concepts of the understanding are constitutive for experience, then there must be a connecting (judging) which is not due to experience but is still indispensable for it. One finds such a connection as soon as one disregards the contents of all concepts and concentrates exclusively on the form of the conceptual connection. Because the conceptual connection occurs in judgment, its form is none other than the form of judging. The connection which is independent of all experience yet directed to possible experience lies—the second step in the Metaphysical Deduction—in the forms of judgment freed of content. Since judging is due to the understanding, the mere form of judging, which disregards all content (empirical content as well), is an act of pure understanding. The pure concepts of the understanding, the categories, thus correspond exactly to the mere forms of judgment. Kant has now, even before the detailed enumeration of the categories, reached an important goal of the Metaphysical Deduction. He has shown how to discover the categories: with the help of the forms of judgment.

In accord with his systematic interest, Kant seeks a complete list of all forms of judgment, a so-called table of judgments, in order to obtain from it a similarly complete list of all categories, the table of categories. Kant extracts the table of judgments—the *third* step of the Metaphysical Deduction—from formal logic since the latter considers only the form of judgments irrespective of all content. Kant is of the opinion that there are exactly four points of view (classes) belonging to the form of judging (connecting) and that for each point of view there are exactly three forms of judgment—for a total of twelve. Each judgment falls under one of the three possibilities for all four classes of judgment and is hence determined in four ways with respect to its form.

A first point of view for the classification of judgments is *quantity*, the magnitude of knowledge. Universal, particular and singular judgments fall under this heading. On the second point of view, the *quality* or value of knowledge, there are affirmative, negative and—introduced here by Kant—infinite (limitative or restrictive) judgments. In formal logic, infinite judgments (e.g. "The soul is immortal") are part of the set of affirmative judgments. In transcendental logic, however, says Kant, they form a group of their own; for the subject (here, the soul) belongs to the infinite set of things to which the predicate (here, mortality) is not attributable, without the concept of the subject (the soul) thereby being "in the least increased, or determined in an affirmative manner" (B 98).

On the third point of view, the *relation* of knowledge, there are categorical, hypothetical ("if . . ., then . . .") and disjunctive ("either . . .

or . . .") judgments. The fourth point of view, *modality*, has a "quite special function" for Kant since it contributes nothing to the content of a judgment but has to do only with the value of the copula (is) in relationship to thinking (B 99f.; an antecedent of this exceptional characterization is to be found in Locke, *An Essay Concerning Human Understanding*, book IV, chap. 1). According to judgments of modality, the asserted state of affairs—for instance, the divisibility of all bodies—holds factually ("assertorically"), possibly ("problematically") or necessarily ("apodeictically").

The table of judgments as the principle of the Metaphysical Deduction has been criticized since the first discussions of Kant. According to the speculative criticism of Fichte and Hegel, the table of categories is not considered to be really justified or is even seen as dependent on the structure of the language in which Kant speaks—at least on the Indo-European language type, to which German belongs. Kant indeed presents the table of judgments as a a finished product, which he explains but does not further justify and which he essentially extracts from the formal logic of the age. The criticism of its being fortuitous is hence justified. It does not, however, disqualify the entire deduction but only its third step, although an important goal has already been reached with the second step. Moreover, to the claim that the table of judgments is dependent upon the historically determined structures of language, one could reply that even though not all natural languages make use of the complete system of logical forms, they cannot contain distinct logics which contradict one another; this argument is admittedly controversial. Finally, there are attempts toward a systematic reconstruction according to which Kant's table of judgments and thus also his table of categories is perhaps not without mistakes and certainly not unproblematic but still more well-founded than is often assumed (cf. Bröcker 1970, 42–48; Reich, 1932). But these attempts cannot disperse all objections (critical from the point of view of modern logic is, for example, Strawson 1973, 74–82).

In the *fourth* step of the Metaphysical Deduction Kant assigns a corresponding category to every form of judgment. At first glance this correlation appears simple and plausible, but upon closer examination, one confronts several difficulties. Why, for example, does the causal relation correspond to the hypothetical judgments although the relationship between cause and effect need not be formulated in a merely hypothetical manner ("If it rains, then the street will get wet") but can also be formulated assertorically ("The rain makes the street wet")? The answer here is relatively simple: In the causal relation at least two events are connected with one another. More difficult is the question why the category of unity is correlated with universal judgments and the category of totality with the singular judgments.

Table 5.1 The Forms of Judgment and the Categories

Forms of Judgments (B 95)	Categories (B 106)
	1. Quantity
Universal	Unity
Particular	Plurality
Singular	Totality
	2. Quality
Affirmative	Reality
Negative	Negation
Infinite	Limitation
	3. Relation
Categorical	Inherence and Subsistence (*substantia et accidens*)
Hypothetical	Causality and Dependence (cause and effect)
Disjunctive	Community (reciprocity between agent and patient)
	4. Modality
Problematic	Possibility—Impossibility
Assertoric	Existence—Non-existence
Apodeictic	Necessity—Contingency

According to the table of categories there are four times three categories, thus twelve distinct basic concepts of the pure understanding which are clearly distinguished from one another and stand in certain relationships to one another. The individual categories can on the main be found in traditional ontology—for example, the fundamental concepts of Wolff and Baumgarten are important—and are thus a part of pre-Critical philosophy. Kant's achievement lies in deriving them from the table of judgments and in explaining the much more extensive stock of basic concepts in circulation at the time. The philosopher separates the basic concepts of the pure understanding from all pure but derivative concepts (the concepts of force, action and being affected, for example, can according to Kant be derived from the category of causality). Kant further sets aside everything that belongs either to intuition—the Transcendental Aesthetic—or to the domain of the ideas, the unconditioned, and thus not to the Transcendental Analytic but to the Transcendental Dialectic.

At least the category of reality deserves a brief explanation, since it will be important for the criticism of the ontological proof of the existence of God. The first category of quality does not coincide with the second category of modality: Kant understands reality not as real existence, a modality, but literally and in agreement with affirmative judgment as *realitas*, the thingness or thing-content of something, its positive attributes.

5.4 THE TRANSCENDENTAL DEDUCTION OF THE CATEGORIES

The Task

The Transcendental Deduction no more intends a formal logical justification—a derivation of statements, the conclusions, from other statements, the premises—than does the Metaphysical Deduction. Without infringing upon the formal rules of deduction, the Transcendental Deduction explains "the manner in which concepts," the categories, "can relate *a priori* to objects" (B 117). By tracing the categories back to their origin in a regressive analysis, the Transcendental Deduction demonstrates that without the categories no objects, and thus no experience, is possible and that for this reason the use of the categories in experience is legitimate (cf. B 116f.).

There are two possibilities for understanding why the categories are indispensable for objects. Either the categories are due to the objects or the objects are due to the categories. But all objects of experience are *a posteriori* whereas the categories are by definition valid *a priori*. The categorial basis of objects thus remains impossible as long as the origin of the categories is sought in "experience and reflection upon experience" within the framework of an empirical, psychological deduction (B 117). Experience can at most indicate the "occasioning causes" because of which the categories are brought forth by the understanding. And Kant accredits the "celebrated *Locke*" with having shown in his "physiological derivation" of the categories from sensible impressions the occasions on which the understanding comes to *possess* pure

knowledge even though Locke errs as to the methodological significance of the pure concepts of the understanding (B 118f.).

Since the categories cannot be justified by experience, there
remains only the other possibility, which brings about the Copernican
revolution: like the pure forms of intuition, the categories arise from
the *a priori* constitution of the subject, from mere thinking. The Metaphysical Deduction discloses the pure concepts of the understanding;
the Transcendental Deduction shows that they are indispensable for all
knowledge. The pure forms of thought, the categories, are not mere
figments of thought occurring only in the fantasy of philosophers.
They form the necessary building blocks of all objectivity. The categories have a (transcendental) ontological meaning; the *modi cogitandi*
prove to be *modi essendi*.

Kant does not include all empirical judgments, experience in the
broader sense, under the kind of experience for which the categories are
constitutive; he includes only a subset, experience in the strict sense,
which is quite different from another subset, the perceptual judgments.
A mere perceptual judgment such as, "If I carry a body, I feel a pressing
of weight" (B 142), contains no category but rather the logical connection (if A, then B) of two perceptions (A: I carry a body; B: I feel a
pressing of weight). The relationship between subject (body) and predicate (heavy) is not formed according to pure laws of thought but
according to empirical laws of association (Hume's "psychological
habit"). The connection holds factually but is not further justified; it
holds fortuitously and not necessarily. Regardless of how many times
one makes the same perceptual judgment, it still does not lead to an
objective necessity grounded in the object itself. Perceptual judgments
have at best relative (comparative) generality but never absolute universality. They depend upon the empirical condition of the subject; they
are valid only subjectively, that is to say, privately. Judgments of experience, however, ("the body is heavy") connect the subject, the body, with
the predicate, weight, through a category. Weight is seen as an attribute
(accident) of the thing (substance), the body. The asserted relation, the
weight of the body, is no longer considered to be a subjective opinion
but to be objective knowledge. The relation is recognized as necessary
(apodeictic) in the strict sense and universal, that is to say, publicly
valid. The "transformation" of perceptual judgments into judgments of
experience occurs with the help of the categories. It is thus the pure
forms of thought which make that objective knowledge possible which

Plato and Aristotle called *episteme*, to be distinguished from doxa, and which Kant calls experience in the strict sense.

With the Transcendental Deduction of the Categories, Kant created a quite original yet extremely difficult theory. He succeeds only with great pains in arriving at a fairly satisfactory account. Except for the section on the paralogisms in the Transcendental Dialectic, the Transcendental Deduction of the Categories is the only chapter which Kant completely rewrote for the second edition. It is true that the new version contains not only the idea for a proof but also its main elements. But one still misses the sort of clarity which allows step-by-step development of the main thought, a branching out of the argumentation, and a treatment of potential misunderstandings and objections. Even in the second edition, the inner complexity of the task leads to a twisted entanglement of Kant's ideas with repetitions, previews and afterthoughts which require of the reader a great deal of interpretatory skill. Important philosophers and Kant experts such as Heidegger (1973, § 31) prefer the first version of the Deduction. An introduction into the main ideas of the *Critique* cannot burden itself with a comparison of both versions. I follow the second edition, whose drastic changes Kant himself deemed necessary.

The Transcendental Deduction acquires a preliminary structure when one follows Kant's division of the argument into two steps (cf. B 144f. and B 159), preceded by a preparatory consideration: In section 13 and 14 Kant indicates the direction in which the argumentation must proceed; the origin of the categories is not to be sought in the objects but in the subject. In the first step (§§ 15–20) Kant shows that all unification originates in transcendental self-consciousness, which needs the categories for determinacy. While the first step explicates the significance of the categories—no objective knowledge without the categories—the second step (§§ 22–27) shows, in connection with the treatment of three objections, the limits of their application: the cognitive value of the categories is restricted to objects of possible experience (cf. the title for § 22). Kant's argument is complicated by the fact that the first step comes "from above"—from the understanding and its activity of connecting—and the second "from below"—from empirical intuition and its unity. Nowhere in the Transcendental Deduction does Kant discuss the content of the various categories; Fichte's corresponding criticism (*Second Introduction to the Science of Knowledge*: "Zweite

Einleitung in die Wissenschaftslehre," 6) is correct; Kant's only goal is to demonstrate the objective validity of the categories in general.

The First Step: Transcendental Self-Consciousness as the Origin of All Synthesis

The first step in the Transcendental Deduction is divided into two parts. Kant begins by showing that all variety of representations can only achieve unity through transcendental self-consciousness (§§ 15–17). He then shows that it is the categories which lend unity its necessary determinacy (§§ 18–19). Kant concludes with an explanatory summary through which the two-part argumentation becomes more clear (§§ 20–21).

First Part. All knowing consists in the connection of a variety of representations (intuitions or concepts) into a unity. The connection—Kant calls it synthesis—can never be brought about by the senses, for they are merely receptive. Therefore, the connection cannot be due to the pure form of sensible intuition. The unifying connection stems not from the object but from the subject, and (1) from a source of knowledge distinct from sensibility, which (2) is not receptive but itself active. It is the spontaneity of the action of the understanding—a first result of Kant's argumentation—which brings about all synthesis (B 130).

On Kant's view, the desired origin or supreme principle of all synthesis is to be understood as that action of the understanding on which all forms of synthesis are commonly based. One finds this principle by disregarding the different sorts of connections and instead focusing on the action of connecting as such. Kant thus reaches the main goal of the first step in the proof: the source of all synthesis lies in an original synthesis, in a unifying connection that *precedes* all (empirically or categorically) determined connection without itself depending upon a prior connection.

Since the original unity precedes all different forms of unity, it cannot be identical with the category of unity; it is unity on a higher level. Because the categories create unity in a pre-empirical manner, this holds all the more for that source of unity in which the categorial unity originates. As the condition for all unity, and thus for all knowledge— for without unification no knowledge is possible—original synthesis is not just valid *a priori*. It has the standing of a transcendental unity of consciousness. As transcendental unity it effects no concrete combination of a manifold of representations; that occurs through empirical or pure concepts. Original synthesis is the prerequisite which makes all empirical and categorial combination possible.

Despite some difficulties in understanding, original or transcendental synthesis is not a secret accessible only to adepts. Original synthesis means only that the entire manifold of intuition must be connected in order to become knowledge, that, further, the connection is not given in intuition but must be effected by thought, and, finally, that the act of thinking is only possible due to a connection prior to the categories: On the first level of synthesis the material of intuition receives the unity of a concept, for example, body or weight. On the second level concepts are connected into the unity of a judgment with the help of the categories ("The body is heavy"). On the third level even the unity produced by the categories rests upon a common property and unity, the transcendental unity of apperception or of self-consciousness.

According to transcendental apperception or transcendental self-consciousness, the knowledge of objects forms an inseparable unity with its relationship to a self. To consciousness belongs not only an object but also the possibility of being conscious of one's consciousness of the object. Kant speaks of the fact that all consciousness includes potential self-consciousness in a famous passage at the beginning of section 16. "It must be possible for the 'I think' to accompany all my representations; for otherwise something would be represented in me which could not be thought at all, and that is equivalent to saying that the representation would be impossible, or at least would be nothing to me" (B 131f.).

The "I think" is the irreducible representation which remains the same throughout all representing of changing contents. Kant calls the irreducible resresentation "I think" the "original synthetic unity of apperception" (§ 16). Even the manifold of sensible intuition, then that of concepts and of the categories, too, is necessarily subject to this condition. From the Transcendental Aesthetic, we are familiar with the supreme principle of the possibility of all intuition: In relation to sensibility, all multiplicity of intuition is subject to the formal conditions of space and time. Now, in relation to understanding, a second supreme principle is added: All multiplicity of intuition is subject to the conditions of the original synthetic unity of apperception (B 136).

Because synthesis is not possible without transcendental self-consciousness and because without synthesis, the variety of intuition never acquires the unity and determinacy of an object, original synthetic unity is the objective condition of all knowledge. The transcendental unity is also called objective unity since it is the condition of the possibility of objectivity and "must be distinguished from the *subjective* unity of consciousness, which is a *determination* of *inner sense*" (B 139).

Modern thought is drenched with the idea of the ego as the source of knowledge. In Kant's case this idea is not connected with rationalist or empiricist metaphysics but with a transcendental critique of reason. Through this critique the final authority of the subject as the principle of knowledge receives a more radical justification and a greater significance which is at the same time methodologically more convincing. Although transcendental apperception underlies all knowledge, it is not for Kant a (thinking) substance (*res cogitans*) as it is for Descartes. To ward off any substantialist misunderstanding right from the beginning, Kant does not speak of the ego but of the "I think," and this "I think," like the ideas of reason (chapter 7), is not known but only thought. (A detailed criticism of Descartes follows in the Paralogism chapter of the Transcendental Dialectic; sect. 7.)

When Kant says of the "I think" that it must be able to accompany all of my representations, he refers to the simple and yet highly significant circumstance that representations are not my representations by force of the content represented but instead because I conceive them, because I can become conscious of them. "I" is not, however, to be understood here in the sense of empirical psychology. With the remark that the "I think" must be able to accompany all of my representations, Kant ascribes to transcendental apperception a necessity which unmasks any interpretation along empirical, psychological lines as a misunderstanding. The "I" of transcendental apperception is not the personal ego of a certain individual. Whereas the individual self belongs to the empirical ego, which lives and breathes in the world over a certain time, the transcendental "I think" is methodologically positioned prior to all experience; it is the origin of the unity characteristic of all judgments. Transcendental apperception is the subject of consciousness as such and is thus one and the same in all consciousness and self-consciousness.

Second Part. The first part of the first step in the argument leads to transcendental self-consciousness as the origin of any synthesis of a manifold; the connection with the categories recedes into the background. The second part starts by identifying transcendental self-consciousness as an objective unity and reaches its climax with the thesis that the manifold of a given intuition falls necessarily under the categories (§ 20 with references to § 19).

In his argument Kant refers back to the logical form of all judgments, here to the copula "is," which combines subject and predicate into the unity of a judgment. The copula stands here for every form of connection and disregards all determinacy brought about by various empirical and pure concepts. The copula—according to Kant's sketch of an argument—is evidence for the objective and necessary unity of apperception. Even if the judgment ("Bodies are heavy") is empirical in content and hence fortuitous, the connection of subject and predicate is justified by the facts and in this sense objective and necessary. The objectivity and necessity of a connection is due—as we know from the Metaphysical Deduction—to the categories. For this reason the connection of a manifold achieves the unity of transcendental self-consciousness only with the help of the categories. The categories thus prove to be the condition of the possibility of all objectivity. Disregarding many questions of detail, we can thus say that the goal of the Transcendental Deduction has on the whole been reached. The categories, which according to the Metaphysical Deduction are pure concepts of the understanding but possibly only figments of thought, now prove to be objectively valid. Subjective yet pure thought is a necessary building block of objectivity. Subjectivity and objectivity have the same origin: transcendental self-consciousness, which is consummated in the pure forms of synthesis, the categories. With the unity of subjectivity and objectivity, Kant overcomes Descartes' dualism, which makes a strict distinction between subjective thought (*res cogitans*) and the objective world of spatio-temporal objects (*res extensae*). Despite Kant's argumentation, this dualism stubbornly lives on both in everyday thought and in science.

Excursus: Transcendental Arguments

Under the title "transcendental arguments" we find in analytic philosophy since Strawson thoughtful attempts to revive Kant's transcendental reflection in a more moderate form.[1] In evaluating these attempts, one cannot forget that the notion of the transcendental is specified not only by the Transcendental Deduction in the Analytic of Concepts. Moreover, "transcendental" does not refer in Kant to an argument or a type of argument, nor even to a certain method; Kant speaks of a critical, not a transcendental method. It is a research program that is transcendental, or more precisely. critically transcendental. This program is connected with the question of the scientific status of metaphysics and examines the necessary conditions without which objective things and knowledge cannot be conceived as possible. According to Kant, it can only be realized through a progressive and increasingly rich analysis of the object of experience. In opposition to a number of overestimations of the Transcendental Deduction of the Categories, one must thus recall the equal significance of the Metaphysical Deduction as well as that of the Transcendental Aesthetic and the Analytic of Principles, not to mention that of the Transcendental Dialectic.

The guiding principle of the transcendental research program and of specific transcendental claims is possible experience (cf. B 811). Transcendental Apperception, too, can be considered as proven if experience appears impossible without it—that is, if there is no alternative to it. The lack of an alternative is thus proposed in the analytic discussion of Kant as a characteristic of transcendental arguments. The special character of the transcendental is not, however, captured here. All knowledge that is strictly necessary in accord with the classical idea of science lacks any alternative. So strictly speaking, the discussion does not concern transcendental arguments but—more generally—the notion of truly necessary knowledge. Adhering to the classical idea of science, Kant demands much more than the non-existence of alternatives merely as a matter of fact; for him, necessary knowledge can have no alternative even in principle. In this case not only alternatives which have as yet been proposed but also those which are at all conceivable are excluded. According to the analytic philosophers, this requirement is invariably too strong—not only in the case of transcendental apperception.

On Bubner's view, however, the fundamental inconceivability of alternatives can be defended with the argument of relation to the self; for despite the variety of experience, every subject finds in itself the unity of self-consciousness. But, one must ask of Bubner, how are we to understand the phrase "to find in oneself"? An empirical fact cannot be meant since that would not be an objective unity but instead the subjective unity explicitly rejected by Kant. Should we instead consider an argument more of the following sort: "Whoever doubts or disputes the unity of self-consciousness confirms its legitimacy through his action;

for doubting and disputing are representations of a subject and therefore elements of a self-consciousness"? On this interpretation Bubner's
argument is similar to Descartes' argument from doubt ("I doubt;
therefore, I think; therefore, I am") and subject to the same criticism; it
is not specifically Kantian.

In Bubner's idea of relation to the self one of the elements of transcendental reflection is overlooked or at least does not become sufficiently clear. Even if no experience is possible without the unity of
self-consciousness, this unity has transcendental standing only if it is
valid *a priori*. Kant shows this by referring to the unity of self-consciousness as the origin of the categories: If the categories themselves
are not due to experience, then their origin most certainly is not.

The Second Step: The Restriction of the Categories to Possible Experience

The first step of the Transcendental Deduction shows first that all
sensible intuition requires unifying thought in order to become knowledge and, second, that the ultimate basis of unification lies in the transcendental "I think," which, third, cannot exist without the greater
determinacy of the categories. The categories are therefore indispensable for the constitution of objects and of objective knowledge. They
are, as Kant more succinctly states, objectively valid. But the goal of the
Transcendental Deduction consists in the demonstration of the objective validity of the categories, and the question arises why Kant does
not end his discussion of the categories here.

On a first reading one could think that Kant really has finished
his deduction; sections 22–27 make a few explanations and additions
but add nothing new; the conclusions drawn in section 26 coincide
with those of section 20. On the other hand, the second part presents
more than just notes to the first part; it thus does contain something
new. But what is it that is new? According to Henrich (1973), the dispute of more than 150 years concerning the structure of the Transcendental Deduction can be resolved by dividing the argumentation into
two steps, which explain the necessity of the categories first for those
sensible intuitions which "already contain unity" and then for all sensible intuition. Brouillet and Wagner have criticized this reconstruction.
According to Wagner, the first step says that the unity of sensible intuition is due to the categories, and the second that there can be no sensible intuition not subject to the categories. Not just theory but even its

"base," perception, rests upon the universal categorial function. But the fact that Kant clearly distinguishes perception and experience and that it is indeed the categories which make a merely perceptual judgment into a judgment of experience, speaks against this interpretation.

If according to the heading of section 20 "all sensible intuitions are subject to the categories, as conditions under which alone their manifold can come together in one consciousness," then the first step already explains the indispensability and universality of the categories for objects and knowledge of objects. The second step can only show that the categories can be utilized solely for the construction of objective reality. On this interpretation the Transcendental Deduction of the Categories takes on the twofold task of the critique of reason: the first part shows the range of the categories, the second their limits. The first step proves that all knowledge is possible only with the aid of the categories; the second step, that categorial knowledge does not extend beyond the domain of possible experience. Beyond objects of possible experience the categories have no use (B 147f.).

Kant completes the second step while discussing three possible objections. The first and most important objection comes from pure mathematics (§ 22). Mathematics is an *a priori* science but does not represent empirical knowledge; it is hence just the sort of thing which Kant wants to dispute: categorial knowledge of an object beyond all possible experience. Kant agrees on one point: categories are used in mathematics. Geometry is not possible through the pure intuition of space alone but only through the connection of a variety of geometrical concepts by means of categories. (The theorem of Euclidean geometry that the sum of the angles of any triangle is 180 is with respect to quantity universal, with respect to quality affirmative, with respect to relation categorical and with respect to modality apodeictically valid; so it is due to the categories of unity, reality, substance and necessity.) The fact that Kant only incidentally mentions the categorial component of mathematics (B 147) confirms that this point has already been clarified in the first step of the Deduction. Only the seeming consequence that there is an application of the categories outside of possible experience is drawn into question.

Since mathematics investigates only the form and not the material of intuition, we acquire through this science "*a priori* knowledge of objects . . . only in regard to their form" (ibid.). Without the material of empirical sensation there is no knowledge of the real world; mathematics is on its own only formal knowledge. Mathematics cannot itself decide whether there can be things which must be viewed in the form studied by mathematics and whether objective reality, nature, or a part thus has a mathematical structure. But since knowledge is for Kant always knowledge of objective reality, it follows that mathematics does not on its own constitute knowledge—unless nature has a mathematical structure. Kant does not thereby depreciate the independent value of mathematics but merely observes that mathematics alone says nothing about reality. Since reality, as Kant will show (sect. 6), is on its own account quantitative—and hence has a mathematical structure—the qualifying assumption holds. Mathematics provides the form of empirical knowledge. Therefore, empirical knowledge relies upon mathematics, and the categories have no other *epistemological* value in the case of mathematics than for objects of *possible* experience.

A second objection (§ 23) which one could make against the limited range of the categories appeals to the possibility of assuming an object of non-sensible intuition and making all those statements which are contained in the assumption that nothing belonging to sensible intuition attaches to the object. Only negative specifications are thus possible: the object is not extended, has no duration in time, and so on. Solely negative specifications do not, however, lead to "genuine knowledge" of the object. Moreover, none of the categories can be applied since they are mere *forms* of thought which remain empty without the material of sensible intuition.

According to a third objection (§ 25), transcendental self-consciousness contains self-*knowledge* which is valid independently of intuitions because it is a transcendental prerequisite for all thought. But here, too, the limited range of all knowledge and its appearance character are preserved. For transcendental self-consciousness is only self-*consciousness* that I am but not self-*knowledge as to what* I am. Such knowledge is not possible without intuition and its categorial combination. (Between the second and the third objection, in the "obscure § 26," Kant introduces two kinds of synthesis, which are both transcendental in character and with the aid of which the first step is completed in a different manner by means of the second.)

Kant closes the Transcendental Deduction with the conclusion (§ 26): Experience is knowledge through the combination of perception; the conditions of the possibility of the combination, and thus of experience, are the categories (B 161). Without the categories the indeterminate variety of sensible impressions cannot become objective reality, or nature: the connection of appearances according to laws. To phrase it differently: The categories prescribe "laws to nature" (B 159), not empirical laws of nature, to be sure, but the categories do constitute the *a priori* prerequisite for all empirical laws of nature.

6.

The Analytic of Principles

With the completion of the Transcendental Deduction of the Categories, Kant's guiding question concerning the possibility of objective experience and the possibility of synthetic *a priori* judgments appears to be completely answered. The combination of a manifold of intuition in accord with concepts makes synthetic judgments possible; its combination in accord with *pure* concepts (the categories) makes synthetic *a priori* judgments possible. The Transcendental Analytic, the logic of truth, is thus apparently complete, and the truth claims of empirical assertions have been explained in general terms. Only the Transcendental Dialectic, a logic of illusion rebuking each illegitimate use of the categories (thus rejecting the illegitimate claim to knowledge on the part of speculative metaphysics), seems to be missing. But in fact, the Transcendental Analytic contains a second book, the "Analytic of Principles," which comes after the Analytic of Concepts. Here Kant examines a third cognitive faculty: judgment, the capacity to subsume things under rules (concepts of the understanding). Subsumption is possible due to a new class of representations, the schemata. They are products of imagination (B 179ff.) and mediate between sensibility and understanding. In the first part of the Analytic of Concepts, Kant presents the schemata of the pure concepts of the understanding: in the second part, he describes the synthetic judgments which follow from the pure concepts of the understanding under the conditions of the schemata. These judgments are the principles of pure understanding (B 175).

The second book of the Transcendental Analytic is very difficult to understand. Many scholars view the question as to the possibility of synthetic *a priori* judgments as answered; they therefore consider Kant's justification of the schemata as intermediaries between intuition and thought to be superfluous (Prichard 1909, 141ff.; Kemp Smith, 334–342; Warnock 1949) as well as obscure and confused (F. H. Jacobi, Schopenhauer and more recently Walsh 1957, 95). If the theory of schemata, which Kant characterizes as important and indeed indispensable (cf. *Prol.*, § 34), is still to make sense, then one must apparently assume a discrepancy in Kant's program. The conceptually indeterminate manifold given in intuition and the concept of the understanding which determines it are no longer two mutually dependent parts of cognition distinguished only by transcendental reflection. They are two relatively independent elements of knowledge and require a third element as an intermediary. But then the concept of the understanding cannot perform the task assigned to it in the Transcendental Aesthetic and the Analytic of Concepts. It cannot form material by combining a manifold of intuition into a determinate unity, since such forming assumes two interlocking items which, without need of a third item, explain the possibility of *a priori* knowledge solely by their collaboration.

Such objections cannot stop at the schematism theory. If the schemata are superfluous, then the synthetic *a priori* judgments following from the schemata, namely the principles of the pure understanding, are, too. Reciprocally, whoever considers the principles to be a meaningful theoretical segment of the Critique must first make sense of the theory of schemata.

On a different interpretation, the chapter on schematism treats the new and important problem of the application of the categories and solves the problem so well that the Transcendental Deduction of the Categories becomes superfluous (Paton 1936, II 17ff.). On another interpretation, the schematism theory makes sense only if it leads to absolute idealism (Daval, 1951 295). But this consequence would contradict the basic position of the *Critique*. In short, however one proposes to interpret the Analytic of Principles, particularly the schematism theory, one seems always to come to a dead-end.

6.1 THE THEORY OF SCHEMATISM

Although Kant deals with the schemata of pure concepts, the basic idea also becomes clear if we consider empirical concepts. One can even go so far as to claim that there can be transcendental schemata as intermediaries for pure concepts only if all concepts require schemata due to the fundamental necessity of a mediating representation between intuition and concept.

Empirical concepts are rules which provide a manifold of given sense impressions with unity and determinacy. In the chapter on schematism, Kant speaks of "giving determinacy," of "subsumption" of what is given by the senses under a concept, and of "application" of the concept to what is given by the senses (B 176 and passim). Kant's talk of subsumption and of application has, however, misled scholars such as Prichard and Warnock into identifying the relationship of intuition to concept with that of the particular to the general or with that of a subset to the set of which it is a part. We are in fact dealing with the relationship of an indeterminate material to its determining form. In Kant's example (B 176), the plate is thus not a subset of circles but rather material (e.g. porcelain, clay or tin) formed in the pattern of a circle—that is, round.

A concept is nothing but the form of material given by the senses, and what is given by the senses is nothing but the material of a determining form. Since intuition and concept thus fit one another and make up a whole, one is tempted to consider a third instance, as presented in the chapter on schematism, to be superfluous. A closer look demonstrates the contrary: A third instance is indeed needed. Concepts are merely possible forms for the material of intuition, and in knowledge, which is supposed to comprehend reality, it is of critical importance not to wander about in free fantasy and make use of any concept whatsoever. One must instead utilize the correct concepts, namely those which correspond to the material at hand: This is a chair; that is a table, closet or bed. Judgment, which makes use of the schemata, is the ability to apply concepts correctly.

Judgment decides whether or not the given manifold of intuition falls under the rule generated by the understanding. It thus constitutes an additional cognitive faculty, which performs the necessary mediation between the other two faculties, sensibility and understanding. Judgment provides neither the material nor the form (the concept) but rather ensures that the concepts applied really do characterize the given states of affairs. To do so, it matches the material of intuition with the appropriate concept and identifies this material as something falling under this and only this concept: this is a chair and not a table, closet or bed. Judgment makes the correct application of concepts possible.

In the empirical sphere, judgment enables a doctor, for example, to apply the medical rules learned during his studies, to determine what is wrong with the patient, and to consider how to help him. Judgment thus enables the doctor to make a diagnosis correct in the present circumstances and to start an appropriate therapy. Because one requires, in addition to the knowledge of medical rules, the ability to apply the right ones in the changing reality of diseases, a good student of medicine is not yet a good doctor. The same is true for a craftsman, a teacher, a lawyer or an engineer. The "possession" of a concept and competence in applying it appropriately are not—as Warnock (1949, 80) claims in opposition to Kant—the same. The capacity to structure the widely varied concrete reality of life in accord with the concepts and rules learned, the capacity to judge, is missing (cf. "Commonplace," VIII 275f.).

In order for judgment to fulfill its task and to match concepts appropriately with the given material of intuition, it requires a representation having both intuitive and conceptual character. Kant calls such a representation a *schema* (Greek for form); through it intuitions are conceptualized or concepts made intuitive. Nonetheless, one should not confuse a schema, say, that of a dog, with a picture. For concepts, and likewise schemata, are general, whereas pictures provide a view of one particular figure. A picture shows, for example, a friend's Belgian sheep dog but not that which is true of all sheep dogs and for all other breeds, crosses and age-groups of dogs and which makes it possible to call both the four-legged ball of fluff in the yard and the neighborhood mutt dogs. In a schema, neither the empirical view of a particular thing nor the isolated concept of the universal is represented but instead the "'listing' of the rule for obtaining the picture" (Heidegger 1973, 93; cf. B 179f.).

There is a schema not only for empirical concepts but also for the pure sensible concepts of algebra and geometry. Kant uses the example already discussed by Locke and Berkeley: the triangle (B 180). We have a general intuition of a triangle which is neither a right triangle nor one having no right angle, which is neither isosceles nor equilateral nor do its segments all differ in length. Graphically representing all triangles, this intuition precedes any picture.

The schemata of the pure concepts of the understanding form the third group. They are supposed to make the appropriate application of the categories to appearances possible and thus to complete the transcendental theory of categories. It is for this reason not correct to consider, as Henrich does, the Transcendental Deduction of the Categories to be the keystone of the *Critique of Pure Reason*. It is indeed true that the Transcendental Deduction performs such fundamental tasks as the proof (1) that the categories are indispensable for objects and the experience of them, (2) that transcendental self-consciousness is their source and (3) that knowledge beyond experience is impossible. But Kant likewise comes across indispensable elements of all experience in the Transcendental Aesthetic, and there he reaches the conclusion that knowledge beyond the subjective forms of intuition is impossible. Moreover, one should not overlook the significance of the Metaphysical Deduction of the Categories, and one should not ignore the fact that without the transcendental schemata, the justification of systematic empirical knowledge remains incomplete. The Metaphysical Deduction shows that there are pure concepts of the understanding, the categories; the Transcendental Deduction shows that without them no experience is possible; and the theory of schemata shows how they are appropriately applied. The theory of schemata thus neither repeats nor replaces the Transcendental Deduction of the Categories. One finds, however, in this theory in connection with the principles the completion of the Transcendental Analytic. The question as to the possibility of synthetic *a priori* judgments is finally answered only with the schematism theory together with the system of all principles of the pure understanding, which builds upon the theory of schemata. Heidegger thus rightly points out the great significance of the theory of schemata and develops a brilliant interpretation which concludes with a division of the argument into seven parts (Heidegger 1973, 108f.). Recently, Allison and Gram (chap. 4–5) have emphasized the particular importance of this part of the *Critique*. Nonetheless, however original interpretations overrating a part of the *Critique of Pure Reason* may sound, one has only understood its intention and its structure when one has grasped the various parts both in their own right and in their indispensable contribution to the whole.

Just as the schemata of empirical concepts are representations belonging both to the conceptual (rational) and to the intuitive realm, the schemata of the pure concepts are representations which are pure concepts and yet sensible. The transcendental schemata are pure intuitive concepts or pure conceptual intuitions. Kant specifies them more closely as transcendental determinations of time. Following his argument in three steps: (1) the category is a pure synthetic unity of the manifold, (2) the unity is due to inner and not to outer sense, and (3) the intuitive form of the manifold of inner sense is time. It is hence time which as a pure intuition provides a view prior to all experience, and the transcendental schemata consist in transcendental determinations of time—not of space. Insofar as the transcendental determinations of time rest upon an *a priori* rule, they resemble a certain category. Insofar as they are determinations of time, they correspond to pure intuition and can provide the necessary mediation between intuition and a pure concept.

In accord with the four points of view for the division of the categories, there are four possibilities for the pure view of time: the time-*series* with respect to quantity, the time-*content* for quality, the time-*order* for relation and the *scope* of time with respect to modality. Kant does not name the corresponding schemata for all categories; he gives only a few examples with increasingly summary explanations.

Kant sees the schema of magnitude in number. In other words, numerical concepts (1, 2, 3, 4, . . .) are generated by applying the category of quantity to time as a form of intuition. To this claim one could object that one cannot count only those things which succeed one another in time, as events do, but also things which are simultaneous or, like the categories, do not even exist in time at all. Yet this objection disappears when one considers that the transcendental schemata are based on the pure form of temporal intuition, on mere succession and not on empirical time, which can be measured with a clock. Thus in counting, regardless of what is counted, the quantity is viewed as a pure succession: first one, then another one, which together with the first one gives two, then yet another one, which makes three altogether, and so forth.

A brief explanation of the schemata of substance and of causality shows that Kant's Transcendental Schematism is not a superfluous baroque attachment to his critique of reason but is instead drawn from the nature of the problems treated: in order to be able to say in the case of empirical processes, for instance, the street getting wet, that it is the street which goes through transformations of its condition, one must recognize one and the same subject (the street) in both a dry and a wet state as the substratum which undergoes a change in what "attaches" to it (inherence, attributes). One must recognize one and the same subject as first dry, then wet. Recognition presupposes that the subject, the street, has duration through time. The schema of substance must hence be the representation of a substratum for something which attaches to it, insofar as being a substratum manifests itself in the pure image of time. This is the image of permanence (substance), which at the same time provides the image of change in the permanent, of attributes. The durability of the real through time, despite changing attributes, is precisely the schema of substance (B 183).

To be able to apply the category of causality to a manifold of intuition, one cannot merely claim of events in time that they succeed one another: the street's getting wet follows upon the rain. The mere succession still does not justify, as Hume shows and Kant agrees, a causal connection. One must additionally claim that, because it occurs according to a rule (e.g., Water makes dry things wet), the succession is founded not on subjective sensibility but on the nature of things. The schema of causality is thus, as Kant says: the succession of appearances when the succession is governed by a rule (ibid.).

6.2 THE PRINCIPLES OF PURE UNDERSTANDING

The theory of schemata reveals the sole intuitive conditions under which the categories can be applied to appearances. The immediately following "System of all Principles of Pure Understanding" presents the supreme judgments brought forth *a priori* by the understanding under the conditions of the transcendental schemata (B 187). The principles are those fundamental statements about reality which are possible prior to all experience. They comprise the final step in the transcendental theory of the constitution of experience and form the "constructive" climax of the critique of theoretical reason.

The principles have great significance both historically and systematically, for they deal with problems central even for non-scientific knowledge, and certainly central for the specialized sciences and for philosophy: the durability of substance and the principle of causality. Moreover, the principles treat such a decisive development as the modern mathematization of the natural sciences—for example, Kepler's planetary laws, Galileo's laws for falling bodies and above all Newton's system of theoretical mechanics. According to the Axioms of Intuition and the Anticipations of Perception, natural scientists do not make use of mathematics by chance but of necessity, for mathematics is the indispensable form of all objective knowledge of nature. What is more, Kant claims "that in any particular theory of nature, only as much *genuine* science can be found as there is *mathematics* in it" (*MOS*, IV 470). Kant thus allows only the alternative: either a mathematical science of nature or none at all. A non-mathematical (pre-mathematical) study of nature is not for him a (strict) science.

Against Kant's thesis that there is no real science without mathematics, one could bring to bear the branch of biology which since Aristotle and his school has investigated the variety of forms. In the eighteenth century, for example, it is G. E. L. Buffon (1707–88) who resists the tendency in the study of nature to quantify and to set up abstract relations. He favors qualitative descriptions. The "victory of technology," in which (on the basis of the mathematical natural sciences) the interest of man in dominating nature goes wild—with effects which no longer seem entirely beneficial—perhaps also speaks against Kant's thesis that mathematics is necessary for science. And the post-Kantian development of historical linguistic and social sciences may also make us skeptical of Kant's view. On the other hand, they do not fulfill Kant's criterion for a "genuine science": strict necessity. Moreover, the introduction of quantitative methods into these sciences is constantly attempted. (Regarding the expansion of the Kantian conception of science, sect. 12.)

Kant's "principles of pure understanding" make up not only the final step in the transcendental theory of the constitution of experience but also constitute the first philosophically justified structural principles for research in the specialized sciences. They form both the conclusion of the analytic part of the *Critique* and the beginning of a metaphysics of nature, which Kant works out in the *Metaphysical Origins of Science*. The principles of pure understanding must nonetheless be distinguished from the specific principles of mathematics and the natural sciences. Located on a more fundamental level, they specify the basic structure to be followed by the principles of the specialized sciences. The principles of pure understanding do not regulate certain states of affairs in nature but nature as nature. They state the principles which constitute nature as such. They are according to Kant explicitly or implicitly asserted in every judgment of natural science. Specific scientific propositions, even fundamental propositions of the specialized sciences, cannot be derived directly from the philosophical principles of pure understanding. The latter principles are guidelines for judgment in scientific research, which relies primarily neither on formal logical derivations nor on the gathering of facts but represents instead a manner of judging rationally in practice.

It is repeatedly asserted in criticisms of Kant that the principles are supposed to legitimate those synthetic *a priori* judgments necessary for the justification of Newton's physics. Recently, it has most notably been Popper (*Conjectures and Refutations*,[5]1974, 192) and Stegmüller (1967, 14ff.) who want to make the *Critique of Pure Reason* into an early treatise on the theory of science. Kant is accredited here with the great achievement of developing a metatheory which, in contrast to Hume's skepticism, provides Newtonian mechanics with a sure philosophical basis. This interpretation is nonetheless fatal, for it places Kant's thought in the sphere of classical physics; thus, with the progress of physics, Kant's first critique of reason can be viewed as having only relative value or can perhaps even be rejected entirely. There are indeed several brilliant attempts to "save" Kant—for example, by von Weizsäcker for the physical laws of conservation and by Beck (1973) for Heisenberg's indeterminacy principle. But in the theory of science, we still cannot avoid the consequence: Because Newtonian physics has been rendered obsolete by the theory of relativity and by quantum theory, Kant's principles of pure understanding appear to have ultimately failed. We must dismiss the Analytic of Principles just as we previously—purportedly because of modern mathematics—dismissed the Transcendental Aesthetic. Both parts of the *Critique* retain at most the significance of an historical model. In fact, the principles intend no more than the Transcendental Aesthetic to justify a particular historical form of modern science but instead to justify all objective knowledge. Although Kant is convinced of the correctness of Euclidean geometry and of Newtonian mechanics and repeatedly cites them as examples, they still do not form an integral part of the transcendental critique (see above, sect. 3 and 4). They are examples of synthetic *a priori* knowledge, whose possibility Kant intends to explain. In the "Principles," Kant seeks to prove the truth neither of Euclidean geometry nor of Newton's laws of motion. He does claim that it is not left to the discretion of the natural scientist whether or not to look for laws and to formulate them mathematically. (On the compatibility of Kant's "critical idealism" with the theory of relativity and quantum theory cf. E. Cassirer, *On Modern Physics*,[2] 1957.) Kant begins with the supreme principle of all analytic judgments, the principle of contradiction. He is, however, only interested in this principle as something with which to contrast the principle of synthetic *a priori* judgments. The formulation of the principle of contradiction, "no predicate contradictory of a thing can belong to it" (B 190), is unsatisfactory since it does not introduce an independent definition but itself includes a reference to contradiction.

Experience, in which Kant is interested, begins beyond analytic propositions. It rests upon the synthetic unity of appearances, without which there would only be unconnected pieces, merely a rhapsody of sense impression. Kant unites the conditions of synthetic unity familiar from the Transcendental Aesthetic and the Analytic of Concepts in the supreme principle of all experience: the conditions of the possibility of experience are at the same time the conditions of the possibility of the objects of experience (B 197). The constitution of objects and the constitution of experience are essentially one.

Only the table of individual principles, which Kant draws under the guidance of the table of categories, brings new insights. Following the four groups of categories, Kant develops four moments of knowledge: intuition, perception, experience, and empirical thought in general. The later moments build on the previous ones. The first three correspond roughly to the three stages of knowledges in Hegel's *Phenomenology of the Mind*: sensory certainty, perception and finally force and understanding. For each of the four moments Kant discovers a particular form of synthetic *a priori* knowledge: axioms for intuition, anticipations for perception, analogies for experience and postulates for empirical thought in general. For each kind of knowledge valid independent of experience, Kant gives at least one principle.

Kant calls the principles of the axioms and anticipations mathematical principles and those of the analogies and postulates dynamical principles. The mathematical principles demonstrate the legitimacy and indeed the necessity of mathematics. Understood as the science of the construction of magnitudes (*quanta*) and of mere magnitude (*quantitas*) (cf. B 745), mathematics becomes the first element in the constitution of all objects of experience and of knowledge about such objects. In this sense, it has objective validity: states of affairs which cannot be represented as magnitudes do not hold objectively. The dynamic principles make the natural sciences possible insofar as they go beyond the "application" of mathematics, assert the existence of objects, and yet still remain in the domain of *a priori* knowledge. For physics, Kant calls this domain "dynamics" (the theory of movement).

6.3 THE MATHEMATICAL PRINCIPLES

In order to understand something as a magnitude, one must represent it as a multiplicity of units. Kant claims in the passages concerning the mathematical principles that one knows *a priori* that such a representation is possible for all appearances. He distinguishes two kinds of representation, depending on the way in which the appearance is given: for intuition extensive magnitude and for perception intensive magnitude.

The first moment of knowledge is *intuition*, which shows appearances extended in space and time. Insofar as one concentrates on intuition alone and disregards all else, appearances are spatially or temporally extended. They have an extensive magnitude. An extensive magnitude such as the number 3 is a whole consisting of parts (3 = 1 + 1 + 1). It is additive in nature, and the representation of the parts precedes that of the whole: the number 3 presupposes the numbers 1 and 2.

The science of the forms of intuition, including extensive magnitudes, is mathematics. Its principles are axioms: in Euclidean geometry, for example the propositions that between two points only one line can be drawn and that two straight lines do not enclose any space (B 204). The principle for all intuition is thus a principle for all principles (axioms) of mathematics. It says: "All intuitions are extensive magnitudes" (B 202).

The principle of the axioms of intuition has a twofold significance. It directly underlies all principles of mathematics and indirectly underlies all knowledge of nature, for all objects of natural science are given in intuition and thus have an extensive magnitude. Since the scientific investigation of extensive magnitudes occurs in mathematics, mathematics is the first formal principle of all knowledge of nature. Natural science is applied mathematics. But it does not follow from this fact, as Kant claims, that everything geometry says about the pure intuition of space and time "undeniably" holds for empirical intuition (B 206). This stronger claim is correct only under the assumption that there is only one geometry; since the discovery of non-Euclidean geometries, this assumption can no longer be made. But it remains true that physics depends upon geometry. The geometry utilized in physics has to be possible from the standpoint of pure geometry without its being the case that every mathematically possible geometry is physically valid.

Although Kant takes his examples from Euclidean geometry, his principle of the axioms of intuition is not bound up with any specific axioms and is thus also valid for mathematics since Kant's time. Kant's transcendental claim says only that all objects of natural science are spatio-temporally extended, that they are thus quantifiable (representable in mathematical terms), and that anything which in principle (not just for present science) resists quantification is to be excluded from the realm of possible objects of strict natural science. Merely collecting, describing, and even explaining states of affairs remains pre-scientific until it finds a mathematical form.

The second principle, the principle of the anticipation of *perception*, is often neglected in interpretations of Kant. In fact, an important step is made here in showing the fundamental significance of quantification, and thus of mathematics, for the constitution of objects. The second principle describes the condition under which the understanding gains an objectively valid perceptual judgment ("This room has a temperature of 14 degrees") from subjective sensations ("I am cold"). The condition is intensive magnitude.

Perception is for Kant the empirical consciousness in which sensations are added to the form of intuition. In contrast to the forms of intuition, which are subjective, the sensations teach the subject of knowledge something which does not stem from the subject but from the "external world," something which really exists. (The exact source of sensation is for Fichte and Schelling the Achilles' heal of the *Critique* and remains unexplained by Kant.) In perception, the appearance, which is extended in space and time, acquires its particular attributes (qualities, properties). These attributes guarantee the reality, in the literal sense of the truly existent thing-content, of spatio-temporally extended things.

Kant calls the *a priori* components in sensations anticipations. This expression, a translation of the Epicurean word *prolepsis* (from the Greek *prolambano*: I anticipate), designates the common form underlying various different sensations. In contrast to Epicurus, Kant does not view the form as an empirical one but as the basic form of all sensations, which is valid prior to experience. One must, however, ask whether there are, in the case of perceptions, *a priori* components at all, since sensations (of colors, temperatures, sounds) are only empirical and always different. Perceptions are thus the best examples of subjective fluctuation.

For each sensation there is, according to Kant, a greater or lesser impression. A color sensation can decrease in intensity until it finally disappears altogether. Kant is thinking here of a continuous decrease (B 211f.); he could not take into consideration the insights of quantum physics into basic discontinuities at the subatomic level. But even presupposing them, Kant's claim that sensations are stronger or weaker without ever taking on the value 0 appears to be correct. If a sensation were nill, it would have ceased to exist. This means that all sensations, regardless of their empirical content, have a certain strength. It is not, however, a spatio-temporal extension (extensive magnitude) but a "degree of influence on the senses" which constitutes intensive magnitude (B 208). Such magnitudes are, for example, the degrees of temperature, of hardness or of brightness, and also weight (mass).

Every object of possible experience is, according to the second principle, by its very nature a quantity in an additional respect and thus relies upon mathematics, the science of construction of quantities. Mathematics hence constitutes not only the principle for the form but also that of the *a priori* content of all objectivity. Even the thing-content, the reality of natural objects, can be mathematically determined. As soon as the experience of nature makes the claim of universality and necessity, it cannot get around mathematics as a constitutive element. Thus, according to Kant, mathematics has objective validity in two senses: every state of affairs which is supposed to be valid beyond merely subjective representations must be describable as a magnitude both in its intuitive form of spatio-temporal extension and in its sensory content of visual, aural and other attributes.

6.4 THE ANALOGIES OF EXPERIENCE

Experience builds upon perception. In experience a variety of perceptions appears in a necessary temporal combination. Kant calls the *a priori* principles which make the necessary combination possible analogies (Greek for relations, relationships). This expression comes from the language of mathematics. Whereas there, it designates the identity of two quantitative relations ("a:b = c:d" or "a:b = b:c"), philosophy understands analogy as the identity of two qualitative relations—here, the identity of the relationships of perceptions to one another.

Because there are three possibilities for temporal combination (permanence, succession and coexistence), there are also three forms for the relationship of perceptions to one another and thus three analogies: (1) the principle of the permanence of substance, (2) the principle of succession in time according to the law of causality and (3) the principle of coexistence according to the law of reciprocity or community. The principle that experience is only possible through the representation of the necessary connection of perceptions is common to all three analogies (B 219).

The Permanence of Substance

In the first analogy of experience, Kant discusses a principle which is recognized even by common sense and which has always played a great role in philosophy: the principle of the permanence of substance. According to Kant, this principle is a synthetic *a priori* proposition without which no knowledge of nature is possible.

The claim that substance is permanent is unproblematic, for permanence belongs to the very concept of substance. To this extent the proposition is analytic. Problematic is the application of the concept of substance, understood as permanence, to appearances. Only the claim that something permanent underlies all appearances and that the various appearances are nothing but changing attributes of it, has synthetic *a priori* character.

Kant's proof of this claim consists of an assumption and five arguments. Kant assumes that there are changing appearances and claims first that it is not possible to conceive of change without a set frame of reference. He secondly identifies the frame of reference as the single temporal order in which all change (the coexistence, the succession and the reciprocity of appearances) is represented. Time itself does not change but persists; it is absolutely permanent. But time cannot be the substance we are looking for since it, according to Kant's third argument, is not perceived in its own right and hence cannot form the basis for the changes of appearances in the realm of perception. So, fourthly, the substratum of all change must be located in the objects of perception. Since, fifthly, the substratum of all properties is substance, it follows that it is substance which persists through all change in the appearances. Hence, there must always be something in experience that relates to the appearances as enduring substance does to its changing attributes (properties).

The principle of the permanence of substance says that change can be experienced only in relation to a substance, and not absolutely. On the other hand, only a change in the appearances of substance can be known—and not its coming-to-be or passing-away. Permanent substance is thus the indispensable condition under which appearances can attain the necessary unity of an experience. The principle of permanence provides an important clarification of the notion of change: In coming-to-be and passing-away (e.g., a street becomes wet and then dries out again), that which comes to be and passes away does not change, but its attributes do: wetness and dryness. The change is one way for the substance to exist, which succeeds another way for it to exist: the dryness succeeds the wetness. Thus everything which changes is enduring, and only its states change. Although it sounds paradoxical, it is correct to say that only the permanent (substance) is changed, whereas the changeable (wetness, dryness) experiences no transformation at all but instead undergoes a permutation: one property, wetness, stops and gives way to another, dryness.

Kant views the analogies of experience, in contrast to the mathematical principles, as regulative rather than constitutive. In other words, they make no statements about the appearances themselves but provide a rule for finding something in the world of appearances. The principle of permanence thus requires empirical research to understand nature in terms of substance and attributes and to find out what has the character of an attribute and what has the character of a substance. In Kant's time, following the French chemist Lavoisier (1743–94), weighable matter was viewed as the ultimate substance. Kant's more detailed explanations hence point in this direction. Nonetheless, the first analogy does not, as is often supposed (e.g., Körner 1965, 471), refer to the permanent as matter or as material substance but instead leaves it to natural science to determine how exactly one must think of permanent substance. Kant's first analogy does not depend upon the progress of physics. The requirement that we must look for relations of permanence and change in order to have objective experience also underlies the present conception of energy and mass as two forms of the same substance.

In the second edition of the *Critique*, Kant amends the principle of permanence and says that the quantity of substance in nature as a whole neither increases nor decreases (B 224). In the first analogy, Kant does not show that substance can be described as a quantity; however, he could appeal to the fact discussed in the first two principles, that all objects of nature can be described mathematically. Particularly in the second edition, the transcendental principle of the permanence of substance resembles the laws of conservation, which have survived the crisis of classical physics brought about by the theory of relativity and quantum theory. As proof of Kant's continuing significance, von Weizsäcker shows that the first analogy is consistent with the most recent insights of physics into the conservation of energy. Not all arguments from transcendental philosophy for conservation can be found in contemporary physics, but arguments of a Kantian kind have become relevant in present work toward a unified physics and have thus also become subject to critique from the standpoint of physics. There are, however, difficulties involved in the idea that Kant has direct significance for fundamental problems in physics. Despite its similarity to the physical laws of conservation, the principle of the permanence of substance is situated on a different level. The first analogy says that all experience contains the relationship between a substance and its attributes, but it does not determine what substance consists in. Only the *Metaphysical Origins of Science* deal with this question. The metaphysics of corporeal nature developed there relies on a certain (perhaps problematic) concept of matter in addition to the ideas of the *Critique* (IV 470). The *first law of mechanics* (that the quantity of matter remains the same throughout all changes in corporeal nature) can only be justified with the aid of this concept of matter (IV 541). Only this law and its justification are appropriate participants in physical discussions.

The Principle of Causality

The second analogy of experience follows and connects up with the first. It treats changes in the states of substance as they occur in temporal succession, and it claims that they obey the law of causality, which connects cause and effect (B 232). Recent philosophy and theory of science distinguish causal *laws*, a certain kind of physical laws, from the causal *principle*, according to which every event has a cause. Since Kant's second analogy, the law of causality, corresponds to that which today is called the principle of causality, we shall for the sake of clarity speak of the principle of causality with reference to the second analogy.

Like the principle of permanence, the principle of causality has for Kant transcendental significance. It does not declare some appearances to be effects and others to be causes. Nor does it assert that we know or should know the cause for all appearances. It says that a temporal succession of appearances can only be recognized as a transformation of the object and as objectively valid if the succession is not left to the discretion of the perceiver but is instead recognized as adhering to the rule of cause and effect and thus seen (in relation to the given succession of appearances) as irreversible.

According to the principle of causality, experience can exist only as insight into natural connections of cause and effect. There can be no supernatural intervention in natural events, no miracles. The principle does not merely assert that we have not up to now experienced any miracles but claims more generally and more fundamentally that in the circle of objects of possible experience, miracles cannot occur. Since the objectivity of experience is constituted by the connections between causes and effects, a miracle would revoke not only causality but also all objectivity.

To illustrate and justify the principle of causality, Kant compares the perception of an object that is changing with the perception of a change (B 235ff.): if I perceive a house in its permanent form, then I apprehend the various parts not all at once but in succession—first the roof, perhaps then the walls and finally the floor. But I can just as well perceive the parts in the reverse order insofar as I am taking into consideration the permanent form and not changes in the house. From the point of view of the object as something which does not change, the succession of perceptions is indeterminate and arbitrary because it is not governed by a rule of cause and effect.

If, however, I concentrate on a change and see, for example, a ship floating freely on a river, the succession of my perceptions is not left to my discretion but instead depends upon the perceived process. Since the ship is moving downstream, I first see it further up and later further down the river. Governed by the causal rule that a ship floating freely is first further upstream and then further downstream, the temporal succession of my perceptions is necessary, or more cautiously formulated: not subject to arbitrary permutations. Of course, Kant does not claim that the observed process is necessary. The ship could just as well go upstream. But then the succession of perceptions would be determined by a different rule of cause and effect: a ship going upstream is first further down, then further up the river. Relative to this rule, the succession of perceptions is again not subject to arbitrary permutations. (Kant's example is admittedly oversimplified. Scientific research does not stop with the rule of going upstream or downstream but instead looks for the forces active and is only satisfied with an explanation on the basis of the appropriate natural laws.)

To Kant's explanation of the principle of causality, one could object that the perception of a house and that of the free-floating ship do not differ significantly. Both are events which the subject recognizes as such, and in both cases a change in the relative positions of two objects is observed. In one case, the eye moves; in the other case, the ship moves from upstream to downstream. This objection is correct in its assertion but incorrect in its assumption. The perception of the house can indeed be understood as a sequence of events, but then that which is perceived is no longer the house in its permanent form, as it is in Kant's case, but the eye that perceives the house. Kant would view this as a confirmation of the principle of causality: Insofar as the eye perceives the house from the roof down, it necessarily moves from the top to the bottom and not vice versa. This necessity is based on the objective determination of the change. The eye perceives the house in a downward and not in an upward direction.

According to the Analytic of Concepts, the connection of perceptions and the determinacy of the connection (first top, then bottom and not vice versa) are not products of intuition or sensation. The determinacy of the connection and its necessity in this respect cannot be perceived. It is attained by the understanding, which provides the category of causality for cases of temporal succession (cf. B 234).

Generally speaking, every change follows the principle of causality on Kant's view because we can conceive a succession of appearances as an objective occurrence, that is, as a transformation of the thing perceived and not of the perceiver, only if we can think of the succession of appearances as a temporal sequence the order of which is irreversible because the later state follows from the earlier state according to a rule of cause and effect. The earlier state is not just before ("lightning comes *before* thunder"); it is the cause ("it thunders *because* there was lightning"). Every succession of appearances lying in the object itself and not in hallucinations of the subject, every objective change, is only possible if it occurs according to a rule of cause and effect ("wherever it thunders, there was lightning"). The succession of appearances governed by rules is the schema of causality. Therefore, every objective change occurs according to a connection of cause and effect ("thunder is the effect for which the cause is lightning").

A frequent objection to Kant's thesis that the principle of causality is universally valid points to modern quantum theory as a counterexample. According to this theory, events in the subatomic realm can be described only by probabilistic laws. The principle of causality appears to be unnecessary in contemporary physics (e.g., Körner 1966, 47). According to Heisenberg's indeterminacy principle, the knowledge of an event E_1 specifies only the probability for the occurrence of another event E_2. For this reason contemporary physics, in contrast to Newtonian mechanics, can no longer do without probabilistic laws. Modern physics, people say, is no longer strictly determinist, like classical physics, but instead indeterminist.

A first defense of Kant could appeal to the fact that the second analogy, on the basis of the knowledge of the time, could not take subsequent developments in microphysics into account and that outside of microphysics, the causal laws of Newtonian mechanics are still valid. But this attempt at a defense has the disadvantage that Kant argues for the principle of causality as a condition of the possibility of all experience. The objection to Kant's view can be better met with a different argument: Kant's principle of causality does not assert the predictability of events but rather their explainability. His second analogy does not say that every event has completely predictable effects but that events which are to be considered objective are due neither to supernatural intervention nor to subjective hallucinations. They can always be explained as the effect of certain causes even though science in its present form may not yet have the required explanations. Although Kant's thoughts concerning natural science are strongly influenced by Newton's deterministic mechanics, his principle of causality is situated on a higher, transcendental level and is in no way bound up with a "*universal determinism*," as Stegmüller (1967, 10) assumes. The principle of causality is not rendered obsolete by modern probabilistic laws. Quantum physics means only that one must conceive the rules of cause and effect in the subatomic realm differently than one does in classical physics. In any case, Kant's principle of causality provides no information as to the sort of laws in which causal connections are to be grasped in physics and no information as to the content of such laws. Because the principle of causality is a transcendental principle and not a principle of natural science, one does not have to look in its defense for good epistemological reasons which make "our knowledge of indeterminacy appear as parasitic upon our knowledge of causal determinacy" either (Beck 1973, 172).

Like the first analogy, the second analogy, and the third, which is not treated here, has regulative and not constitutive importance. The principle of causality is a rule for spelling out appearances in their temporal succession so that they can be read as determinate objects and objective experiences. Whoever wishes to know nature is required to view all events as effects and to investigate their underlying causes. What the causes are in each particular case can be discovered only empirically (cf. B 165). Every determinate causal relation, even the form of rules of cause and effect, is due to experience and to the scientific theory of experience—not to transcendental necessity. Not only the mathematical side of the modern science of nature but also its character as an empirical investigation of causes receives from Kant a philosophical justification. The transcendental critique of reason does not put shackles onto the science of nature but liberates it to carry out an ongoing process of research.

6.5 THE POSTULATES OF EMPIRICAL THOUGHT

The combination of the three previous moments of knowledge—intuition, perception and experience—is performed by empirical thought, which has to do with the three modalities of knowledge: possibility, actuality and necessity. The postulates proposed by Kant for empirical thought show the *a priori* conditions under which the state of affairs asserted in a judgment is possible in an empirical (not just logical) sense, those under which it is actual and those under which it is necessary:

1. That which agrees with the formal conditions of experience (with respect to intuition and concepts) is *possible.*
2. That which is bound up with the material conditions of experience (sensation) is *actual.*
3. That which in connection with the actual is determined in accordance with universal conditions of experience, is *necessary* (exists necessarily). (B 265f.)

The formal conditions of intuition and of thought do not bring us further than (empirical or real) possibilities. Only sensation can establish actuality; only sensation can teach me that there really is something corresponding to my representations.

⟨∞⟩

Kant appends the "Refutation of Idealism" to the explanation of the second postulate. In Descartes' "problematic" version, idealism declares inner experience to be beyond doubt (*cogito erao sum*) but the existence of external objects to be "doubtful and *indemonstrable*" (B 274). Berkeley's "dogmatic" idealism regards "the things in space as merely imaginary entities" (ibid.). According to Kant, this view assumes that space is a property of things in themselves, an assumption refuted in the Transcendental Aesthetic (sect. 4). Against Descartes, Kant brings to bear "that even our *inner* experience . . . is possible only on the assumption of *outer* experience." My own existence, perceived by inner sense, presupposes something permanent outside of me and hence presupposes the existence of external things. We therefore have experience and not just imagination of external objects, too (B 275f.).

With the postulates of empirical thought, Kant provides the final answer to the main question of the *Critique*, the question of the possibility of synthetic *a priori* judgments. Synthetic *a priori* judgments are possible in that knowledge does not adapt itself to the objects but the objects adapt themselves to knowledge. The subject of knowledge itself furnishes nature with the transcendental laws formulated in the synthetic principles of pure understanding. The objects of nature are thus our own creation. That which is to be known becomes a determinate object only on the basis of constitutive *a priori* acts. In short, it is an appearance (phenomenon) and not a thing (object) in itself (noumenon, literally: that which is thought).

The notion of a thing in itself has given rise to many misunderstandings. It is a methodological concept and not, as is frequently assumed, a metaphysical notion. It is not a leftover of dogmatism worthy, as Nietzsche says, "of Homeric laughter" because the thing in itself only veils knowledge of true reality—that is, of illusion. In the theoretical realm, the thing in itself does not designate a world beyond, a true world hidden behind the appearances. The thing in itself belongs instead to the set of concepts necessary for an adequate understanding of the possibility of empirical knowledge. The expression "thing in itself" or, more exactly, "thing viewed in itself (and not as appearance)" points to the fact that that which is known is not due exclusively to the subjective determinants of knowledge. There is a "participant" which belongs neither to empirical nor to *a priori* subjectivity. This item, which is independent of the subject and without which no knowledge is possible, must be assumed even though we cannot at all specify it more closely nor know it in any way. The thing in itself is "merely a *limiting concept*" (B 311; cf. *Prol.* § 57) for theoretical reason; it is the completely indeterminate cause of sensation, the mere *x*. However, it has been claimed ever since the earliest criticisms of Kant that even a *limiting* concept must still be a *concept*. The German Idealist movement is sparked by this claim (sect. 13).

According to a philosophical tradition which goes back as far as Parmenides and Plato, we only grasp "true being" when thought has liberated itself from all limitations of the senses. True being, for Plato the Idea, reveals itself only to pure thought while knowledge gained through the senses learns only about "defective being" or "appearance." Kant reverses this evaluation for the theoretical realm: the appearances viewed by the senses and the understanding are for us the only objective beings, and thought alone is not capable of knowledge. That which exists in itself, independent of sensibility and the understanding, is not true and objective being. It is indeterminate and completely hidden. According to the critique of reason, there is no place in the theoretical sphere for a thing in itself in the positive sense of that which truly exists. Objects can no longer be divided up into objects of the senses (phenomena) and objects of the understanding (noumena). Although the understanding does, in contrast to empiricism, limit sensibility, it does not have its own sphere of knowledge, as rationalism believes.

Kant also contradicts the skeptics, who deny all metaphysical truth. There really are such truths. But—Kant adds to the dismay of traditional metaphysics—metaphysics never extends beyond experience. It provides no entry into extrasensual domains but instead clarifies the conditions of the possibility of all experience. All *a priori* knowledge is subservient to *a posteriori* knowledge, that is, experience.

7.

The Transcendental Dialectic

7.1 THE LOGIC OF ILLUSION

Following the Transcendental Analytic, Kant returns to the problem which prompted the critique of reason in the first place: metaphysics must exist, but it can create only the illusion of being true. Accounting for the necessity of metaphysics and understanding the illusion it creates, belong to the tasks of the Transcendental Dialectic, which forms an indispensable continuation of and not a useless appendix to the transcendental justification of experience.

Kant shows in the Transcendental Dialectic that the attempts of pure reason to conceive a world beyond the appearances as the true realm of being inevitably fail. All attempts of traditional philosophy to gain knowledge in the field of (speculative) metaphysics are doomed to failure. Reason can prove neither that the soul is immortal and the will free nor that there is a God. Everything so passionately sought by traditional metaphysics loses its philosophical basis. But, Kant consoles us, the opposite position cannot be demonstrated either. It cannot be proved that there is not an immortal soul, a free will and a God. (Speculative) reason can adopt neither a positive nor a negative stance on God, freedom and immortality. Does Kant want us simply to ignore these questions? Is he a predecessor of positivism, which, considering it to be sheer nonsense and utterly meaningless, dismisses metaphysics right from the start?

According to Kant, metaphysics does not arise from a chance inspiration, and even less does it arise from intentional deception. It represents more than a transitory, aberrant phase in the development of occidental thought (cf. B xxxi). Metaphysics is based on the interest of reason in finding the unconditioned. Knowledge receives an indeterminate material from intuition. The understanding gives determinate unity to this material with the aid of concepts and principles. Finally, reason strives to bring supreme unity to conceptual knowledge. But the supreme unity is only reached with a condition which itself is no longer conditioned. This condition is the unconditioned. By means of the unconditioned, which Kant also calls the (transcendental) idea, the understanding is brought "into thoroughgoing accordance with itself" (B 362). The unconditioned produces a systematic unity of all experience. The search for such a thing thus seems to be a matter of course and indeed an inevitable continuation of all knowledge. The search is in the natural interest of reason.

Kant allows the interest of reason to unfold before annihilating its claim to knowledge. The thoroughgoing accordance of understanding with itself is necessary neither for its constitution nor for the performance of its epistemological task. Only subjective necessity, and not objective necessity, underlies the progress of knowledge toward the unconditioned. The understanding seeks, "by comparison of its concepts, to reduce their general use to the smallest possible number" (B 362).

Kant's reference to reason as the supreme force of *knowledge* (B 355) is misleading. For the main point of the Transcendental Dialectic consists in the insight that reason can conceive the unconditioned but can have no knowledge of it. The transcendental ideas deal with something "to which all experience is subordinate, but which is never itself an object of experience" (B 367). Whereas the understanding produces the primary unity without which nothing objective can emerge from the indeterminate manifold of intuition, reason creates a secondary unity. It brings the unifying concepts of the understanding into yet another unity, which is not, however, necessary for the constitution of objects. It cannot expand our knowledge.

Reason is quite successful in its search for supreme unity. It discovers not just one transcendental idea but, in accordance with Wolff's division of special metaphysics, three ideas: the unconditioned in the sense of the absolute unity of the thinking subject (the object of rational psychology); the unconditioned in the sense of the totality of things and conditions in space and time (the object of transcendental cosmology); and finally the unconditioned in the sense of the absolute unity of the condition of all objects of thought, that is, in the sense of a supreme being (God as the object of natural theology). But reason pays a high price for its success: it must feign knowledge where there is none. In conceiving an absolute subject, reason falls prey to fallacies (paralogisms); in the case of the totality of things and conditions, it involves itself in contradictions (antinomies); and with regard to God, it speaks of proofs which can all be refuted. Knowledge of the unconditioned thus proves to be spurious knowledge. It is mere illusion.

The illusion does not, however, stem from subjective misunderstandings, logical fallacies or intentional deception. It thus cannot be eliminated simply by more exact reasoning. We have to do here not with sophistic but with speculative or transcendental illusion, with ambiguities of thought which stem from the nature of reason itself. This ambiguity has to do with the *a priori* conditions of knowledge and is only understood after critical reflection on the connection between reason and knowledge.

Like an optical illusion, transcendental illusion can be understood but not eliminated: a stick held in the water seems crooked even to the physicist, and not only to the uninformed layman does the moon seem larger when it is rising than it does at its zenith. Although everyone perceives phenomena in the same way, scientists and, in a different way, men with relevant practical experience understand the causes and do not let themselves be misled. They perceive the stick in the water as crooked and the moon near the horizon as larger but realize that the stick is in fact straight and that the moon stays the same size. Similarly, the philosopher cannot make the transcendental illusion disappear, since reason continues to have a metaphysical need for something unconditioned. The philosopher can, however, keep us from taking the illusion for the truth and thus being tricked by it.

Transcendental illusion occurs when one views the natural continuation of thought toward the unconditioned as an extension of the pure understanding, considers such results of thought to be objectively valid, and believes oneself to have found substantive, comprehensive knowledge. In fact, the unconditioned is lacking in both conditions of objective knowledge: sensible intuition and conceptual understanding. Since the Transcendental Aesthetic and the Transcendental Analytic establish these two conditions, speculative illusion can only be understood on the basis of the theory developed in these parts of the *Critique*.

As long as the constitutive elements of all experience are not explained methodologically, reason is completely delivered over to its natural interest in knowledge of the unconditioned. It allows itself to be deceived into thinking that it can overstep the limits of possible experience. Only the transcendental critique allows us to unmask the claim of metaphysics to knowledge of the unconditioned as a spurious presumption.

The expression "illusion"[3] designates putative knowledge which, upon looking more closely—but only after looking more closely—proves spurious. Transcendental illusion is thus to be seen not just negatively as the paradigm of false consciousness; the Transcendental Dialectic does more than merely destroying metaphysics. Putative knowledge consists of propositions which can be convincing. The Paralogisms, the Antinomies and the purported proofs of the existence of God contain propositions which seem plausible at first.

The positive significance of the Transcendental Dialectic extends further. Even the dissolution of transcendental illusion does not lead to a general rejection of the transcendental ideas of pure reason. Kant gives them a new methodological function. They do not have a constitutive function with respect to knowledge and thus can neither make experience possible nor expand it. But they do have a regulative significance. Experience necessarily shows us only parts or segments of reality. Reason seeks to put these fragments together into a whole and is correct in doing so. The whole, however, is never given to us but constantly demanded of us. It is the goal of the ongoing process of research and not the object of a particular science called metaphysics. Because all experience has a fragmentary nature and because every new experience pieces the fragments together into larger fragments—but never to a complete whole—science, the methodical acquisition of experience, is a never-ending search for knowledge. The whole is like the horizon, of which only children believe that one can reach its edge. The idea that the whole of experience is not merely the horizon of the search for knowledge but a topic in its own right gives rise to transcendental illusion and has fooled philosophy for a very long time.

The Dialectic of the first *Critique* has not only a theoretical and negative significance but also a practical, positive meaning. Because the existence of God, freedom and immortality can be neither proven nor refuted, the Dialectic severs "the root of *materialism, fatalism, atheism*, free-thinking *agnosticism. fanaticism*, and *superstition*" (B–xxxiv), which believe in the refutability of the aforementioned claims. Moreover, the limitations of theoretical reason clear the field for pure practical reason. The destruction of "bad," speculative metaphysics prepares the ground for a "good," practical metaphysics. According to this metaphysics, the ideas of God, freedom and immortality are postulates of practical reason rather than objects of knowledge for theoretical reason: "I have therefore found it necessary to deny *knowledge*, in order to make room for *faith*" (B xxx). With faith, Kant means here the recognition of pure practical reason. And pure practical reason is simply morality, which Kant conceives in terms of freedom. The traditional metaphysics of being thus gives way to a new metaphysics of freedom.

7.2 THE CRITIQUE OF SPECULATIVE METAPHYSICS

7.2.1 *The Critique of Rational Psychology*

The first illusion to which reason falls prey is the opinion that it can gain substantive knowledge about the self or the soul by mere thought—by reason alone without any experience at all. The discipline of metaphysics which is based on this illusion is the rational theory of the soul, also called speculative psychology. Its main goal lies in the demonstration of the immortality of the soul. It is thus not a theoretical but a practical goal.

Even Plato contrasted in his *Phaedo* the unity and simplicity of the soul with the multiplicity and complexity of bodies. He further demonstrates the immortality of the soul in four series of arguments. Following Plato's example, Mendelssohn wrote a dialogue called *Phaedo, or On the Immortality of the Soul*[4] (1767). Kant refers explicitly to this dialogue. When modern philosophy asserts, as Plato does, a dualism of body and soul, it follows in the footsteps primarily of Descartes. In his search for the ultimate foundation of all knowledge, Descartes in the *Meditations* (1641) calls all putative knowledge into doubt and finds in the act of doubting the undoubtable certainty of the thinking ego: I doubt, therefore I am ("dubito, ergo sum"). Since doubting is a form of thinking, Descartes can also say: I think, therefore I am ("cogito, ergo sum"). I exist as a thinking being (*res cogitans*), to be strictly distinguished from all corporeal things in the external world (*res extensae*). Fascinated by the "cogito" argument, many philosophers have agreed with Descartes—for example, Wolff and Baumgarten during the German Enlightenment.

In the Transcendental Deduction of the Categories, Kant confirms Descartes' basic idea. The "I think" is indeed the necessary condition of all knowledge; moreover, it is the apex of transcendental philosophy. But Kant ascribes an entirely different significance to the "I think." It is not an object of inner experience, a substance, nor is it an attribute, the opposite of substance. It has neither existence nor nonexistence. For substance and attribute, and existence and non-existence are categories. Because it is the origin of all categories, the transcendental "I think" is categorically indeterminate. Moreover, the constitution of objects and of objective knowledge about them requires (sensible) intuition. But there is no intuition for the transcendental "I think." Thus there is no objective knowledge of the self (the soul) and no valid proof of its immortality. The soul is not, however, mortal. Since it does not have the character of a substance, the question as to its immortality is simply meaningless.

According to Kant, Descartes and all representatives of rational psychology make four basic assertions. But the arguments which are supposed to support these assertions are all wrong. They are fallacies. The critique of speculative psychology, which attempts to make synthetic *a priori* judgments about the soul, thus carries the title: the Paralogisms (fallacies) of Pure Reason.

Rational psychology claims: (1) the soul (the thinking being) is substance (paralogism of substantiality), (2) the soul is simple (paralogism of simplicity), (3) the soul is a person (paralogism of personality), and (4) the existence of all objects of outer sense is doubtful (paralogism of the ideality of the relation to the outside world). Further claims are derived from these main theses: for example, the immateriality, incorruptibility, spirituality and above all the immortality of the soul, the latter being the real aim of rational psychology.

The basis for all other arguments is the paralogism of substantiality. Kant intentionally puts it into the form of a sylloglsm, in which the conclusion follows from two premises:
That which cannot be thought otherwise than as subect does not exist otherwise than as subject. and is therefore substance.
A thinking being, considered merely as such, cannot be thought otherwise than as subect.
Therefore it exists also only as subject. that is, as substance. (B 410f.)

In a valid syllogism, the connection of two concepts (A, C) is demonstrated by producing a middle term (B), which connects the outer terms (A, C) with one another (sect. 5). The conclusiveness of the syllogism relies on the identity of the connecting middle term. But in the paralogism of substantiality, as in the other paralogisms, the middle term has a different meaning in the first and in the second premise. In the first premise (B_1), it refers to transcendental self-consciousness, the formal "vehicle of all concepts" (B 399); in the second (B_2), it refers not to a transcendental but instead to an objective ego: the real self as object of inner experience. The transcendental "I think" is not, however, objectifiable since it is the condition of the possibility of all objectivity. The arguments of speculative psychology thus lose their validity because they rely on an ambiguity in the middle term.

Analysis of the function of the transcendental "I think" gives rise only to the following claims: (1) that it is always a subject and never a predicate, (2) that it is a simple subject from a logical standpoint, (3) that it retains its identity in the face of the manifold of appearances, and (4) that it is distinct from external objects. These valid propositions are all analytic in character. Having now been cleansed by the critique of reason, philosophical psychology purports to make synthetic *a priori* judgments concerning the "I think." Philosophical psychology cannot do more than explain the concept of transcendental self-consciousness. The synthetic propositions corresponding to the analytic judgments—(1') The ego is substance, (2') simple, (3') a person, and (4') exists without doubt—are valid only under the assumption of a corresponding intuition. But this intuition is sensible in character and hence empirical. Such propositions, if they are true, are thus valid *a posteriori* and not *a priori*. They belong to a branch of empirical psychology which according to Kant is possible but not the business of philosophy.

Rational psychology originates in a misunderstanding. It views the transcendental unity of consciousness, which underlies all categories, as the intuition of an object; it then applies the categories of substance, unity, and so on. In fact, the unity of consciousness is only the formal unity of thought. Without an additional intuition, there is no object and no knowledge. The dialectical illusion of the paralogisms rests upon reification (hypostatization): the completely indeterminate notion of a thinking being is made into a "real object existing . . . outside the thinking subject" (A 384). Such reification is unavoidable as long as one does not (on the basis of the Transcendental Analytic) know that without intuition no object, no knowledge, and thus no objective self is possible. For this reason, the fallacies of speculative psychology cannot be eliminated with the tools of formal logic alone. Only the transcendental critique of reason provides the means for understanding the ambiguity of the middle term of rational psychology and for unmasking its claims to knowledge as illusory.

Kant's critique of rational psychology has important implications. The paralogism of substantiality, for example, rests upon the widely accepted notion that body and soul are two independent realities. As long as one accepts this dualism, the question comes up as to how these two substances affect one another and how they can be unified in man. This so-called mind-body problem has puzzled philosophers ever since Plato and Descartes. With his critique of the paralogism of substantiality, Kant shows that the problem proceeds from a false assumption. Because the basis for all knowledge, the self or soul, is not a substance at all but instead a transcendental "I think," the problem is solved by dissolution. The mind-body problem is in this respect a spurious problem.

7.2.2 *The Critique of Transcendental Cosmology*

What happens to reason when, in its quest for completeness, it views the world as a completed whole? It then fails even more clearly than in the case of the thinking ego. The attempt to extrapolate the fragments of human experience into a totality of all appearances and to make objective statements about the totality demonstrates the utter hopelessness of speculative metaphysics. Reason becomes entangled in antinomies. Antinomy means literally "conflict of the laws" (B 434); for Kant, it means that human reason is governed by two conflicting laws: the law of tracing everything conditioned back to something unconditioned and the law of seeing every condition as itself conditioned. In a second meaning, antinomies (in the plural) are pairs of sentences which obviously contradict one another (e.g., the world has/does not have a beginning in time) but which can be proven conclusively from the two laws of reason without resorting to sophisms. In the field of (in Wolff's terminology: transcendental) cosmology (Greek for the theory of the world), reason involves itself in contradictions, a scandalous situation which first woke Kant from his "dogmatic slumber" and "drove" him to the critique of reason (cf. *Letters*, 781/426).

It was well known that metaphysicians, particularly the rationalists and the empiricists, contradicted one another in their central claims. Kant's new idea was to seek out the contradictions systematically and to present equally plausible proofs of both opposing claims, so that the contradictions appear necessary.

Because the claims are advanced in a purely speculative manner, the resolution of the contradictions cannot be achieved with the aid of experience. Astronomy, for example, examines the age of our universe, which it estimates as being several billion years. It thus supports the thesis of the First Antinomy: The world has a beginning; and it rejects the antithesis: The world has no beginning. However, the universe dealt with in astronomy is only relative and does not include absolutely everything. Even ignoring empirical errors and theoretical controversies, there still remain questions of the following sort: What exists before the beginning of matter as determined by astronomers, and Where did "primordial matter" come from? Since speculative cosmology investigates the absolute totality of appearances, that is, something unconditioned, empirical research provides no help. The natural sciences cannot resolve the Antinomies. Philosophy must itself take on this task.

Kant shows that the Antinomies can only be overcome with the aid of transcendental philosophy. He thus saves reason from giving in to skeptical despair (B 434). The metaphysical speculations which Kant discusses in the chapter on the antinomies have not only theoretical but also practical interest, for they—so it seems—determine the foundations of morals and religion: The first antinomy investigates the spatial extension of the universe and the duration of its history; it concerns the question of whether the world has a beginning in time, and thus may have been created by God, or whether the world instead, as Aristotle claims, exists "since eternity." The second antinomy deals with the world's ultimate, absolutely simple building blocks: atoms in the sense of the Greek philosopher Democritus or monads in the sense of Leibniz. The third antinomy concerns the opposition between freedom and complete determination and is thus critical for the foundations of ethics. The fourth antinomy, which according to Al-Azm refers to the Leibniz-Clarke correspondence, discusses the existence or non-existence of a perfect being and thus leads into the critique of speculative theology.

The cosmological ideas of the unconditioned (the absolute completeness of appearances in four respects) can be thought of in two ways: (A) as the absolutely last member in the series of appearances and (B) as the whole of the series, so that the members of the series are conditioned and only the infinite series itself is unconditioned. The conflicting claims of speculative cosmology result from the twofold interpretation of the unconditioned. Interpretation A corresponds to dogmatic rationalism, interpretation B to empiricism. Kant calls the rationalist position the thesis and the empiricist position the antithesis. Since there are, in accordance with the four groups of categories, four cosmological ideas, Kant obtains four pairs of conflicting assertions (table 6.1).

Table 6.1 The Four Antinomies

Thesis	Antithesis
1. (Quantity)	
The world is limited in time and space.	The world is infinite in space and time.
2. (Quality)	
Every complex substance in the world consists of simple parts, and nothing exists except what is simple or composed of simple parts.	No complex thing in the world consists of simple parts, and nowhere in the world does something simple exist.
3. (Relation)	
In addition to causality according to the laws of nature, a causality through freedom is necessary for the explanation of the appearances.	There is no freedom, but everything in the world occurs exclusively according to laws of nature.
4. (Modality)	
A necessary being belongs to the world either as a part of the world or as its cause.	No absolutely necessary being exists, neither in the world nor as an external cause of it.

Kant investigates the truth of speculative cosmology by waiting. Since equally strong reasons support both the thesis and the antithesis, he allows free and unhindered competition of the opinions, without himself taking sides. Kant calls this procedure the skeptical method but distinguishes it from skepticism. Whereas skepticism, in asserting the fundamental impossibility of reliable knowledge, advocates its own specific academic doctrine, the *skeptical method* neither accepts nor rejects anything immediately. The conflicting positions have the right to discuss freely. The ensuing discussion is supposed to bring the "point of misunderstanding" to light. The point of difference is to be revealed as a "deceptive appearance," and a new certainty becomes possible (B 451f.).

In accordance with the two conflicting laws of reason, the arguments in this dispute prove to be equally strong. Each side succeeds in refuting its opponents and thus concludes that only its own claims are true. An indirect or negative proof of this sort is logically sound—on the assumption that thesis and antithesis form an exhaustive alternative: *either* the world has a beginning in time or it exists "since eternity"; *either* there is causality in the form of freedom or all events, including human actions, are completely determined; and so on.

The assumption that there are only two possibilities, one of which must be true, does not, however, hold here. There is a third possibility, which only comes to view with the aid of the transcendental critique of reason. Kant calls this previously unnoticed possibility *transcendental* or *formal idealism*. On this view the unconditioned can be conceived but not known. The ideas of pure reason have a transcendental but not transcendent significance. In the form of regulative principles, they relate to experience and are not objects existing in themselves. In contrast to material or empirical idealism, formal or transcendental idealism recognizes the objects of outer intuition as real. In contrast to transcendent idealism, however, it is aware that knowledge is directed only toward appearances and not toward things in themselves since the *a priori* structure of knowledge stems from the subject.

Transcendental idealism is justified in the Transcendental Aesthetic and the Transcendental Analytic and receives indirect but forceful confirmation in the critique of transcendental cosmology. The attempt to gain knowledge of the world by mere thought without the aid of intuition ensnares reason in contradictions. Acceptance of the Transcendental Aesthetic and Analytic, on the other hand, resolves the contradictions: if the world is a whole existing in itself, then it must be either finite, as rationalism claims, or infinite, as empiricism claims. Since the claims contradict one another, the assumption must be wrong that the world is a whole existing in itself.

Faced with the unresolved controversies about how to conceive the world as a whole, Kant neither seeks a reconcilation of empiricism and rationalism nor gives in to skepticism, which demands that we confess our ignorance because an answer to the controversial question is not within our power. Kant provides an incisive solution, which refutes rationalism, empiricism and skepticism: The cosmological ideas do not have constitutive but only regulative significance. They do not say how the world appears as a whole but give a rule for investigating nature in such a way as to attain comprehensive knowledge. The world, as the totality of appearances, does not exist in itself but comes to light more and more (but never entirely) through empirical research.

Since research never comes to an absolute conclusion, it is, for example, wrong to say that the world has a beginning in time or that it consists of absolutely simple parts. This error manifests itself in microphysics, which calls certain particles atoms—that is, indivisible particles—then discovers after further research that atoms are divisible into protons, neutrons and electrons, and later sees that even these are not the smallest particles. There is no end in sight to the discovery of smaller and smaller particles. The instruments required (accelerators, electron microscopes, etc.) set at most a technological or pragmatic limit to research. On the other hand, empirical research into the history of the universe and into its constituent parts surely cannot ever reach complete infinity; so, it is also wrong to assume that the world has an infinite past or that its parts are divisible *ad infinitum*. The antitheses are thus just as wrong as the theses.

In the first two, mathematical antinomies, both the claims and their opposites are incorrect: both sides overlook the fact that the potential infinite constitutes a mean between the finite and an actually existent infinite: infinity not as given but as the possibility of continuing beyond any given finite limit. In the other two, dynamic antinomies, both claims are true according to Kant. This difference between the mathematical and the dynamic antinomies does not follow from the nature of the antinomies themselves but from an additional problem which attaches to them. One can indeed formulate the dynamic antinomies in such a way as to correspond exactly to the mathematical antinomies. The third antinomy then reads: Thesis: There can be a first cause, which itself has no further cause but is instead causality through freedom, for everything which happens in the world. *Antithesis*: There is no causality through freedom; instead, everything that happens follows only the laws of nature.

Here, too, the thesis is false. For freedom in the sense of a cause which itself has no cause cannot occur in the sphere of empirical events. For experience, all events, even human actions, can be investigated as to their causes. From an empirical standpoint, human action is *potentially* determined. Methodological determinism follows from the principle of causality, which holds for all experience. Methodological determinism is not, however, to be confused with the dogmatic determinism propounded today by strict behaviorists, which denies that there can be causality through freedom at all. The dogmatic version of the antithesis does not contain the necessary restriction, "in the sphere of possible experience of nature," and is thus just as false as the thesis. Freedom, without which morals, according to Kant, cannot exist, thus remains conceptually possible. At the same time, Kant determines the only possible location for the philosophical concept of freedom: outside of possible experience. Outside is the world of the purely intelligible, which plays a legitimate role only in ethics.

As in the case of the Paralogisms, Kant is able to reduce the various antinomies to a single dialectical argument. The major premise is a conditional sentence, and the minor premise asserts the truth of the condition: "If the conditioned is given, the entire series of all its conditions is likewise given; objects of the senses are given as conditioned; therefore, etc." (B 525)

In this argument, as in the paralogisms, the middle term is taken in two different meanings. The major premise takes the conditioned transcendentally as the (infinite) regress in the series of conditions. The minor premise, however, takes the conditioned empirically, as if the totality of conditions actually existed. In contrast to empiricism and rationalism, the cosmological ideas do not signify fundamental concepts of nature but rather principles of empirical research. They mean in a negative sense that research never reaches an absolute limit: There can be no unconditioned empirical condition which constitutes the condition of all conditions. Like the paralogisms, the antinomies also wish to unmask false consciousness and to de-objectify an idea falsely objectified in dogmatic metaphysics. As soon as the unconditioned is placed outside the sensible world, the ideas become transcendent. Contrary to illegitimate reifications on the part of metaphysics (rationalism) and positivism (empiricism), the ideas are transcendental in character: they have significance for the structure of all objective knowledge. They remind science that all current knowledge, even the most recent and most comprehensive scientific knowledge, remains fragmentary, a mere torso.

In addition to this negative result, Kant's critique of speculative cosmology comes also to a positive conclusion. While the world is not hypostatized as something existing in itself, the idea of the world as a complete set of appearances remains to spur the natural sciences on in the endless process of research. The totality of appearances can never be completely measured. The cosmological ideas thus leave empirical research open in a much more fundamental sense than that of the rather trivial fallibilism of contemporary epistemology and theory of science. Kant does not merely claim that no scientific statement is completely free of error and of bias. He teaches further that for empirical research, there is no microscopic or macroscopic final object designating the ultimate limit of human knowledge. Unhappy metaphysics, in conflict with itself, makes way for happy, harmonious research in the specialized sciences.

7.2.3 *The Critique of Natural Theology*

Theology forms the supreme discipline of traditional metaphysics. God, its central concept, which is defined in philosophy as the supreme being, traditionally represents the crown of human knowledge. Questions concerning God, the original being, have priority over all other metaphysical topics.

Although questions about God developed primarily in the context of religious discussions, they also rank among the oldest philosophical topics. Ever since Plato and Aristotle, the most brilliant thinkers have attempted to illuminate the essence of God by means of natural reason. In the history of the philosophical investigation of God, Kant's thought marks a watershed. Kant brought about a revolutionary paradigm change in philosophical theology. (A critique of religion leading to philosophical atheism is, of course, older than Kant and a position which he rejects. For the Enlightenment period, cf. d'Holbach, *Système de la nature*, 1770, part II.)

Kant's new orientation in theology consists of four parts. *First*, Kant rejects all natural theology and its attempts to know God objectively, in particular its attempts to prove the existence of God. In agreement with tradition, Kant recognizes God as the supreme aim of all thought, but he denies that this aim is an object to which existence or nonexistence can be attributed. *Second*, the transcendent idea of God is replaced by the transcendental ideal, which, as the principle of completeness of knowledge, concludes the metaphysics of experience and has little to do with religious ideas about God. *Third*, in agreement with the moral interpretation of the Enlightenment (cf. Lessing, *The*

Education of the Human Race[5]), the first *Critique* prepares the way for a moral theology, which is carried out in the works on the foundations of ethics (sect. 11). Kant's paradigm change for philosophical theology lies in taking pure practical, moral reason rather than theoretical reason as the primary source of legitimate questions about God. *Fourth*, in his work on religion, Kant presents an interpretation of basic propositions of the Judeo-Christian faith in light of his moral belief in God (sect. 11).

Kant's new paradigm for philosophical theology destroys the old paradigm, according to which the existence of God can be proved speculatively (theoretically). Kant was not originally convinced of the impossibility of all proofs of the existence of God. In 1755 (I 395f.) and even as late as 1762 (II 70ff.), he held to the objective reality of God without hesitation. But in the 1760s he begins with the de-objectification of God which culminates in the first *Critique*: God is the rationally necessary ideal of objective knowledge but not an objectively known idea.

Kant is not satisfied with simply examining previous essays in natural theology. He claims to discuss comprehensively all possibilities for speculative theology. He thus, in contrast to Hume (*Dialogues Concerning Natural Religion*, 1799—posthumously), first surveys all conceivable proofs of the existence of God. There are, corresponding to the possible reasons for God's existence, three. The reason for the existence of God is either experience in the sensibly perceivable world or, disregarding all experience, a mere concept. And in the realm of experience, the reason lies either in a specific experience, that of the order and harmony of the world, or, disregarding all notions of harmony, in the indeterminate experience that *something* exists.

All three proofs can look back on a long history. The proof from the harmony of nature, which Kant calls the physico-theological proof, is considered to be the oldest, most clear, and "the most accordant with the common reason of mankind" (B 651). It can be found in philosophy, for example, to some extent in Aristotle (*Metaphysics*, book XII, chap. 7, 1072a26–b4), and also elsewhere, and we cannot say who first came up with it. St. Paul, for example, appeals to the physico-theological proof when he says in Romans 1:20 that ever since the creation of the world, God can be seen in created things. In the Middle Ages, Thomas Aquinas advocates this proof (*Summa theologiae*, part I, question 2, art. 3, 5th way; cf. *Summa contra gentiles*, book I, chap. 13, 5th proof); in modern times, Paley (*Nature of Theology*, 1802), although Hume has previously rejected it and Kant's *Critique* is also earlier than Paley's work.

The proof of the existence of God from existence in general is known as the cosmological proof. It stems from philosophy and goes back to Plato (*Laws*, book X, chap. 2–9) and Aristotle (*Metaphysics*, book XII, chap. 6–7; cf. *Physics*, book VIII). Kant, however, argues somewhat differently than, say, Aristotle. Moreover, Aristotle's brief and rather sketchy argumentation has more the character of a model than of a strict proof. Proceeding from movement, Aristotle says that nothing can be moved without a mover. After noting the eternal rotation of the first heavenly sphere, he concludes that there must be an unmoved mover. This first mover of everything which is moved is the causal foundation of nature in the sense that it constitutes the supreme object of all desire (the latter being a physico-theological aspect of the "proof").

Because Aristotle's claim that the world is eternal contradicts the Judeo-Christian notion of a creation, the cosmological proof could be accepted in the Middle Ages only with certain modifications. The first three of the five arguments cited by Aquinas (*Summa theologiae*, part I, question 1, art. 3) to show that belief in God is rational take the form of cosmological arguments (cf. *Summa contra gentiles*, book I, chap. 13). In the modern age, this proof has been advocated by Locke, for example (*An Essay Concerning Human Understanding*, book IV, chap. 10).

The proof of the existence of God on the basis of mere concepts, in abstraction from all experience, is called the ontological proof. It is the most recent. It stems from philosophy and goes back to St. Anselm of Canterbury's *Proslogion* (1077–78). Even after Kant, the ontological argument did not lose its fascination. The philosophers Hegel and Maurice Blondel as well as the theologian Paul Tillich all considered it to be true.

Kant shows that all three proofs fail. But he does not conclude that God does not exist. The negative claim, Kant says, is just as impossible to prove as the positive claim. Kant thus rejects not only speculative theology. He likewise distances himself from speculative atheism, which claims to demonstrate the non-existence of God. Kant's thesis is not, "There is no God," but rather, "God does not admit of objectification." In relation to any objectifying manner of speaking, God is "something completely different." More exactly: we cannot make any theoretical statement about God at all.

Many scholars, such as Bennett (1974, 228), overlook the fact that Kant does not begin with the destruction of all speculative proofs of the existence of God. Kant first asks about the motives of theoretical reason for proving the existence of God. Kant's most radical claim in connection with natural theology is not that the existence of God cannot be proved theoretically but that theoretical reason cannot even legitimately *ask* whether or not God exists. For since "existence" is a category, the question of God's existence assumes that God is something which can be categorically determined. The question thus confuses a transcendental idea with a transcendent concept. The notion of absolutely complete knowledge, which reason cannot do without, is replaced by the concept of a potentially existent object. It is not the steps in the various proofs but the titular concept "existence of God" which ensnares speculative theology in dialectical illusion.

Natural theology does not deal with the God of religious worship, the "God of Abraham, Isaac and Jacob." It investigates the "God of the philosophers." Before Kant, philosophers conceived God primarily by extrapolating from concepts of substance and properties. They thought of God as being the supreme substance, as being the paradigm for all things, and as being the supreme property—as omnipotent, omniscient, and so forth, that is, as the most perfect being. Kant adds a "step backward" to the traditional method. Then, God is not a supreme object which (even beyond all experience) *exists*. For theoretical reason, God is no longer a transcendent being but instead a transcendental ideal. God is an *a priori* representation *within* the realm of experience but behind its back, so to speak, and still necessarily bound up with experience. The transcendental ideal is a principle necessary in order to make the sciences, understood as comprehensive and systematic experience, possible.

Kant's "step backward" behind experience changes the methodological significance but not the content of the representation of God. God no longer plays the role of a determinate object but remains as the totality of all possible predicates. God is on the one hand the very essence (*ens erfectissimum*) and on the other hand the source of all possibilities (*ens realissimum*). The twofold idea of totality, Kant says, is not only consistent but also, for reason, necessary. Reason looks for complete knowledge. In order to know an object completely, one must be familiar with all possible predicates, and one must also know which predicates are attached to the object and which are not. The interest of reason in complete knowledge hence presupposes an essence and source of all possible predicates. This is the idea of a perfect and most real being, which Kant designates as the transcendental ideal.

As in the other parts of the Dialectic, reason here, too, becomes entangled in dialectical illusion as soon as it takes the transcendental ideal of a totality of all predicates as a constitutive principle for the knowledge of objects. Under these circumstances, reason first, making the totality of predicates into an object, reifies it, then, claiming the totality to be an object existing outside of the thinking subject, hypostatizes it, thirdly, referring to it as a person, personifies it, and finally specifies the purportedly objective person through the categories of reality, substance, causality and necessity of existence. In fact, the transcendental ideal is a mere idea of reason, and the categories are valid only for possible experience. They are "entirely without content when I venture with them outside the field of the senses" (B 707).

The Ontological Proof

Kant begins his detailed refutation of all proofs of the existence of God with the *ontological argument*, which excludes any empirical considerations. It deduces the existence of God solely from his concept. In his *Proslogion* (chap. 2-4), St. Anselm conceives God as the absolutely supreme being ("ens quo maius cogitari nequit": the being in comparison to which none can be conceived as greater). This specification, says Anselm, is accepted even by those who deny the existence of God. They claim only that such a being exists only in thought (*in intellectu*) and not in reality (*in re*). Anselm objects that it is contradictory to think of God as the supreme being and to deny his existence. For an existent supreme being would be superior to an absolutely supreme being which does not exist. But an absolutely supreme being does not by definition allow of superiority; so the notion of an absolutely supreme but nonexistent being is contradictory. Existence is attached to the absolutely supreme being.

Anselm's contemporary Gaunilo already viewed this brilliant argument as fallacious. And Thomas Aquinas does not accept it either (*Summa contra gentiles*, book I, chap. 10–11; *Summa theologiae*, part I, question 2, art. 1). Descartes, on the other hand, takes up the ontological argument in his *Meditations* (5th meditation) but also advocates another proof, which is related to the cosmological argument. Since Descartes, the ontological proof has often been repeated, for example by Spinoza (*Ethics*, part I, propositions 7–11), by Leibniz (*Nouveaux Essais sur l'Entendement Humain,*⁶book IV, chap. 10; *Monadology*, sections 44–45), by Christian Wolff, and by Baumgarten. Descartes defines God as the most perfect being (*ens perfectissimum*). God is the being to which all perfections, that is, all positive or desirable attributes, attach to the highest degree. He considers existence to be a necessary element of perfection and correctly concludes that existence necessarily attaches to God. Descartes, too, received thorough criticism from contemporaries such as the scientist and philosopher P. *Gassendi* (*Disquisitio metaphysica*, 1644).

Kant shows with great conceptual clarity where the error in the ontological argument lies: not in the idea of God, which Kant accepts, but rather in the assumption that existence is a perfection, that is, a positive or desirable property. To bring out the underlying error, Kant distinguishes between various senses of "is." Whereas natural theology naïvely fails to consider what "is" means in the sentence, "God is (exists) ," Kant sees that "is" in the sense of existence is a grammatical (logical) predicate but not a "real predicate" (B 626; cf . *The Only Possible Basis for a Demonstration of the Existence of God*, I, 1, 1: "Existence is not a predicate or determination of any thing at all," II 72) .

According to a stubborn myth (to which Körner, too, adheres, 1955, 120), Kant claimed summarily that "being" in the sense of "existence" is not a predicate. J. Hintikka has objected to this purported Kantian thesis that "existence" is indeed a predicate. However, he adds, this predicate has the peculiarity of being redundant for all descriptive purposes (one could, following Frege, speak of a second-order predicate over and against first-order predicates). If this is what Kant means, Hintikka says, he is completely right (*Models for Modalities*, 1969, 45–54).

Kant not only meant but also explicitly said just that in stating that "being" is not a "real predicate." "Real" does not for Kant mean "genuine, " as it does today. A predicate which is not real is thus not a seeming predicate. In the table of categories, "reality" is a category of quality and means the real content of a thing or what the thing is. If God is defined in the ontological argument as the most perfect or most real being, that means that he lacks no positive real content, that is, no desirable attribute. This is the right notion of God, Kant says, but existence does not designate a possible attribute. The claim of existence adds nothing to the real content of God. God does not have in addition to his omnipotence, omniscience, and so forth, the property of existence. Instead, the claim of existence presupposes the complete concept of God (as a being that is omnipotent, omniscient, etc.) and maintains that there actually is an object with the properties of omnipotence, omniscience, and so on.

Since existence says nothing about the properties of a thing, I cannot by mere thought determine whether or not my notion of God corresponds to something in the real world. In asserting existence, I go beyond the mere concept of God. The statement "God is" in the sense of "God exists" is not analytic but synthetic.

In the case of mathematical objects, the question of existence is answered by construction in pure intuition. But since God is supposed to have objective and hence more than mere mathematical existence, Kant can set this case aside. Objective things, whose existence is determined by means of (sensory) perceptions or by inferences from perceptions, remain. The ontological argument, however, is based on pure thought and has nothing to do with perception or experience. Since we can have no knowledge of the existence of objective things without perception and experience, the existence of God cannot be proved by purely speculative arguments—nor can his existence be disproved speculatively. Limiting itself to pure thought, the ontological proof deprives itself of any criterion for existence.

Kant treats the ontological argument with disdain. It relies upon a conceptual confusion (existence is viewed as a property) and can be unmasked by logical and conceptual means. Nonetheless, it does not represent mere sophistry but rather a dialectical illusion, in which a transcendental idea is confused with a transcendent idea. The critique of reason allows us to clear up the confusion and shows that only perception and experience can guarantee the existence of objective things.

The Cosmological Proof

The second, cosmological proof of the existence of God proceeds from the fact that something exists in space and time, considers this fact to be contingent, and looks for its cause. In this proof, the first step deduces the existence of an absolutely necessary being from the contingency of the world (Greek: *kosmos*); a second step attempts to show the existence of a being which is more real than any other. The second proof seems to be superior to the first because it proceeds from experience and thus promises to fill in the weak point of the ontological argument, namely the lack of a criterion for existence.

The second argument which Descartes combines with the ontological argument in his *Meditations* is related to the cosmological proof: Since an effect, Descartes says, cannot be more perfect than its cause, the notion of an infinite being cannot be a creation of human understanding, which is finite. The notion of an infinite being is without doubt present in understanding. Therefore, an infinitely perfect being, whose image is our representation of it, must exist. This being is called God. In Kant's account, the cosmological proof proceeds from the more general assumption that something exists at all; it proceeds more from Leibnizian than from Cartesian assumptions. No one, including Kant, wishes to contest this assumption. Only the additional assumption that if something exists, an absolutely necessary being must also exist as its cause, is questionable.

The first step in the cosmological argument says: Everything which exists contingently must have a cause, which, if it is contingent, must also have a cause, and so on until the series of contingent causes finally ends at an absolutely necessary cause. Without a cause which, because it is absolutely necessary, requires no further explanation, we would not have a complete explanation. We could not adequately explain the actual existence of the contingent. The second step concludes from the existence of a necessary being, as the result of the first step, that there is a being having supreme reality. This being is God.

In this proof, Kant sees "a whole nest of dialectical presumptions" lying hidden (B 637). One such presumption lies in the fact that the transcendental principle of tracing the contingent to its cause "has significance only in the sensible world; outside that world it makes no sense whatsoever"(ibid.). Descartes, for example, makes this mistake when, in his second argument, he applies the category of causality to imperceptible objects. Moreover, the attempt to apply the category of necessity to objects beyond all experience and to conceive God as an absolutely necessary being involve reason in a peculiar ambiguity: "One cannot put aside, and yet also cannot endure the thought" (B 641). For an absolutely necessary being which exists "from eternity to eternity" still asks itself "*but whence then am I?*" (ibid.). The possibility of further questioning still comes up, and the cosmological notion of God does not achieve its purpose of providing an ultimate support for all being and a final answer to the question of cause. Reason urges us to complete our line of questioning, but we can reach no final conclusion.

Kant considers another objection to be the most important one. Cosmological considerations, he says, can culminate in a proof of the existence of God only if the existence of a being more real than everything else can be derived from the notion of an absolutely necessary being. Experience is no longer mentioned here. As in the ontological proof, one makes inferences here on the basis of concepts alone. Moreover, the concepts of being absolutely necessary and of being real in the highest degree are coextensive, so one can reverse the second step of the cosmological argument ("the being which is most real is absolutely necessary") to obtain the ontological argument: An absolutely necessary being is the most real being, and its very concept implies its existence. The cosmological proof is thus subject to the same criticism as the ontological proof. And it poses as a new proof but in fact is not.

The Physico-Theological Proof

Since neither pure thought nor the experience that something exists can prove the existence of God, there remains only the possibility of basing the proof on a specific experience. The physico-theological proof does just that. It infers from the astonishing order and harmony of nature the existence of a sublime cause with all the power and wisdom necessary to shape the world in a harmonious and orderly fashion. A being with such power and wisdom is perfect; it is God.

Strictly speaking, the third proof consists of three steps. First, from the order and harmony of nature, it infers the existence of a creator of this order and harmony; then, from the empirically observed order, it infers the absolute completeness of order and harmony, which corresponds to an absolutely necessary creator; finally, from the absolute necessity of the creator, it infers its existence.

Although Kant sympathizes most with the physico-theological argument, he raises a number of objections against it, too. For one thing, he detects a fallacious analogy. The proof compares the natural world with the products of human art, such as houses, ships and clocks, and it assumes that natural objects, like human artefacts, are created by a being with an understanding and a will. This assumption makes a fallacious inference from the familiar to the unfamiliar. Besides, human art can only form a given material to suit our purposes but cannot create the original material. The analogy thus leads at most to the assumption of an architect of the world who does his best with materials for which he is not responsible and which are governed by laws which he did not make. Even if one considers the analogy to be legitimate, it establishes only the existence of a demiurge, an *architect* of the world in the sense of Plato's *Timaeus*, but not a *creator* of the world in the sense of the Judeo-Christian tradition.

Above all, the proof can show nothing more than a cause whose wisdom and power are proportional to the observed order and harmony of nature. Now the order and harmony perceived in the world may be amazingly great, and we may through further discoveries marvel at nature more and more. But that still does not justify the claim that the wisdom and power governing the world must be infinite. Experience always resides in the domain of the finite and conditioned; so, the physico-theological proof necessarily fails. *Either* it rests on empirical premises and fails to reach its theological goal, that is, a God which is not just greater than everything familiar to us in power, intelligence and wisdom and not just an architect of the world; *or* one seeks to counterbalance its empirical inadequacies with non-empirical arguments. That is what happens in the second and third steps. The second step corresponds to the cosmological argument, which itself presupposes the ontological argument. Thus, it all goes back to the ontological argument, which, however, has no argumentative strength. Kant shows the impossibility of any attempt to establish the existence of God theoretically. The case of natural theology can be closed. Neither empirical nor purely conceptual arguments nor a combination of the two can demonstrate the existence of God.

Nonetheless, the dialectic of theological reason does not have a purely negative result. It shows that the idea of God contains no contradiction. Moreover, God is not just a possible concept but, within the bounds of a transcendental ideal, one which reason requires. Kant rejects not only speculative theology but also speculative atheism, which claims that God does not exist, and any sort of positivism which considers the idea of God to be unthinkable and unworthy of reason. Since God can be conceived without contradiction but cannot be known theoretically, *philosophical* theology, the only kind of theology possible for pure reason independent of divine revelation, is based upon moral laws (B 664). Kant stays true to his transcendental idealism, restricts knowledge to possible experience, and leaves room for a philosophical belief in God.

7.3 THE IDEAS OF REASON AS PRINCIPLES OF COMPLETENESS FOR KNOWLEDGE

According to the second preface of the *Critique*, (speculative) metaphysics has become questionable because it fails: instead of progressing in scientific knowledge, it becomes entangled in endless conflicts. Metaphysics fails because it attempts the impossible: it seeks knowledge which transcends all experience. And it confuses its wishes with actual possibilities. In the Dialectic, Kant shows just what the confusion consists in: transcentental ideas are taken as transcendent, and regulative principles are taken as constitutive. The ideas of reason—the soul, the world, freedom and God—are possible, and indeed necessary, representations. They belong to the implications of thinking. These implications are not, however, objects but principles of scientific research.

In the case of the ideas, reason is directly occupied only with itself. This occupation of reason with itself is not, however, superfluous. For particular bits of categorically determined knowledge make up objective knowledge but not the systematic combination of knowledge necessary in science. We achieve such combination only when we allow ourselves to be guided by the ideas of reason, which are notions of an absolute whole. The ideas direct the concepts and propositions acquired in experience toward completeness. This orientation has two competing components: the greatest unity of a whole which is combined according to necessary laws, and the broadest extension within the manifold of objects.

This twofold completeness, demanding both unity and expansion of knowledge, can be realized only by means of experience. There are no objective things without the interplay of sensibility and the understanding. The ideas of reason thus do not have a constitutive but only a regulative function. They contribute nothing to true knowledge. Nonetheless, the ideas are not philosophical fictions but rather, it seems, indispensable for a proper understanding of the sciences. The sciences look not only for truth but also for systematic unity and for the greatest possible diversity of knowledge.

Even a brief glance at the history of science shows that Kant's theory of the regulative use of the ideas of reason is not simply grafted onto the actual process of research. Natural scientists thus seek to explain a multitude of forces on the basis of a few fundamental forces and, if possible, on the basis of a single force. In this spirit, Newton united the observations, experiments and special laws of nature developed by Kepler for the movements of the planets, by Galileo for free fall, by Huygens for the wave theory of light, and by Guericke for the pressure and weight of air into a single system of theoretical mechanics. In this century, physicists have reduced the variety of "substances" to one basic substance with two forms of appearance: mass (m) and energy (E), which according to Einstein's equation $E = mc^2$ (where c is the speed of light), are interchangeable. Biologists similarly seek to explain the life processes for all living things in terms of basic biochemical reactions occurring in human beings as well as in plants and in other animals. Psychologists try to find general elements which aid them in deriving the broad variety of psychological events (instincts, wishes, passions, interests and hopes) from a few basic motives and in attributing these events to one identical person. Economists and social scientists, too, seek to derive the phenomena they study from basic unifying concepts and motivational forces, such as the law of supply and demand or the "reduction of complexity" (Luhmann).

Many scientists distinguish between an experimental and a theoretical branch of their fields. In addition to experimental physics, chemistry and biology, scientists also do work in theoretical physics, chemistry and biology; economists and social scientists study both empirical and theoretical economy and sociology. In the theoretical disciplines, scientists seek to combine particular observations into general, unified theories, which explain various phenomena in terms of a single model. In so doing, scientists act according to the idea of the greatest unity. On the other hand, scientists constantly seek to discover new phenomena in the natural and social world. They value not only systematic unity (or, as scientists themselves say, simplicity and elegance) but also the broad variety and multiplicity of the objects of knowledge.

Kant formulates the underlying principle of both tendencies in research. The search for unity corresponds to the transcendental law of the homogeneity of the manifold; the search for the greatest possible extension corresponds to the law of specification or variety. Traditional philosophy, Kant says, accepted both laws when it proposed the rules that the number of principles should not be increased unneccssarily ("entia praeter necessitatem non esse multiplicanda") and that the varieties of being should not be diminished without reason ("entium varietates non temere esse minuendas").

Kant sees that there are two competing, yet complementary tendencies in research. It follows that recurrent historical conflicts as to whether there is more unity or diversity in phenomena are of no use. First, in such conflicts, unity and diversity are viewed as knowable, objective properties of the world while they are in fact subjective principles or maxims of reason (B 694). Second, they emphasize one task at the expense of the other although only both principles, taken together, lead to the absolute completeness sought by reason.

Scientific research rests upon notions of the unity, the diversity, and (a third principle) the continuity of the natural and social world. Nonetheless, these notions do not come from experience. All experience, and any sum of experiences, is limited. The ideas, however, refer to unlimited, absolute completeness. The ideas are thus due to a faculty extending beyond understanding, which relates to experience. This faculty is reason.

Reason demands a threefold completeness of knowledge: unity, diversity and continuity. But only the understanding can realize this task. The ideas of reason do not designate supernatural causes which could compensate for deficits in natural explanations. On the contrary, they do not allow scientists to be satisfied with faulty explanations and challenge scientists to look always for more accurate reasons. The ideas of reason have heuristic significance and provide impulses for scientific progress: "Thus all human knowledge begins with intuitions, proceeds from thence to concepts, and ends with ideas" (B 730).

Kant's theory of the regulative ideas of reason can be read as a contribution to the new logic which Bacon and many others demanded. In the course of the modern scientific awakening, a "new organon" of the sciences (Bacon, *Novum organum*, 1620) becomes important as a replacement for the "old organon" (Greek: instrument; designation for Aristotle's logical writings). As an art of discovering new things (*ars inveniendi*), the new organon stands in opposition to the traditional "art of demonstration" (*ars demonstrandi*). In the Dialectic, however, Kant does not formulate fixed rules for the new art but only general principles of judgment. These principles make progress in our knowledge of reality appear meaningful and rational while allowing progress to follow its own dynamics.

Since no experience or sum of experiences can yield absolute completeness of knowledge, the ideal of completeness is a goal which governs research but can never be reached. In painting, the vanishing point lies outside of the picture but determines its perspective. Similarly, scientific research is determined by the ideas of reason without ever being able to reach absolutely complete knowledge. Whenever someone views the vanishing point of research as an object in its own right and believes that the principles of scientific progress can establish speculative metaphysics as an objective science, dialectical illusion occurs. The ideas of reason in fact designate the goal toward which scientists always proceed but never completely completely reach. They are like an horizon which recedes at each forward step. One never arrives at its edge and never comes to a final stop.

If the sciences are obligated to strive for an unattainable completeness, must we not view scientific research as a pointless Sisyphean task? This conclusion seems plausible but is by no means necessary. Due to the forms of intuition and to the categories, objective scientific knowledge and scientific progress are possible. Only absolutely complete knowledge is excluded.

Lessing preferred the eternal search for imperfect truths to the possession of a perfect truth since the possession of such a truth would extinguish mental activity. Kant shows that we need not fear mental inactivity since completeness never obtains even though it is constantly sought. The systematic unity of knowledge is not an actual but a "projected unity" (B 675). The ideas remind the sciences of the limitation of even their most recent knowledge and point at the same time to the endless, infinite nature of the research process.

Guided by the question of "the final purpose of the natural dialectic of human reason," Kant claims in the "Appendix to the Transcendental Dialectic" that one may think of the ideal of systematic unity and absolute completeness of knowledge as an intelligence which, lying outside of the world, created it (B 697ff.). With this claim Kant seems ultimately to contradict the main thesis of the Transcendental Dialectic, to fall back into the errors of metaphysics, and, hypostatizing, to make a transcendental maxim of research into a transcendental object. Strawson (1973, 231) considers Kant's idea of an extramundane intelligence which directs the world and contains the "therefore for every wherefore" to be a "pardonable indulgence of a kind of *fatigue of reason*," which temporarily reverts back to a primitive and comforting model. But Kant develops this thought in a theoretical rather than a practical context; it is thus not intended as a comfort. Moreover, Kant explicitly refers to the thought as a mere "analogy" and speaks of a figurative description of the idea. He does not speak of an existing object. The notion of an extramundane intelligence is required, Kant says, in order to conceive complete knowledge as a meaningful aim for theoretical reason. If we are to view the attempt of science to combine fragmentary bits of knowledge into a systematic unity and order as meaningful, then we must think of nature in such a way that it allows us to approach this goal. We must assume that nature does indeed have a systematic order. But such a systematic order is only possible if we view nature as we would if it was due to a supreme, extra-mundane intelligence, "which, acting in accordance with wise purposes, is the author" of the unity and order of the world (B 725).

Kant does not ultimately himself objectify the transcendental ideas, as is demonstrated by the fact that it makes no difference to him whether we say that God wanted the unity and order of the world to be such or that nature wisely ordered the world in such a way. The idea which theoretical reason has of God remains a part of Kant's transcendental metaphysics of our knowledge of nature. This idea coincides with the idea of harmony in nature. It cannot be realized by an intuition but only by (endless) progress in our search for knowledge.

PART III

What Ought I to Do?
Moral and Legal Philosophy

అలోఅలోఅలోఅలోఅలోఅలో

The transformation in philosophical thinking brought about by Kant relates not only to knowledge but also to action. The special status of science in the realm of knowledge attaches in the domain of action to morals or ethics. In the theoretical sphere, science claims to have universal, objective validity; in the practical sphere, it is ethics which makes this claim. Kant accordingly transforms practical philosophy by providing a new foundation for morals.

Prior to Kant, the origin of morals was sought in the order of nature or society, in the desire for happiness, in God's will or in moral sentiments. Kant shows that the claim of morals to objective validity cannot be conceived in any of these ways. In the practical sphere, as in the theoretical, objectivity is only possible through the subject. Morals originate in the autonomy, the self-legislation, of the will. Since autonomy means the same thing as freedom, Kant provides a philosophical foundation for freedom, the key concept of the modern age.

Kant's new foundation for morals has more than a mere historical value. Kant actively participates in the current discussion on the justification of moral norms, and rightly so, for he fulfills the two criteria for a stimulating conversationalist. *First*, he agrees with the minimal conditions generally accepted in contemporary ethics. Like the proponents of utilitarian ethics and of the principle of universalization (Hare, Singer) as well as Rawls, Kohlberg, Karl-Otto Apel, Jürgen Habermas, and constructivist ethics, Kant opposes ethical relativism, skepticism and dogmatism. Kant, too, assumes that moral judgment and action do not stem from personal feelings, from arbitrary decisions, from cultural and social origins, from tact, or from habit and convention. Instead, he considers human action to be governed by ultimate obligations. Toward others and toward oneself, one has the responsibility of fulfilling these obligations.

Kant bases moral argumentation on a supreme moral principle. The controversy with Kant begins at the point of dispute in contemporary ethics: the exact specification of the moral principle. Here, Kant fulfills the *second* criterion for a stimulating conversationalist. Resting upon autonomy and the categorical imperative, his ethics represents the most significant alternative to ultilitarianism. Not only with regard to its high level of reflection but also with regard to its elaborated conceptual apparatus, which distinguishes between law and morals, between the empirically conditioned and the pure will, between legality and morality, between technical, pragmatic and moral commitments, and between the supreme and the highest good, Kant's alternative is virtually peerless. Kant's major works on ethics are thus still worthy of a substantive investigation and not just an historical description.

Kant's significance in contemporary discussions of ethics also has its disadvantages. Not only the general public but also philosophers often deal with Kant fragmentarily, and gross misunderstandings distort even the fragments. Ever since Schiller and Benjamin Constant, Kant has been accused of rigorism. Ever since Hegel, it has been repeatedly claimed that, in contrast to Aristotle, he lacks a concept of practical activity. Kant's practical reason is purportedly a sort of theoretical reason put into service in practical contexts. Furthermore, his ethics is claimed to rest upon a dubious dualism separating the moral from the empirical world. Such a dualism cannot grasp the unity of action. Also beginning with Hegel, Kant has been accused of examining merely subjective obligations, which, in addition, he fails to consider historically. "Substantive morals" (another Aristotelian ingredient) and historicity are demanded instead. Max Scheler accuses Kant of having an ethic of conviction (*Gesinnungsethik*) and, appealing to Nietzsche and Husserl, of excessive formalism. Nicolai Hartmann has reinforced the latter criticism. Finally, Kant's ethic of duty is considered to be in part responsible for "Prussian obedience."

Most of these accusations disappear as soon as one recognizes the purpose of Kant's argumentation as critical reflection on actions.

(Other objections are perhaps more justified and lead in any case to the German Idealist movement.) In the *Groundwork of the Metaphysic of Morals* and in the *Critique of Practical Reason*, Kant wishes only to disclose what the consciousness of a moral agent always (dimly) contains (*GMM*, IV 389, 397 and passim). Kant carries out his reflection on moral action with characteristic rigor, although even during the critical period, he is constantly amending his ideas and does not always attain final clarity. With Kant, moral reflection on actions finds its first principle: the categorical imperative and the autonomy of the will.

But Kant is not satisfied with a mere reflection on principles. Contrary to the accusation of excessive formalism, in the *Metaphysic of Morals* he seeks out the obligations which, with the aid of autonomy and the categorical imperative, can be shown to be moral. In so doing, he mentions exactly the substantive morality which many scholars find only in Aristotle or Hegel. At the same time, Kant does not have the tendency of Hegel, Marx and Critical Theory to neglect the personal "substance" of morality for the sake of its social substance. Kant's *Metaphysic of Morals* has two parts, corresponding to the division of Aristotle's practical philosophy into ethics and politics. While the *theory of law* investigates the consolidation of morality in social institutions, the *theory of virtue* treats its intensification in the subject of action and in his character. The supposed oppositions "Aristotle versus Kant" and "Kant versus Hegel," which have become commonplaces in histories of philosophy, are in desperate need of revision.

Even the principle of happiness (*eudaimonia*), which has dominated Western ethics ever since Aristotle, is not entirely rejected in Kant's ethic of autonomy. As the highest good, it occupies a secure position among the ethical postulates. We also find in Kant extensive thoughts on the philosophy of history. These thoughts no longer deal with the question, "What ought I to do?" but with the question, "What may I hope for?" A comprehensive assessment of Kant's practical philosophy would also have to take into account works such as the *Anthropology from a Pragmatic Point of View* and the lectures on *Education*,[1] in which Kant interprets the educational process as a kind of bridge between empirical human nature and morals, which belong to the intelligible sphere. Even worldly wisdom and the art of living have a place in Kant's thought, but, in accordance with the principle of autonomy, they are far from central. Since Kant, they have been situated on the periphery of philosophical ethics.

8.

The Critique of Practical Reason

Kant's new foundation for ethics results from the critical examination of practical reason. Practical reason is nothing separate from theoretical reason. There is only one reason, which is utilized either practically or theoretically. In general, reason means the capacity to transcend the sensible realm of nature. The transcendence of the senses in knowledge is the theoretical use of reason; their transcendence in action is its practical use. With the distinction between the theoretical and the practical use of reason, Kant accepts Hume's distinction between descriptive and prescriptive sentences. Practical reason, as Kant says for short, means the capacity to choose one's action independent of sensible determinations such as instincts, desires, passions, and sensations of pleasure and displeasure.

Kant does not moralize but speaks instead a plain, cognitive language—not a normative one. Instead of moralizing, he begins with a morally neutral phenomenon: the capacity not to act according to the given laws of nature but instead to conceive of laws (e.g. relations of means and ends), to accept these laws as principles, and to act accordingly. The capacity to act according to representations of laws is also called the will, so practical reason is simply the capacity to will (cf. *GMM*).

The will is nothing irrational. It is not a "dark force from murky depths" but something rational. It is reason with respect to action. The will distinguishes rational beings such as man from natural beings such as animals, who act only according to laws given by nature—not according to representations of laws. Occasionally, we take the expression "will" in a broader sense and mean any impulse from within, as distinguished from external constraint. Then, natural beings have a will, too, insofar as they follow their own instincts and desires. But for good reason, Kant takes the expression in a more strict sense. For natural beings, instincts and desires have the significance of laws, according to which such beings necessarily act. Since their inner impulses are inner constraints, natural beings have a will in at most a metaphorical sense. They follow their own impulses but not their own will. They obey the "will of nature." Only the capacity to act according to one's own conceived laws establishes a will of one's own. Such a will assumes the ability to distance oneself from natural impulses and to suspend their efficacy as determining causes, even if they are not extinguished.

In the practical sphere, as in the theoretical, Kant makes a clear methodological distinction between dependence upon sensory causes and independence of them. He thus distinguishes between empirically conditioned and pure practical reason. While empirically conditioned practical reason is in part determined externally by instincts, desires, habits and passions, pure practical reason is independent of all empirical conditions and completely self-sufficient.

Kant claims that "all moral concepts have their seat and origin in reason completely *a priori*" (*GMM*, IV 411) and that morality in the strict sense can only be understood as pure practical reason. Hence, in the practical sphere as compared to the theoretical, the aim of the argument is reversed. In knowledge, Kant rejects the presumptions of pure reason; in action, he rejects those of *empirically conditioned* reason. Kant dismisses the claim of moral empiricism that one can only act on the basis of empirically determined causes and hence that even the principles of morals are dependent upon experience.

Kant sets four main tasks for himself in the justification of ethics: He specifies the concept of morality (8.1) and applies it to the situation of finite rational beings. This application leads to the categorical imperative (8.2). He shows further that morality originates in the autonomy of the will (8.3) and seeks finally to prove the reality of morality by drawing upon the fact of reason (8.4). Having rejected ethical empiricism, Kant sees the proof of the reality of morality as a refutation of ethical skepticism. He adds the theory of postulates, which points toward the philosophy of religion (11.1).

8.1 PERSONAL MORALITY

The *Groundwork of the Metaphysic of Morals* begins abruptly. The very first sentence makes the provocative claim that only a good will is good without qualification. With regard to this claim, it is not only the thesis itself that is significant. The underlying question as to what is good without qualification as well as the identification, implicit in this question, of the "morally good" with the "good without qualification" are also important. The implicit identification defines the notion of moral goodness. In the *Groundwork*, Kant thus does not proceed, as is usually assumed, from the notions of the good will and of duty. He begins with a hidden definition, that is, with a meta-ethical and not with a normative proposition. This proposition specifies the concept of morality and distinguishes it from all other notions of goodness. A thorough defense or critique of Kant's ethics must start here.

According to Kant's explanation (*GMM*, IV 393f.), whatever is good without qualification is not good in any relative sense but good absolutely. Morality hence cannot denote the functional (technical, strategic, or pragmatic) suitability of actions—or of objects, circumstances, events and capabilities—for given purposes. Nor can it designate correspondence to the customs and mores or to the laws of a society. In all of these cases, goodness depends upon favorable circumstances. Absolute goodness, however, is by definition independent of qualifying conditions. Thus, it is unconditionally good, good in itself and for no further purpose.

The concept of unqualified goodness appears as the necessary and sufficient condition for an investigation of the good. The concept is necessary, Kant says, since, considered alone, all qualified goodness is ambivalent: if its conditions, in particular the intentions, are good, then the conditioned is good, too; if not, it is bad. Hence, unconditioned goodness is the presupposition required for conditioned goodness to be good at all. On the other hand, this concept is sufficient for an investigation of the good, since unqualified goodness cannot possibly be surpassed.

Kant's notion of absolute goodness, reminiscent of the ontological notion of a most perfect being, is not automatically restricted to certain aspects of action. The normative notion of unqualified goodness is valid not only for the personal but also for the institutional side of human action. It can also be applied to the law and the government. Because we can distinguish these two aspects of human action, there are two basic forms of morality: on the one hand, personal morality and on the other, the rational concept of political justice as morality in the social sense.

Although the idea of morality also relates to the law and to forms of government, Kant deals in the *Groundwork* and in the *Critique of Practical Reason* primarily with the personal side of morality. This imbalance has nurtured the misunderstanding that his theory of justice is either detached from the new critical foundation for ethics or viewed from the standpoint of personal morality. The first interpretation would mean a reversion to Kant's pre-Critical theory of justice; the second would mean moralizing on justice in a philosophically and politically dubious manner.

Right from the start, the *Groundwork* seeks to restrict morality to the personal side of action. Only the good will is seen here as absolutely good, and as possible rivals, only personal characteristics, such as mental talents, temperament, good luck, and character, are considered. All of these rivals, Kant shows, are not absolutely good but instead ambivalent. They allow of both good, desirable use and detrimental, bad use. It is, by way of contrast, the will, which, depending on whether it is good or bad, decides which direction their use will take. As a result, the alternatives are only conditionally good. The condition for their goodness lies in the good will, which itself is not good due to still other conditions but good in itself. In contrast to traditional moral philosophy, absolute goodness does not consist in a supreme object of the will (cf. *CPrR*, V 64), such as Aristotle's happiness, but in the good will itself.

What the good will consists in, Kant shows with the aid of the concept of duty. But "duty" and "good will" do not have the same extensions. A good will implies duty only under the condition of "certain subjective limitations and obstacles" (*GMS*, IV 397). Duty is morality in the form of an imperative. This form of morality makes sense only for those subjects whose will is not good in and of itself. It is irrelevant for purely rational beings, whose will, like that of God, is exclusively good, by nature and necessarily (cf. *CPr R*, V 72, 82). One can speak of duty only when, in addition to rational desires, there are competing natural inclinations, that is, when there is a bad will in addition to the good. This situation maintains for any rational being dependent upon sensible determining causes. Man is such an impure, finite rational being. Insofar as Kant explains morality with the aid of the concept of duty, he seeks to understand man as a moral being.

There are three ways of fulfilling moral duties. First, one can perform his duty while being ultimately guided by self-interest. This is the case for a businessman who, for fear of losing his customers, gives honest advice even to inexperienced buyers. Second, one can act in accordance with duty due to an inclination toward the duty, as is the case when one helps someone in need for reasons of sympathy. Finally, one can accept his duty purely "out of duty."

The good will is not present in all cases where one does his moral duty because of any determining causes *whatsoever*. A person's morality does not consist in mere compliance to duty, which Kant calls *legality*. For the compliance of an action to duty (its moral correctness) depends on the determining causes for which one fulfills the duty. Mere compliance is thus only conditionally, not unconditionally good. The (meta-ethical) criterion for morality is met only if one does what is morally correct for no other reason than because it is morally correct. An action is good without qualification only if it fulfills duty for the sake of duty. Only in such cases does Kant speak of morality.

Since morality does not consist in mere compliance to duty, it is not situated on the same level as observable behavior and the rules thereof. In contrast to legality, morality cannot be ascertained from the action alone but only from the determining cause of action, the will. Many philosophers nonetheless attempt to conceive morality solely in terms of norms, values or rules for resolving conflicts. This is the case for ethics of values, for utilitarianism and for the contemporary principle of universalization, and it also holds for the communicative ethics of Apel, Habermas and the Erlangen School and, above all, for ethological and sociological derivations of ethics. None of these attempts can constitute a moral theory in the sense of a theory of goodness without qualification with respect to an acting subject. They lead at most to moral correctness but not to moral goodness. They explain legality but not morality.

As an indirect justification of their own theory, critics of Kant often object that an ethic of personal morality and of the good will reduces morality to the pure subjectivity of good convictions. This objection, which attributes to Kant an ethic of conviction, contains a twofold criticism. First, it is claimed that Kant promotes a world of inactive introspection which is indifferent to success in the real world and—as Marx says in the *German Ideology* (part III, 1, 6)—corresponds "completely to the impotence, suppression, and misery of the German bourgeoisie." Second, it makes it too easy for action or inaction to be assessed as good and correct. In the sense of the often criticized, and presumably misinterpreted aphorism of St. Augustine, "dilige et quod vis fac" ("love, and do as you wish"), good convictions depend only on a clear conscience and lack any objective standard of measure.

As popular as the objection that Kant has an ethic of conviction may be, it rests on a misunderstanding of Kantian ethics. On the one hand, according to Kant, willing does not consist in a mere wish but in the summoning of all means—to the extent to which they are in our power (*GMM*, IV 394). The will is by no means indifferent toward its expression in social and political reality. It is not above and beyond reality but rather the ultimate determining cause—insofar as the cause lies in the subject. To be sure, the expression of the will may, due to bodily, mental, economic and other imperfections, fall short of what is willed. For example, help may be too little or too late despite supreme efforts. But man can never escape this danger. His action and inaction occur in a context dependent upon natural and social conditions. The agent's will does not alone determine this context and cannot even grasp the context in its entirety. Because morality relates to the sphere of responsibility of the subject, to what is in his power, observable success, as the bare result of an action, cannot be the measure of personal morality. Personal morality cannot be determined by looking only at the action as such but only by considering the underlying will. Any moral philosophy which, to distinguish itself from a "mere ethic of conviction," takes actual success to be the decisive criterion makes people responsible for conditions which they cannot determine completely. Misjudging the human condition, such a philosophy brings no improvement but is instead, when applied rigorously, fundamentally inhumane.

On the other hand, this criticism overlooks the fact that for Kant, legality is not an alternative to morality but instead its necessary condition. In contrast to Max Scheler's distinction between an ethic of conviction and an ethic of success (Scheler 1966, part I, chap. III) and to Max Weber's division between an ethic of conviction and an ethic of responsibility (*Gesammelte politische Schriften*,[2] [3]551ff.), Kant's distinction between morality and legality does not separate two mutually exclusive ethical stances. Morality does not compete with legality but instead contains more strict conditions. A moral action is, first, morally correct; it fulfills duty. Second, it makes the fulfillment of duty its determining cause. Morality thus does not fall short of legality but instead intensifies and surpasses it. Finally, Kant proposes as an objective criterion for personal morality the categorical imperative, whereby strict objectivity is itself the essential criterion. The accusation that Kant advocates introspection into one's own subjective conscience without any objective standard of measure cannot be upheld.

8.2 THE CATEGORICAL IMPERATIVE

The categorical imperative is one of the most famous—and most thoroughly misunderstood—elements of Kant's thinking. Even among philosophers, it is often distorted to the point of caricature. Frankena[3], for example, asserts that according to the categorical imperative, maxims such as tying one's left shoestring first or whistling in the dark when alone are moral duties. Others view the categorical imperative as a test for compliance with duty—that is, for the legality of an action and not for its morality. Still others accuse Kant of completely ignoring all utilitarian consequences of dutiful action and thus of being indifferent to the welfare of man. Finally, the categorical imperative is considered to be convincing only as an empirical, pragmatic principle and not as a pure imperative of reason.[4]

The Concept of the Categorical Imperative

With the categorical imperative, Kant proposes an ultimate criterion for judging personal morality and, with appropriate changes, for morality as a whole. But one should not overlook the fact that the categorical imperative does not just make a morally neutral proposal. It does not impartially show what moral obligations consist in and then leave it to the discretion of the agent whether or not to recognize such obligations. As an imperative, it is an "ought." It demands that we act in a certain way, and this is the only demand which, as the term "categorical" specifies, is valid without qualification. The formulation of the categorlcal imperative hence begins unconditionally with "Act. . . ." Only secondarily does the categorical imperative say that moral action consists in maxims capable of universalization. First and foremost, it demands that we act morally. In its shortest form, it could hence say, "Act morally."

The categorical imperative follows directly from the notion of morality as absolute goodness, which implies, first, that it is categorical and, second, with reference to finite rational beings, that it is an imperative. More precisely— therein lies Kant's insight—the categorical imperative is none other than the notion of morality under the conditions holding for finite rational beings. In the categorical imperative, Kant applies his fundamental meta-ethical thesis to beings of a human sort.

Since limited rational beings such as humans do not automatically and necessarily act morally, morality for them has the character of an obligation rather than a fact. Despite the secondary possibility of reinforcing certain dispositions of character and of establishing a normative environment, morality is primarily imperative in nature. The fact, which Aristotle and Hegel cannot deny, that not every character nor every institutional environment is moral demonstrates the imperative nature of morality. One should not, however, take the imperative aspect of morality too restrictively and limit it to explicit commands and interdictions. The imperative aspect may also be hidden, as, for example, in Biblical parables, where it at most appears in the supplementary "Go forth and do likewise." Intentionally abstaining from commands and interdictions and from any form of moralizing, ethics can also work with examples and models or can, as in hermeneutical ethics, draw our attention to the ethical substance already realized in the world. But in both cases, we still have to do with forms of behavior and with ways of life which are considered to be morally correct but do not rank as natural laws, which are recognized necessarily and without exception.

Moreover, in speaking of an obligation or an imperative, Kant means more than just any command at all. Right from the start, he excludes the arbitrary orders of a superior force. The command to close a window or not to smoke are imperatives in Kant's sense only if they have a purpose, such as health, which makes the relevant action appear obligatory or prohibited. Imperatives respond to man's basic practical question, "What ought I to do?" not with external or inner compulsion but instead with principles of reason—of a sort which the agent need not necessarily accept (*GMM*, IV 413). Even non-moral imperatives constitute practical necessities, that is, obligations for action which are valid for everyone and differ from the pleasant, which is due merely to subjective sensations (ibid.).

Kant shows that the basic question as to what I ought to do can be understood in three ways. There are thus three distinct classes of answers, which contain the same number of classes of principles of reason. The theory of practical argumentation sought today is, according to Kant, divided into three parts (classes), which are not situated on the same level but instead build upon one another. They signify three stages of practical reason or, one might say, of the rationality of action. The three levels of reason or of rationality differ not in rigor but in the scope of reason. In the case of the first two levels (the hypothetical imperatives), the strict necessity attaching to all reason is bound up with contingent presuppositions. On the third level (the categorical or moral imperative), all limiting presuppositions are excluded. The categorical imperative and morality are not irrational. On the contrary, the idea of practical reason or of the rationality of action finds its ultimate consummation here.

The technical imperatives of skill, which comprise the first level, require the necessary means for an arbitrary aim. Whoever wants to become rich, for example, must strive for an income far exceeding his expenditures. The pragmatic imperatives of cleverness, which make up the second level, prescribe actions which contribute to happiness, the aim of limited rational beings. Diets, which promote health, belong to this group. It is common to the first two levels of rationality that although an objective obligation is given without qualification, the corresponding action is required only under the condition of subjective intentions. Anyone who would like to become rich must seek an income exceeding his expenditures, but this does not at all imply that one should place importance upon a large income. This command only maintains when one actually resolves to become wealthy. But such a resolution is not necessary.

The first two levels are hypothetical imperatives whose validity is limited by a presupposition: "*If* I would like *x, then* I must do *y.*" Their hypothetical aspect does not, however, depend upon their grammatical form. The categorical command, "Do not smoke too much," is still a hypothetical imperative because it is conditioned upon an interest in health. And the hypothetical sentence, "If you see someone in need, then help him," contains a categorical imperative. The premise ("If . . . need") does not restrict the validity of the command to help but only describes the situation in which the command is relevant.

Following the criterion of unqualified goodness, moral obligations are valid unconditionally. Such categorical obligations, which rely on no presuppositions, make up the third, unsurpassable level of rationality. Because an imperative belonging to this level obligates without any qualifications, it is valid universally: necessarily and without exception. Strict universality thus constitutes the hallmark and the criterion for morality.

The objection from followers of Aristotle and Hegel that Kant has no notion of practical activity can now be answered. Although Kant uses the expression *Praxis* (practical activity) sparingly, he has quite a sophisticated substantive conception here. In addition to his structural analysis of action with the aid of the concept of will, his distinction between personal and political practical activity (virtue and law), and, in the sphere of personal activity, his separation of legality and morality, there are three basic forms of practical activity implicit in Kant's ethics. They correspond to the three forms of imperatives. While technical action contributes to arbitrary aims and pragmatic action supports the natural desire for happiness, moral action has a value which is not merely functional.

The elements already treated define the categorical imperative. Objective obligation and the lack of necessity in following it correspond to its imperative aspect, and its strict universality demonstrates its categorical character. Nonetheless, these elements do not yet lead to Kant's precise formulation in the *Groundwork*. We are still missing the restriction of the *Groundwork* to the domain of personal, in contrast to political, activity. The missing ingredient is contained in the concept of a maxim, so the categorical imperative says in its basic form, "*Act only on that maxim through which you can at the same time will that it should become a universal law*" (*GMM*, IV 421).

In addition to this basic form, Kant recognizes "three ways of representing the principle of morality" (IV 436). They relate to the form, to the material and to the complete determination of the maxims. Since the existence of things makes up the formal concept of nature, the categorical imperative can also read, "*Act as if the maxim of your action were to become through your will a universal law of nature*" (IV 421). The second, "material" mode of representation proceeds from the nature of reason as a goal in itself: "*Act in such a way that you always treat humanity, whether in your own person or in the person of any other. never simply as a means, but always at the same time as an end*" (IV 429). According to the third, complete representation, "*All maxims proceeding from our own making of law ought to harmonize with a possible kingdom of ends as a kingdom of nature*" (IV 436).

The categorical imperative is not undisputed as a criterion for morality. Ever since Jeremy Bentham (1748–1832) and John Stuart

Mill (1806–1873), utilitarianism has been the most influential ethical position in the English-speaking world. In Germany, discourse is presently advocated as a criterion for morals. Both utilitarianism and discourse ethics presuppose, however, that the desired criterion for morality obligates not only under certain qualifying conditions but universally. They thus both rely on the concept of the categorical imperative as the ultimate criterion for morals. Abstract as the categorical imperative may sound, it represents the supreme form of all obligation and the consummation of practical rationality.

Maxims

The categorical imperative relates only to maxims and not to rules of any sort whatsoever (not, for example, to morally irrelevant rules). Kant understands maxims as subjective principles of action (as early as *CPR*, B 840) which contain a general determination of the will and have several practical rules under them (*CPrR*, § 1; cf. *GMM*, IV 420f.). (1) As *subjective* principles, they differ from individual to individual. (2) As determinations of the *will*, they do not designate formal types attributed to the agent by an objective observer. They are principles recognized by the actor as his own. (3) As *principles* which have several rules under them, maxims denote the manner in which one leads his life as a whole—in relation to certain basic aspects of individual and collective life, such as being in need of help, being tired of life, or being insulted. Through their relationship to certain spheres of life and to situational types, maxims differ from the higher level of generality of Aristotle's forms of life (*bioi*) or Kierkegaard's modes of existence. Maxims are basic attitudes which provide a common direction for a variety of specific aims and actions. One follows a maxim when one lives according to a resolution of being considerate—or of being inconsiderate—of reacting vindictively or magnanimously to insults, or of providing aid or behaving indifferently in cases of need.

Maxims specify the guiding principles for judging entire spheres of action, for example, for judging helpfulness or indifference in all cases of need. In the rules of action subsumed under a maxim, the principle is applied to recurrent situational types within the corresponding sphere of action. Practical rules of this sort, such as stopping when you see a car stalled, have to do with the changing conditions of life. Depending on the situation and the abilities of the agent, the practical rules vary, even when they follow the same maxim. A non-swimme will thus help a drowning person differently than a strong swimmer would. In spite of constant principles of judgment, there must be different rules (norms) for helpfulness or indifference, for consideration or the lack thereof, or for vidictiveness or magnanimity. For this reason, an ethic of maxims, and not an ethic of rules or norms, as is frequently proposed, is the appropriate form for moral philosophy. Since Kant in his critique of practical reason is more interested in the refutation of ethical empiricism and skepticism, he does not himself emphasize or even adequately explicate the significance of an ethic of maxims. Closer consideration, however, shows its fourfold superiority over an ethic of norms:

1. Because the general principles of the will ignore the changing circumstances of action, the maxims are distilled from concrete actions as their fundamental normative pattern. In this way, the norm becomes recognizable as determining cause without our being distracted by changing situational factors. Without resorting to ethical relativism or to a rigorous dogmatism of rules, one sees how human action can vary and yet still have the common quality of morality or immorality. A maxim is precisely the factor of unity which speaks against relativism, and the necessity of appropriately applying the maxim to the specifics of a situation is the other factor, which opposes normative dogmatism. Maxims provide only a general outline. For concrete action, "contextualization," involving interpretation and judgment, is necessary. It is moral, practical judgment which, in accordance with maxims, performs this task.

2. Since maxims have to do with general principles for living, they do not transform a person's biography into an endless list of rules nor into infinitely many individual acts. Maxims combine the parts of life into uniform wholes, the morality of which is tested by the categorical imperative. While the instillment of practical rules makes education seem more like indoctrination, maxims, as guiding normative principles, make rational self-determination possible and give sufficient leeway for differences in temperament, in abilities, in social and cultural circumstances, and in situations experienced.

3. Because maxims disregard changing personal and social circumstances, they reflect a man's character. Not norms in the sense of concrete rules of action but instead maxims make up the principles for living on the basis of which one can morally judge a person. Such moral judgments are to be distinguished from judgments of physical, mental,

or spiritual qualities. Moral judgments attribute to a person the qualities of vindictiveness or magnanimity, of consideration or the lack thereof, of egoism, rectitude, and so on. Hence, for questions of moral identity, education and judgment, maxims are much more appropriate objects of investigation than norms.

4. Finally, only an ethic of maxims is capable of providing a standard on which to measure personal morality. Only the examination of the ultimate principles determined by the self allow us to judge whether an action merely complies with duty (legality) or is done out of duty (morality).

Universalization

The universality present in every maxim is a subjective (relative) universality and not objective (absolute or strict) universality, which holds for any rational being whatsoever. Universalization, the second aspect of the categorical imperative, tests whether or not the subjective perspective given by a maxim can also be conceived and willed as an objective perspective for a community of persons. From the broad variety of subjective principles (maxims), the moral ones are separated from the non-moral ones, and the agent is enjoined to follow the moral maxims.

According to a popular objection, Kant's ethics is indifferent toward the actual welfare of concrete human beings and is thus inferior to utilitarianism, which defines morality in terms of general well-being. At first glance, this objection appears to be justified. Kant's idea of universalization explicitly excludes the consideration of effects and the assessment of actions in light of their influence upon well-being. Nonetheless, upon closer examination, the objection proves to be unjustified. The consideration of effects is excluded from the justification of moral maxims but not from their application to concrete action. Here, they are not just legitimate but usually indispensable. Not in opposition to but quite in agreement with utilitarianism, Kant considers the promotion of the well-being of others to be morally obligatory, and in order to fulfill this obligation, one must consider the effects of his actions upon the well-being of his fellow men. Utilitarianism neglects to justify philosophically the well-being of others as the guiding principle for the consideration of consequences. Kant, on the other hand, offers the categorical imperative, with its test of universalization, as a justification of this principle. Furthermore, Kant does not view the well-being of others as our sole duty. Finally, Kant deals with a question ignored by utilitarianism: Under what *a priori* conditions is a subject capable of morality? The answer lies in the autonomy of the will. From a Kantian perspective, utilitarian ethics thus appears not entirely wrong but rather morally and philosophically incomplete. It is not so much an alternative to Kant as it is an abbreviated, fragmentary ethical theory.

Examples

In the *Groundwork of the Metaphysic of Morals*, Kant illustrates the procedure of universalization with the aid of four examples. Although they are only examples, the two main aspects of Kant's system of moral obligations come to light here.

First, Kant recognizes obligations not only toward others but also toward oneself. Morals cannot be reduced to social morals, nor is all virtue united in the single virtue of (personal) justice. Kant thus criticizes Aristotle and agrees with Stoic and Christian views. As the principle of all obligations toward oneself, Kant cites one's own perfection: the cultivation of intellectual, emotional and physical capabilities as well as the cultivation of morality (*TV*, VI 386f.). As the principle of social obligations, he cites the happiness of others (VI 387f.).

Second, following tradition, Kant distinguishes the "perfect" duties, which allow no leeway, from the "imperfect" duties, which do allow some leeway for behavior. The leeway does not reduce the validity of a duty, such as loving one's neighbor. In the face of limited possibilities, it merely allows us to favor one sphere of application (such as that of parents or children) over another.

The combination of both divisions yields four classes of duties (table 8.1). In the *Groundwork*, Kant discusses for each class the negative example of a maxim not capable of being universalized (IV 397ff., 421ff., 429ff.).

Table 8.1 Moral Duties

	Perfect duties	Imperfect duties
Duties to oneself	Forbiddance of suicide	Forbiddance of not developing one's abilities
Duties toward others	Forbiddance of false promises	Forbiddance of indifference toward the need of others

The test of universalizability has two forms. The first, stricter form has to do with the perfect duties and considers whether or not a maxim can even be *conceived* as a universal law. According to Kant, one arrives at a contradiction when, for example, one makes the maxim of killing oneself due to dissatisfaction with life to a universal law. Kant assumes that the biological function of unpleasant sensations is "to stimulate the furtherance of life" (*GMM*, IV 422). Unpleasant sensations indicate a lacking (hunger, for example, indicates a lack of energy) and motivate us to eliminate this lacking (for example, to eat). Dissatisfaction with life is a kind of unpleasant sensation. Taken as a universal law, suicide due to dissatisfaction with life would then mean that the same sensation serves toward two contradictory tasks: the furtherance and the destruction of life (ibid.).

The second and weaker form of the idea of universalization tests whether or not one can without contradiction *will* a maxim as a universal law. An exact understanding of the criterion of "not being able to will" makes for a good deal of difficulties; Does Kant, as R. P. Wolff (1973, 169) and N. Hoerster (473) claim, make the dogmatic assumption that certain human aims, such as the cultivation of abilities and talents, are matters of natural necessity? Or is Kant thinking of a contradiction of the sort, "No one can will to do something against his will?" If we take Kant seriously, we must seek the contradiction in his concept of the will or, what is the same, of practical reason. According to Kant, the will, or practical reason, consists in the ability to act not according to laws but according to representations of laws—that is, according to objective reasons. It does not matter whether these reasons are technical, pragmatic, or assertoric in nature. In any case, one has the ability to act according to reasons only if one is not committed to the subjective sensation of pleasure. This is exactly the case in Kant's first example of not being able to will: unwillingness to cultivate one's abilities. One can of course without contradiction conceive of a world in which human life is devoted "solely to idleness, indulgence, procreation, and, in a word, to enjoyment" (*GMM*, IV 423). But as a rational being, one cannot will such a life, for having practical reason, or will, means overcoming the merely subjective world of pleasure as the ultimate cause of action.

The universalization demanded by the categorical imperative should not be confused with contemporary principles of universalization such as those advocated by Hare and Singer. For one thing, the contemporary principle is applied directly to actions, whereby the purpose of an ethic of maxims is lost. For another, the consideration of effects is not only allowed but also required. The difference between Singer's empirical, pragmatic interpretation of universalization and the purely rational considerations of the categorical imperative becomes clear from the case of *false promises*.

In the case of false promises, Kant is not, as is often assumed, concerned with the injunction to keep promises under all circumstances. Neither a child who promises something beyond its means and abilities nor an adult who is forced to break his promise is immoral. Kant is not concerned with the observable sequence of events, in which a promise is made and then kept or broken, but is instead concerned with honesty as the subjective principle determining the will. He asks whether it is morally permissable for someone in need to give a promise that he does not intend to keep (*GMM*, IV 402, 422). The false promise, like the famous example of the denial of a deposit (*CPrR*, V 27), is seen as an instance of lying and deceit.

On the empirical, pragmatic interpretation, promising is a socially binding rule of action, or institution. Such institutions define advantages and obligations. They create expectations and enable us to adapt our own actions to those of others. They thus make an ordered society possible. Breaking promises, it is said, undermine the credibility of the institution, and if everyone breaks them, there will soon be no one who believes them. Thus, upon universalizing the breaking of promises, the institution of promising, and with it the possibility of rational association, dies out.

This reasoning is correct but does not exactly capture the problem. From an empirical, pragmatic standpoint, it does not matter where the general loss of faith comes from—whether it comes from dishonesty or from not being able to keep a promise, despite good intentions, due to unforeseen difficulties. Whereas the second reason is not morally reprehensible, the categorical imperative is concerned solely with the moral aspect and with the maxim of dishonesty underlying false promises.

On a pragmatic interpretation, no logical contradiction occurs. A world in which, after repeated disappointments, one no longer trusts promises, or, in the extreme case, does not trust any statement at all, may not be desirable, but it is not inconceivable. One only recognizes the logical contradiction when, following Kant's reasoning, one concentrates on the maxim itself rather than on the (unpleasant or desirable) consequences. What is the meaning of an intentionally false, dishonest promise?

Whoever gives a promise undertakes an obligation toward others and abstains from making its fulfillment dependent upon egoistic or utilitarian calculations. It does not matter whether a promise, as an obligation, reflects stupidity or slyness, responsibility or irresponsibility of the promisor. Nor does the obligatory nature of a promise depend upon whether the institution of promising is morally acceptable or should instead, like certain games of chance, be outlawed. If a promise means an obligation, then an intentionally false promise means that one takes on an obligation but yet does not accept it. A promise which one gives with the intention of breaking it rests upon an inconsistent maxim. An intentionally false promise cannot be conceived as a universal law and thus proves to be morally reprehensible.

Because the categorical imperative implies the strictest form of universality, Kant has been accused of moral rigorism, according to which maxims such as not lying must be obeyed under all circumstances. In his famous dispute with the French writer and politician Benjamin Constant, Kant indeed claims that one does not have a right to lie even to those who are unjustly pursuing someone ("On the Putative Right to Lie for the Love of Man,"[5] 1797). Nonetheless, Kant does not advocate a dubious rigorism here. As the title of this piece shows, it treats a problem of *rights*, while the moral problem (the duty to be honest) is set aside (VIII 426, note). Constant had raised the question whether or not someone has a *right* to truthfulness under all circumstances—hence, the extreme case that the inquirer intends to murder a friend of the person questioned. According to Constant, this case shows that the absolute validity of the duty to be truthful would make all society impossible. For Kant, exactly the opposite is true: it is the right to lie that would make all society impossible. Truthfulness is the basis of all contracts, which would become meaningless if the participants could make use of a "right to lie." Not only specific contracts within the framework of an existing legal and governmental order would become meaningless. Even that original contract, which establishes a legal order and rational principles for human association (sect. 9), loses all meaning. On the other hand, we need not on Kant's view condemn a "liar for the love of man" legally. Kant speaks of a law of emergency (VI 235f.), according to which there are cases which are culpable yet unpunishable. Today, even the most progressive legal systems do not recognize a right to lie for witnesses who are close to the defendant and might thus be tempted to mislead the court. They recognize only the right to refuse to give evidence.

One can of course, departing from the dispute between Kant and Constant, discuss truthfulness as a duty of virtue rather than of law. According to the categorical imperative, a deceitful life is then certainly not permissible. An honest life is required. But the maxim of honesty does not necessarily imply that one must at all times tell everyone "the complete truth." Without being permitted to lie, one may perhaps withhold certain information from the terminally ill or from small children (cf. XXVII 138f., 448). We cannot, however, exclude the possibility (which Kant disallows) that a situation is ambiguous, that various duties are called into play simultaneously, and that they point in different directions.

First, this possibility is not an ethical problem but a problem belonging to the theory of action. It does, however, have the significant ethical implication (which Kant wrongly denies) that there can be a genuine collision of duties (cf. *TV*, VI 426). If in certain situations the duty to honesty clearly conflicts with the duty to help (a clear contradiction occurs much less often than we like to think), then we must weigh the two duties against one another. One may for such purposes seek for higher, more formal principles on which to orient one's decision. But these higher principles must still be moral and cannot appeal to personal advantage or to feelings of sympathy. Otherwise we might lie when a friend or we ourselves are in danger, while we would remain honest in the case of an enemy or of someone whom we do not know. The higher principle which arbitrates the conflict between honesty and helping must be absolutely correct as a moral principle. It must be universally valid. It thus remains a maxim which proves to be categorically binding on the basis of universalization.

8.3 THE AUTONOMY OF THE WILL

The categorical imperative is often seen as the principle of morality. Such an understanding is misleading, since Kant is looking for principles of ethics in two senses. On the one hand, he seeks the concept and highest standard for all moral action. On the other hand, he is concerned with the ultimate cause for being able to act so as to meet this standard. The categorical imperative answers the first question, and the autonomy of the will answers the second. Moral subjectivity, as the condition for the possibility of moral action, lies in the ability to determine oneself by one's own principles. So the two points of view are interrelated. The categorical imperative specifies the concept and law governing the autonomous will; autonomy enables us to fulfill the requirements of the categorical imperative. The idea of self-legislation goes back to Rousseau, who says in *The Social Contract* (I 8) that obedience to a law made by oneself is freedom. But it is Kant who discovers in Rousseau's remark the basic principle of all ethics and who provides a justification for Rousseau's idea.

Kant answers the question of the basic structure of the moral will, a question often neglected in present-day ethics, in two steps. In the *Critique of Practical Reason*, he first eliminates all maxims which arise from a non-moral will and specifies their general principle as determination by another (heteronomy (§§ 2–3). Then he investigates autonomy as the positive content of the remainder (§§ 4–8). This two-step argument is transcendental in a narrow sense, for it investigates the *a priori* conditions which make morality possible. By way of contrast, Kant's presuppositions on absolute goodness and on the categorical imperative, as well as the theory of the fact of reason (sect. 8), are necessary components of the critique of practical reason but are not, strictly speaking, transcendental in nature.

Kant's argument plays upon the content and the form of desire. All objects, states, or activities desired for the sake of pleasure belong to its content. Desire and pleasure do not refer exclusively to the sensual sphere here (food, drink, sexuality, relaxation). Spiritual enjoyment, which comes from intellectual, creative, or social activities, is also included here. Hence, the distinction between lower (sensual) and higher (spiritual) enjoyment, of such importance for pre-Kantian ethics and for J. S. Mill's utilitarianism, becomes irrelevant for the foundations of ethics (*CPrR*, § 3, Remark I). In both cases, the agent is determined by the pleasure expected from his actions. For the will, all action guided by the expectation of pleasure and the avoidance of displeasure (pain, frustration) comes from outside. It comes from the senses rather than (practical) reason and is always empirical. Only from experience can one know what one desires and whether fulfilling one's desire (food, drink, health, wealth, scientific, artistic or athletic activity) is associated with pleasure or displeasure. The corresponding experiences are at most valid in general but never universally valid. Hence, material causes can never yield practical laws, which require strict universality.

The common principle of all material causes is personal advantage: love of the self or one's own happiness. Nonetheless, Kant says explicitly that every limited rational being necessarily wants happiness. Because we have needs and desires, happiness, in the sense of satisfaction with one's entire existence, is not an inalienable possession but instead an inescapable task (*CPrR*, § 3, remark II).

Kant's insight into the significance of happiness makes it understandable that happiness is repeatedly claimed to be the principle of moral action. But Kant also identifies the exact reason why, assuming Kant's definition of happiness, theories binding morality to this principle are wrong. Morality is unconditionally and universally valid, whereas happiness, as satisfaction with the whole of existence, depends upon the (individual, social and genetic) constitution of the subject—upon preferences, instincts, desires, interests, longings and hopes, and upon the possibilities offered by the natural and social environment. Because, in other words, the content of happiness is in many ways empirically conditioned, it cannot serve as a universal law and cannot provide the determining cause of morality.

Aristotle's *Nicomachean Ethics* ranks among the most important philosophical attempts to establish happiness as the basic principle of human action. It is doubtful that Kant's critique is directed against an attempt of this sort, for Aristotle takes happiness not as subjective satisfaction but as the supreme aim beyond which no further aim can be conceived. It thus corresponds more closely to the highest good recognized by Kant in his Postulates (sect. 11). Nonetheless, Kant considers the highest good in the context of an ethic of will, while Aristotle views it from the standpoint of an ethic of aims.

Since according to Kant even spiritual interests rank among the material causes, which are not of a moral character, one must ask whether the entire field of possible determining causes has not been covered, so that there is indeed no place for morality. In the second argumentative step, Kant shows that after the exclusion of all content, the form, and only the form, of all maxims still remains. Hence, the sole determining cause of a moral will lies in the form in which maxims set up laws (*CPrR*, § 4).

What must the will be like in order for it to be determined solely by such a legislative form? The mere form of law is not a possible object of sensibility and thus does not fall under the principle of causality, which applies only to appearances. The mere form of law corresponds to a faculty which transcends appearances and the principle of causality. In the *Critique of Pure Reason*, Kant has characterized the independence from causality as transcendental freedom. Morality thus originates in freedom in the strictest, transcendental sense. The concept of transcendental freedom developed in the first *Critique* means independence from all of nature. In ethics, it turns out to be none other than practical (moral) freedom: self-determination. Free of all causation and external influence, the will establishes the law for itself. Therefore, the principle of all moral laws lies in the autonomy, or self-legislation, of the will. In a negative sense, autonomy means independence from material causes; in a positive sense, it means self-determination or self-legislation (*CPrR*, § 8).

With the justification of action on the basis of autonomy, practical rationality and responsibility gain a new clarity and a more fundamental significance. Not one who is ultimately determined by the forces of instincts, passions, feelings of sympathy and antipathy, or customs, nor who always seeks the best means for reaching the given ends acts completely rationally. In the strictest, moral sense, only someone who follows principles stemming from the autonomous will behaves responsibly.

The claim of morality is directed toward a being which can overcome neither its sensible nature nor its social and historical heritage. Man always remains a creature of needs, history and society. Thus, for him, morality always has imperative significance. It is a categorical commandment, but no human being can always be sure of following it. Morality in the sense of autonomy means recognizing and even affirming one's needs and social dependencies without admitting them as the ultimate determining cause in life. Autonomy entails going beyond mere needs and customs and thus finding one's real self, Kant provokingly claims, as a moral being consisting of pure practical reason.

Going beyond does not mean eliminating everything else. The autonomous action of finite rational beings does not manifest itself in independence from all personal, social, economic and political conditions. One cannot possibly set these various conditions aside. The opinion of certain existentialists that man must begin again from scratch if he wishes to be free misunderstands the Kantian principle of freedom. This principle does not require people to replace vitality, sensitivity and social orientation with an empty rationality—as if a "pure" morality would have to side with reclusiveness, a lack of tradition and history, the critique of convention, and retreat from society and politics.

It is also wrong to think that Kant's idea of autonomy, and of morality in general, leads to excessive moralization and an examination of the morality of one's each and every move. On the contrary, an ethic of maxims has the advantage that the principle of morality does not relate directly to particular actions nor even to rules for action but instead to tried and true principles of life. The assessment of such principles is not, however, left solely to technical and pragmatic considerations. Finally, the view that on the basis of autonomy, one can have no natural inclination toward moral actions is also incorrect. Schiller's famous remark, "I enjoy serving my friends, but I unfortunately have the inclination to do it / And thus it often bothers me that I am not virtuous," ignores Kant's belief that "an inclination to do that which accords with duty (e.g., to do beneficent acts) can greatly facilitate the effectiveness of moral maxims" (*CPrR*, V 118). The man who helps his friends does not live heteronomously unless he serves them *alone* and is indifferent to all others' needs. A person who adheres to the maxims of being helpful, truthful and so forth when his natural inclinations or customs do not require it acts autonomously.

With the principle of autonomy, Kant places philosophical ethics upon a new foundation (cf. *CPrR*, V 40). The basis of morality lies neither in benevolent self-love (Rousseau) nor in moral sense (Francis Hutcheson, 1694–1746, as well as Shaftesbury, 1671–1713, and Hume). In connection with the duty to promote one's own perfection, one should cultivate benevolence and moral sense (cf. *TV*, VI 386f.), but they represent only a factual, fortuitous condition of the subject. They are not universally valid. Rousseau and the philosophers of moral sense remain bound to a sublime empiricism. Morality is based even less on a physical feeling (Epicurus, whom Kant does not consider to be "so base in his practical precepts" as is often assumed: *CPrR*, V 115). Even the perfection of things (the Stoics, Wolff) and the will of God (Crusius, theological moralists) cannot in the final analysis justify moral obligations. For Kant, a maxim is not rational because God sovereignly commands it. Instead, God commands it because God and the maxim are rational. Although empirically speaking it may sometimes be the other way around, from a systematic point of view morality does not follow from faith but instead precedes it.

8.4 THE FACT OF REASON

The idea of absolute goodness, the categorical imperative, and the principle of autonomy constitute necessary elements of a philosophical ethics, but they do not suffice to complete it. Unless he can demonstrate the existence of morality, as the object of investigation shared by all three elements, Kant does not achieve his goal of overcoming ethical skepticism. The latter view can only be refuted if morality proves to be an actual "fact" and does not ultimately rely upon personal, cultural, historical, or genetic illusions.

Despite its central importance, Kant mentions the problem of the reality of morality rather incidentally. Due in part to the imbalance between the substantive significance and the actual treatment of this problem, many difficulties in Kant's solution have not yet been clarified in a generally accepted manner. Kant finds the fact of reason only in the practical sphere—and not in the theoretical sphere. Whereas theoretical reason always relies on possible experience, pure reason occurs in the domain of action—and only in this domain. With the phrase "fact of (pure practical) reason," Kant wishes to point out that morality actually exists. The fact of reason is supposed to confirm the character of Kant's ethics as a reflection of practical reason upon its own nature and upon its realization in the moral dimension. It shows that Kant's ethics is not an impractical theory of abstract obligations. The paradox situation of Kantian, and perhaps all ethics manifests itself in the fact of reason: one reflects upon an existent fact always present in moral consciousness (or moral language, etc.), and this reflection is supposed to lead us to a principle of morals, the standard for normative *obligations.*

The apparent paradox is eased when one considers the specific nature of this fact. It is not an empirical circumstance but rather the fact of reason in practical contexts; it is a fact having the nature of an obligation only in the case of finite rational beings.

Kant does not designate the moral law but rather the consciousness of the moral law as the fact of reason (*CPrR*, § 7, V 31). Kant speaks of a fact because he considers consciousness of the moral law to be something real—not a mere assumption or fiction. We are dealing, Kant says, with the indisputable (apodictically certain) fact that moral consciousness, the consciousness of an unconditioned obligation, exists. Through the consciousness of unconditioned commitments, reason presents itself "as originally creating law (*sic volo, sic iubeo*)" (ibid.).

In the face of repeated scientific and philosophical doubts as to the possibility of morality, the fact of reason is supposed to prove the objective reality of morality and to refute skepticism. According to Kant, the fact of reason shows that ethics is not only possible in a negative sense as a tool of destruction but also in a positive sense as a normative theory of morals. Only if moral consciousness is not sheer self-deception do normative ethical theories lose the status of clever, yet impractical conceptual constructs so that they can contribute to an understanding of the human condition.

Kant considers the fact of reason to be undeniable. In justification of this view, he says that one need only analyze the judgments which people make as to the legitimacy of their actions. The fact of reason is thus supposed to manifest itself in certain judgments. The judgments in which it comes to light are those in which we express the morally correct action in independence of any competing inclination (ultimately, our happiness). In the remark to section 6, Kant gives an example. He asks whether someone who, threatened with immediate death, is required to bear false witness against an honest man could, despite his great love of life, possibly overcome this inclination and refuse to bear false witness. The answer to this question is doubtless, "Yes." It may be understandable under certain circumstances to intentionally bear false witness against an honest man, and we may, reckoning with a surplus of self-love, even expect it. But nonetheless, we still judge false witness to be morally wrong. In order to understand such an evaluation, one must according to Kant appeal to the notion of moral law or to that of the categorical imperative. This notion implies a law valid unconditionally. In other words, the validity of this law does not at all depend even upon the crassest threat to one's happiness. Since we actually do condemn the bearing of false witness, Kant sees the reality of pure reason, which is independent from anything empirical, such as, in this case, inclinations, to be proved in the practical sphere. Pure practical reason, or morality, no longer appears as a lifeless obligation but as a reality which we have recognized from the beginning.

Because we are all familiar with judgments which require us to act in a manner conflicting with our inclinations, we need not search far to discover pure reason. Nor can pure reason in the sense of morality be considered an invention of moralists. The fact of reason, Kant says, has long been "incorporated" into the being of all men (*CPrR*, V 105). It is "written with the coarsest and most legible writing in the human soul"

("Commonplace," VIII 287). But due to the post-Kantian critique of morals and perhaps also due to experiences with inhumanity in our century, some will doubtless not wish to relinquish skepticism entirely.

Since pure practical reason consists in the freedom of the will, the fact of reason forms the third step in Kant's theory of freedom: (1) In the antinomies of the first *Critique*, Kant has shown that the notion of transcendental freedom is conceptually possible. (2) The principle of autonomy from the second *Critique* shows that transcendental freedom is a negative concept which, taken positively, means moral freedom. (3) The fact of reason demonstrates that transcendental, or moral, freedom is real. Further elements of the Kantian conception of freedom emerge in his legal philosophy, his philosophy of history, and his philosophy of religion, as well as in the *Critique of Judgment*. Freedom is a guiding concept which influences Kant's entire philosophy.

Kant's reflections on the fact of reason have methodological as well as substantive significance. They point out indirectly that an appropriate philosophical ethics constitutes a complex task. In the first methodological step (the constructive analysis of concepts), it is crucial to form an appropriate concept of morality and to specify it in accord with Kant as unqualified goodness. In the second step, the concept of unqualified goodness is applied to the situation of finite rational beings. This application occurs in the concept of the categorical imperative. The third step (transcendental reduction) leads to the freedom of the will as the principle of moral subjectivity. Finally, a fourth step, which one can characterize as inductive or hermeneutic in a broad sense, shows that the foregoing argument deals with a reality rather than a fiction. Here, one can pick out a moral phenomenon from human life, such as the conviction that we are obligated to testify truthfully even when threatened with death (the "inductive side"). Then, the moral phenomenon must be "brought under its concept" and interpreted as "duty against inclination" or as the "consciousness of an unconditioned obligation" (the "hermeneutic" side).

It follows from the methodological complexity that only a small part of Kantian ethics is transcendental in the strict sense and, further, that contrary to the moot confessional dispute as to the only true method in ethics ("analytical or hermeneutical," "transcendental philosophy or dialectics," etc.), the philosophical justification of morality constitutes a variegated task which cannot be solved by a single method.

The naturalistic fallacy, introduced by G. E. Moore (*Principia Ethica*, 1903), ranks among the most important arguments for criticizing traditional ethics. Kant is also accused of this fallacy (Ilting). With the argument of the naturalistic fallacy, Moore rejects all naturalistic and metaphysical views of ethics in order to replace them with his own ethical intuitionism. On his view, "the good" is an absolutely simple and thus undefinable object. Strictly speaking, the purported fallacy does not consist in defining "good" in terms of natural or metaphysical "properties" but in identifying various different things (the good on the one hand and the properties on the other) as one. It is thus better to speak of an error or fallacy of identification. Whether this error actually exists cannot be decided logically, as the talk of a "naturalistic fallacy" would suggest, but only on the basis of ethical considerations. Moore makes only a few rudimentary considerations of the required sort. Applied to Kant's ethics, the purported fallacy calls into question not the fact of reason but instead the basic definition of moral goodness. But although the *Groundwork* begins with an explication of moral goodness as unqualified goodness, it is not the entire genus of the good that is defined here but the specific difference of *moral* goodness. Kant thus does not necessarily contradict Moore.

If one wishes to accuse Kant of a logical error in his treatment of the fact of reason, the is-ought fallacy first pointed out by Hume would seem more appropriate (*Treatise on Human Nature*, 1739–40, book III, part I, sect. I). According to Hume, prescriptive propositions, using "ought," cannot be derived from descriptions of fact, using the copula "is." Because Kant speaks of a fact of reason, one might think that he commits such a fallacy. But closer consideration shows that Kant's ethics instead contains a sophisticated proposal for solving the problem of is and ought. First, Kant distinguishes between the domain of theoretical and of practical reason. Whereas theoretical reason examines what is (the laws of nature), practical reason is always concerned with what we ought to do (with technical, pragmatic and categorical imperatives, the laws of freedom). Second, Kant separates empirically conditioned from pure practical reason and defines moral goodness in terms of pure reason. Moral goodness thus cannot possibly be derived from non-moral experience. Third, the fact of reason does not refer to an empirical fact but instead to the way in which a being endowed with practical reason experiences itself. Moral experience manifests itself not in observable actions but in moral judgments of actions. Fourth, Kant does not derive any prescriptive propositions from the fact of reason. In his argument, the categorical imperative does not follow logically from the fact of reason but from the notion of unqualified goodness, applied to the situation of finite rational beings.

In the *Critique of Pure Reason*, Kant has determined that "in respect of the moral laws" experience "is (alas!) the mother of illusion" and that it is thus "highly reprehensible to derive the laws prescribing what I *ought to do* from what *is done* or to limit the former by the latter" (*CPR*, B 375). It is thus necessary to leave the domain of being (nature). Contrary to utilitarianism, to ethology, and to sociological and anthropological views, morality must be defined with *a priori* concepts, which are independent of experience. One of the main tasks in contemporary ethical discussions can thus perhaps be solved by a critical reexamination of Kant. A creative examination of the idea of morality as unqualified goodness, together with the categorical imperative and autonomy as its underlying principles, would have a very good chance of overcoming the problems of naturalism and of the is-ought fallacy.

9.

Political Philosophy

↔↔↔↔↔↔↔↔↔↔

Kant's philosophy of law and of government has not received as much attention as his critiques of theoretical and practical reason. In the history of modern political thought, Kant does not play as significant a role as Hobbes, Locke, Rousseau and Montesquieu before him, or as Hegel, Marx and Mill later on. Even in scholarship on Kant, his political philosophy often recedes into the background. Ever since Schopenhauer's condescending remark that he could explain the *theory of law* in the *Metaphysic of Morals* only as a mark of Kant's senility (*The World as Will and Representation*, book 4, § 62), this theory has been considered to be of inferior quality. According to V. Delbos (1969, 559f.), the breadth and clarity of the other writings is missing. Other scholars (Cohen ²1910, 381ff.; Ritter 1971) are of the opinion that there is no critical, transcendental justification here and that Kant thus remains bound to a metaphysical doctrine of natural rights. Still others criticize Kant as being a theorist of the bourgeoisie (Saage 1973) or accuse him of promoting authoritarian thinking in Germany.

A negative assessment is widely accepted but does not do justice to Kant. Prejudices which are neither philosophically nor politically convincing do enter into his political philosophy and do warrant several points of criticism: the excessive importance placed upon the protection of property in the justification of government, the priority of men over women, discrimination against wage-laborers, and the defense of castration. Also dubious are his treatment of marital and family law, his rejection of a right to active resistance (right to revolution), and his defense of the death penalty. But methodological considerations show

that few of these propositions are situated on the level of the explication of concepts and the justification of principles. On Kant's view, the
latter tasks are the central concerns of the philosophy of law and government (cf. *LT*, preface and § A). The main philosophical task is the
justification of law and government from *a priori* concepts. If we lay the
methodologically problematic elements aside and concentrate on this
central philosophical problem, Kant proves to be a significant political
thinker, who for good reason ranks among the classics of thought about
law and government.

Years before the French Revolution and the *Universal Prussian
Law of the Land* (1794), at the time a highly commendable legal code,
and a generation before the Prussian reforms of Karl Freiherr von Stein
(1757–1831) and Karl August von Hardenberg (1750–1822), Kant
advocates a constitutional government with basic limitations on all use
of power. More than a century before the founding of the League of
Nations, Kant proposes the philosophical principles on which it rests.
In light of his political philosophy, he is quite enthusiastic about American independence (cf. Jachmann in: Groß, 153f.) and about the
French Revolution—at a time when such sympathies involved personal
risk. Like Montesquieu (1689–1755) in France and Adam Smith
(1723–90) in Scotland, Kant is one of the eighteenth century's outstanding theorists of a politics of freedom.

Kant first develops his philosophy of law and of government in
various shorter works: "Idea for a Universal History with Cosmopolitan Intent" (1784); "On the Commonplace: That may be right in theory but is not valid in practice" (1793), "II. National Law" (against
Hobbes) and "III. International Law" (against Moses Mendelssohn);
and *On Eternal Peace* (1795). A comprehensive systematic investigation
occurs only in the *Metaphysic of Morals*, first part, "Metaphysical Origins of Legal Theory" (1797; "legal theory" is to be understood here
neither in the sense of specific laws nor in the sense of jurisprudence
but in the sense of the system of principles of law). Kant's treatment of
this difficult material is overly succinct and is lacking in rhetorical elegance. For this reason and because the theoretical background is completely left out, this is a very cumbersome text, which challenges the
analytic skills of the reader. But the student of this work who also takes
into consideration Kant's "Preparatory Works on Law"[6] (XXIII
207–370) confronts a high degree of conceptual rigor. Kant justifies
limitations of power, sets up a supreme standard for the modern idea of

human rights, and develops a philosophical sketch of civil and public law. This sketch deals with property, with the government as the instance securing property and adjudicating questions of ownership, and with the punishment of crime.

Kant's thought on law and on government also belongs to the tradition of the Enlightenment, which leads from Hugo Grotius (1583–1645) and Hobbes to Samuel Freiherr von Pufendorf (1632–94), Locke, Thomasius and Wolff, and then on to Hume and Rousseau. As in his critiques of theoretical and practical reason, Kant does more than simply integrate various methodological and material elements of previous Enlightenment philosophy. He instead takes a decisive stand. In distilling out the rational elements in his predecessors' views, he adheres to the idea of a philosophy consisting of *a priori* knowledge and to that of a law independent of experience, as envisioned in the critique of practical reason. Kant bases law and government upon principles of pure (legal) practical reason. His political philosophy advocates natural rights in the sense of critically examined rational laws.

Above all, Grotius, Hobbes and Rousseau have a strong influence on Kant, who rejects the combination of heterogeneous Biblical and rational or empirical and historical arguments as well as the empirical leaning in the legal philosophy of Locke and Hume. According to Kant, the law, along with property, government and the punishment of crime as its basic institutions, cannot be derived from experience, which is not only variable but also controversial. Even in the justification (not the application) of law, experience is the "mother of illusion."

9.1 THE RATIONAL CONCEPT OF LAW

The title of the work "*Metaphysic of Morals*, First Part, Metaphysical Origins of Legal Theory" reflects the decisive methodological considerations for Kant's philosophy of law.

The *Metaphysic of Morals* is for Kant the system which follows upon the *Critique of Practical Reason* (*LT*, VI 205). As a part of the *Metaphysic of Morals*, Kant's philosophy of law no longer belongs to the critique of practical reason but presupposes the results of this critique. It is not a pre-Critical, dogmatic theory but a critical one. It develops the rational concept of law which sets the supreme critical standard for any existing law. In contrast to an exaggerated rationalism, which attempts to derive existing law from rationality, Kant recognizes that philosophy is limited to the small task of the clarification of basic concepts and principles. As a science independent of experience, legal philosophy can replace neither the legislator nor the judge or legal expert. On the other hand, the latter all rely upon the philosopher and upon the justification of the *a priori* legal principles on the basis of which a constitution and legal system is seen as reasonable and just.

While the basic concept of law is valid *a priori* (*LT*, §§ A–E), empirical considerations of a general sort enter into the argument when the concept is "applied," particularly in civil law. It is assumed, for example, that human beings have bodies and lives, which can be threatened, that there are objects that can be made into property, that there are men, women and children, and so on. The empirical elements play no role in the justification of the law but only specify its sphere of application. But Kant does not make it sufficiently clear that a philosophical theory of law cannot do without empirical elements. He does see that the notion of law is "a pure concept, which is, however, oriented toward practical activity" (*LT*, VI 205). Philosophy thus cannot design a complete system of law. As in the case of virtue and the philosophy of the natural sciences, Kant speaks only of "metaphysical origins" of law.

In contrast to mathematics, philosophy cannot begin with definitions. They must be developed from the substantive investigation. Law has two substantive aspects: For one thing, it is, like virtue, a concept of reason ("moral concept," *LT*, § B) and not an empirical concept. For another, this concept of reason, in contrast to that of virtue, refers not to inner attitudes (convictions) but to outer social freedom. The first aspect is normative and *a priori* in character; the second is descriptive but not just empirical. The underlying notion of law has no need of empirical elements, but civil law does. Since the concept of law results only from the combination of a normative and a descriptive component, Kant escapes both the naturalistic fallacy, which describes morality in purely descriptive terms, and the normativistic fallacy, which wishes to derive it solely from normative considerations.

Both in interpretations of Kant and in systematic studies, it is often overlooked that only the examination of similarities and differences between law and morals allows us to arrive at an appropriate understanding of law. Contrary to anarchism, it is not a sign of irrationality that laws govern human relations. In contradiction to strict legal positivism and to political decisionism, legitimate legal systems are not arbitrary constructions. They are not, in the sense of Hobbes' "auctoritas non veritas facit legem,"[7] at the free disposal of an absolute sovereign but are bound to general principles of law for their legitimation. On the other hand, Kant rejects the position that the law and the state should promote the citizen's morality (virtue). Such moralizing tends toward totalitarianism.

The descriptive element in the concept of law contains the condition of application: the task solved by the law. The law, Kant says, is supposed to make the association of persons possible, prior to all experience. "Person" is not a general anthropological notion here but instead a specific legal concept. It denotes a legally competent subject, who can be the cause of his actions and is free in this sense. Law has to do with the outward freedom to do as one pleases without being at the mercy of others, and not with inner or moral freedom in the sense of the independence of the will from instincts, desires and passions.

In posing the task of making the association of outwardly free subjects possible, prior to all vicissitudes of experience, Kant emphasizes the importance of the conditions of application and renders the discussion of all additional problems superfluous. After Hobbes, a debate ensues as to why people influence one another, whether this influence is peaceful or violent, and where the roots of violence lie. Kant excludes all of these anthropological questions from the justification of the law. Even the problem of the mutual influence of free subjects upon one another due, for example, to the fact that they share a limited amount of space is irrelevant.

Because law is concerned with outward freedom in a social context, all inner aspects, such as desires and interests, are of legal relevance only if they lead to action and effect outward freedom. The legal community is not for Kant an association due to need but a free community of competent subjects. In contrast to Wolff and Mendelssohn, and also to C. G. Svarez, the main author of the *Universal Prussian Law of the Land* duties of humanity (benevolence) do not fall under the jurisdiction of the law. States which view the utilitarian commandment to promote the general welfare not only as a moral principle but as the constitutive "purpose" of the legal system do not conform to the fundamental task of the law: "The best form of government is not that in which it is most pleasant to live (*eudaimonia*) but that in which the citizen's rights are most secure" (XXIII 257). A government based on the principle of happiness treats its citizens, with their different notions of happiness, as incompetent minors. Furthermore: "The sovereign wants to make the people happy according to his ideas and becomes a despot. The people do not want to give up the universal human right to happiness and become rebellious" ("Commonplace," VIII 302).

In contrast to the now prevalent conception of government, the welfare state does not for Kant have the status of political justice. Hence, such a state should never develop at the expense of constitutional government. As soon as the state gives up or relaxes the preservation of freedom in order to promote happiness, it becomes unjust. In any case, laws serving toward happiness are legitimate in order "to secure the *state of law* . . . both internally and against outer enemies" ("Commonplace," VIII 298). An additional Kantian argument for a community with a social state could be derived from the duty not to humiliate one's fellow man. One should thus think of "benevolence either as a mere obligation or a lesser service of love" (*TV*, VI 448f.). But we are dealing here with a duty of virtue rather than law.

The conditions for applying the law imply finally that only the free action itself and not the underlying conviction counts. Every contract, such as the exchange of commodities for money, is just, as long as both partners act freely and without deceit. It does not matter whether they do not deceive because they would lose the respect of others, including, perhaps, their business partners, and because they might also be punished, or whether they are honest for moral reasons. Quite aware of the difference between law and virtue, Kant sees that questions of conviction have no legal significance. Without explicitly saying it here, Kant excludes snooping into convictions from his concept of law.

The task of making the association of outwardly free subjects possible can be addressed in different ways. One group (the masters) can, for example, subjugate the other (the slaves). We would consider this solution to be unjust since it implies drastic privileges and discrimination. In Kant's non-moral argumentation, however, subjugation does not even represent a solution of the task. Outward freedom is denied to those who are subjugated. Kant investigates the conditions under which the subjects can retain their outward freedom and still live together. In accord with his rational intention (this is where a normative, moral component enters into the argument), he investigates more precisely the purely rational conditions, independent of experience, under which a community of outwardly free subjects is possible. Only conditions which hold universally and thus cannot be denied without contradiction are independent of experience. In a social context, the assumption of unqualified freedom would lead to a contradiction since it allows subjugation and thus the destruction of outward freedom. In the sense of independence from arbitrary power of another, outward freedom is possible in society only if it is limited by the condition of its strictly universal accordance with the outward freedom of all others. The rational concept of law is thus "the essence of the conditions under which the arbitrary choice of one can be united together with the arbitrary choice of another according to the universal laws of freedom" (*LT*, § B). The law of freedom of which Kant speaks here draws our attention to the reliance of a rational legal order on pure practical reason, which is in the relevant respect independent of empirical conditions ("laws of nature") (cf. *LT*, VI 221).

Insofar as the association of competent subjects such as human beings is rational in an emphatic sense and wishes to be moral, it must take on the character of law. The law is not a fortuitous human institution and by no means an arbitrary one. It is necessary. That does not mean, though, that every existent legal stipulation is allowed or even required. On the contrary, Kant's concept of law contains a standard with which we can judge the legitimacy of all existent laws. Only those legal stipulations are rational, or simply legitimate, which allow the freedom of one person to be compatible with the freedom of all others according to strictly universal laws. This standard is the legal counterpart to the categorical imperative in the field of ethics (virtue). It obligates the community of outwardly free subjects to obey universal legal regulations in the same way that the categorical imperative obligates the personal will with the maxims which it has laid down.

With his conception of law, Kant criticizes not only, as we have mentioned, legal positivism but also the personalization of morals, which would demand absolute rationality (morality) only of one's private convictions. On the other hand, Kant rejects all moralization of law, for law, as reason in human association and as political justice, coincides neither in substance nor in purpose with the reason of the acting subject, or personal morality. Logically speaking, the first group of moral duties treated in the theory of virtue, the duties concerning the perfection of the self, do not at all belong to the legal duties. For example, although Kant views suicide as morally wrong, he criticizes attempts to make the preservation of one's own life to a legal duty. And in the second group, the duties toward others, the duties of benevolence, gratitude and sympathy are also only duties of virtue. Only those social commitments required *a priori* for the coexistence of outwardly free subjects belong to the legal duties. The breaking of contracts, theft, or manslaughter, for example, make coexistence impossible. Even in this domain, one is not obligated to recognize these legal commitments freely. One may fulfill them for other reasons, such as fear of punishment.

Due to the fundamental difference between personal and political morality, between morals (virtue) and law, Kant does not derive law from the autonomy of the will as the principle of personal morality but instead from pure practical reason and its criterion of universal legality.

According to Kant, the rational concept of law is closely connected with the authority to use force (*LT*, §§ D–E). He does not see this authority as irrational violence or an immoral usurpation on the part of the legal system but instead as an indispensable *a priori* element of all law. As paradox as it may seem, without the authority to use force, no legal system, which must nonetheless be committed to the coexistence of free subjects, can be conceived.

Ever since Thomasius (*Fundamenta juris naturae et gentium*,[8] 4th ed.: 1718, preface), the interconnection of law and the authority to use force has been almost a commonplace. But it is Kant who first succeeds in proving the connection and thus in solving the fundamental problem in law and government: the authority to use force in the name of the law limits freedom, and no one likes to accept such limitation. For this reason alone, social utopias which abolish all government and all use of force will continue to be conceived. Kant decidedly rejects such conceptions and presents strong rational arguments for his case. Without any additional assumptions, the authority to use force follows immediately from the legal task of making the association of outwardly free subjects possible.

Because the law is the very essence of the conditions under which the freedom of one is compatible with the freedom of all others, every action which, in accordance with universal laws, is compatible with the freedom of all others is legitimate from a legal standpoint. Any interference with this legal authority is illegitimate. Anyone who impedes me in my performance of legal actions does me wrong. Hence, the force preventing illegitimate interference is itself legitimate because it makes freedom of action possible (cf. Hegel, *Philosophy of Right*, § 93). But with his justification of the forcible nature of law, Kant does not open the door to force of any sort whatsoever. Force is only legal insofar as it prevents injustice. Any other use of force is unjust.

The rational concept of law includes not only the authority to use force but also, as its complement, the idea of human rights. Human rights are rights which every human being has as such, regardless of his personal situation, of political constellations and of historical conditions. Because every action compatible with the freedom of all others is legally allowable, "every human being by virtue of his humanity" has a proper claim to such a degree of freedom as "can maintain together with the freedom of everyone else according to a universal law" (*LT*, VI 237). The degree of freedom reconcilable with the freedom of all others is the only human right, or, one might also say, the only standard for measuring all human rights. For Kant as well as Rousseau (*The Social Contract*, chap. I 1), freedom is not acquired. It attaches to human beings prior to all legal acts. It is (in a legal, not a biological sense) innate. But, Kant adds, it is not unqualified freedom that is innate but only outward freedom which is reconcilable with the same freedom of everyone else according to universal laws.

Kant divides his philosophical theory of law, which builds upon the principle of rational association, into the two main fields of civil and public law. In contrast to Hobbes and Rousseau, he treats civil law before public law—so that the legal force of natural rights increases.

9.2 CIVIL LAW: THE JUSTIFICATION OF PROPERTY

Neither in the history of the theory of property nor in Kant scholarship has Kant's theory of property received much attention. And those who deal with this theory at all often sharply criticize Kant as advocating a law of brute force (Schopenhauer). He is further accused of depriving property of any moral foundation whatsoever and of falling short of Rousseau and even of the archliberal Locke (Vlachos 1962, 391ff.). Yet Kant's theory of property contains arguments still worthy of discussion.

Property is an institution whose concept and justification constitutes one of the central problems of politics and its philosophy. We freely dispose over our property almost as we do over our own bodies. Property extends, so to speak, the body beyond its natural boundaries and at the same time defines the limits of the free disposition of others. Private property thus means power in two senses. My property immediately implies power over those things which I possess, and it indirectly implies power over anyone who does not possess them but would like to.

Because property restricts the freedom of others and establishes power, it is often criticized—most severely by "philosophical communism." Such strict communism differs from socialism in that it allows only common property and no personal property at all. The rejection of all personal property frequently occurs in the name of justice and freedom. Kant shows that this position, contrary to its claim of protecting justice and freedom, is fundamentally opposed to law and to freedom. Proudhon will formulate the thesis: Property is theft (*Qu'est-ce que la propriété?*[9] 1840). According to Kant, however, property is not just legitimate (and hence not comparable to theft). It is a rationally necessary institution and an indispensable component of any system of justice, which must count *a priori* as an order of freedom. Kant does not thereby exclude the possibility of voluntarily doing without certain sorts of property. He does not declare life in a monastery or a kibbutz to be contrary to reason. According to Kant, only a legal prohibition, a forced "renunciation" of any sort of personal property contradicts reason.

Kant does not justify the institution of property with empirical, anthropological or historical arguments but instead offers a purely rational justification. Property is not legally necessary because the human species has certain zoological characteristics or because humanity has developed historically for the worst. Nor would property become superfluous if men should improve due to better experience and education. On Kant's view, property follows solely from rational considerations regarding the nature of outward freedom in a social context.

A conceptual clarification precedes the justification of property (*LT*, § 1; cf. §§ 4–5). One can view this clarification as a "metaphysical discussion," for it shows that legal, in contrast to physical, ownership constitutes not an empirical but a pure *a priori* relation. Kant speaks of what is "outwardly yours and mine," so innate freedom (what is inherently yours and mine) can never belong to the sphere of exchange. Life and limb are thus excluded. Surprisingly, though, Kant does not sufficiently emphasize their elementary significance for freedom in his theory of law. He thus himself contributes to the impression that he has a "possessive individualist bias."

Following the relational categories of substance, causality and community (reciprocity), Kant includes three domains under what is outwardly yours and mine: (1) corporeal things outside of myself (a piece of land or commodities), (2) service which have been agreed upon (contracts), and (3) the state of another person in relationship to me (*LT*, § 4). In addition to laws of property (§§ 11–17) and contract law ("personal law": §§ 18–21), laws concerning marriage, children and domestics, which are "personal in an objective manner" (§§ 22–30), also fall under civil law. Kant does not count the spouse, children and domestics as "property," for one can make free use only of corporeal things. No man is "the owner *of himself*. . . , let alone of other human beings" (§ 17). But they do count as "personal effects" (§ 4). A spouse who runs away may at any time be brought back "like a thing" (§ 25).

I can call things, services and states legally mine (*meum iuris*) if the use which someone else makes of them without my permission infringes upon my legal (i.e., compatible with the rational concept of law) freedom of action. It obviously violates my freedom of action if someone forcibly takes an object from me which I have with me and which belongs to me. But my freedom of action is also violated if someone makes use of an object belonging to me during my (physical) absence. Hence, legal property is not limited to physical (empirical) possession. Legal property extends not only to the soil on which I am momentarily lying or standing and to the object which I have with me. It also applies to things with I have set aside or left behind and to the soil I have left—under the assumption that these things actually belong to me. Because physical possession does not coincide with property, Kant introduces the notion of intelligible (rational) possession (*LT*, § 1).

At first glance, the talk of intelligible possession appears to be the product of eccentricity or at least a far-fetched abstraction. But in reality, this concept draws our attention to a constitutive characteristic of property in the legal sense: legal property does not consist merely in present spatio-temporal, empirically observable possession but instead in a non-empirical, conceptual or intelligible relation. The bicycle which I am riding but which I have stolen does not belong to me, nor do I relinquish ownership of my bicycle when I leave it parked. A radical communist would have to claim that personal property is always an injustice or, somewhat weaker, that it is limited to empirical possessions, which someone is carrying or wearing at present. Kant takes

exactly the opposite view. It is an "*a priori* assumption of practical reason to see and to treat every object at my disposal as potentially yours or
mine in an objective sense" (*LT*, § 2[10]).

Kant does not argue pragmatically. He does not say that the
restriction of ownership to empirical possession would allow only the
immediate satisfaction of certain primary desires, that it would endanger their satisfaction over the long term, that it would make little use of
nature, and that it would thus allow human abilities to deteriorate. He
instead makes an *a priori* claim, which, however, does not follow "from
mere concepts of law in general" (*LT*, § 2).

Everything which I have the physical power to use counts as an
object at my disposal (an object of my outward freedom). Using an
object means putting it to service toward my aims. Independent of the
question as to what my purposes and aims consist in and independent
of all anthropological, historical and social considerations, outward
freedom cannot be realized unless it can make use of some objects
(things, services, or states). On the view of a radical critic of property,
there are certain things which, from a physical point of view, can be
placed at the service of freedom but which, from a legal standpoint, no
one is allowed to use. Freedom would thereby deprive itself of useful
objects, which are cut off from the possibility of personal use.

Strictly speaking, as Kant claims in the second step of his argument, the self-deprivation of freedom means its complete dissolution
and a "contradiction of outward freedom with itself" (*LT*, § 2), for
Kant discusses this view as a possible principle of reason. But pure
practical reason recognizes "only formal laws"; thus, it cannot distinguish between legitimate and illegitimate objects. It must either
exclude all objects or allow all objects. The absolute prohibition of
property, however, eliminates outward freedom, the pursuit of aims of
one's choosing. Hence, according to Kant, all objects must without
qualification be allowed as potential possessions.

After the general justification of the institution of property, the
question arises of how ownership comes to be. This question is connected to the problem of how the legal relation of intelligible ownership arises from mere empirical possession. Kant distinguishes three
problems: the empirical acquisition of property, the legal ownership
and the relation connecting the two.

Today, property arises from contracts in the various forms of pur-
chase, gifts, or inheritance. But contractually acquired ownership pre-

suppose that the objects already belong to the person selling, giving, or bequeathing them. The contract is thus a derivative form, and original acquisition cannot rest upon contracts.

In *De iure belli ac pacis*[11] (1625, book II, chap. 2–3), one of the most influential books of the modern age, the Dutch philosopher Hugo Grotius assumes that originally, everyone owned the earth and its fruits. Through original acquisition in the sense of contractual transfer of common property, personal property comes into existence. Against Grotius, Locke makes the claim that people acquired property through labor, which allows us to shape an object so as to satisfy our desires (*The Second Treatise of Government*, 1689, chap. V). Paradigmatic for Locke's theory of labor is farming, the production of food from the soil.

Kant agrees with Locke that primary ownership, contrary to Grotius as well as Pufendorf, does not arise by contractual agreement but only through original acquisition. But Kant considers Locke's further opinion that original acquisition comes from labor to be untenable. Since labor does not create its object from nothing, it presupposes material which must already belong to me if I wish to work on it legally. Labor does not justify the original title to ownership. It is only an outward sign of original possession, which could be replaced by many other, less difficult signs (*LT*, § 15).

Like Grotius, Kant proceeds from the assumption of an original common ownership of land and what is on it (§ 6). This original condition is not to be understood empirically as an early phase in human history but instead as a conceptual construct. It reminds us that the material basis for all civil law does not itself originate in a legal act. The material basis is given to man. At the same time, Kant criticizes the notion of originally unowned land. The earth is not property of none but property of all. The first owner does not come across no man's land but instead finds common property. He has to do with the community of all co-owners and not with objects outside the law.

The right to use the land and its fruits is just as basic as common ownership. Since, in the context of common ownership, the right of one person to use the land conflicts with the same right of all others, these rights would cancel one another if the original common ownership did not already contain the law by which it can become the private property of individual persons. But how can common property become privately owned?

The original acquisition of a certain part of common property can, Kant says, only be conceived as unilateral occupation. This statement has been interpreted as advocating the law of the jungle, but such an interpretation is based on a misunderstanding. First, occupation does not consist in usurpation but in the original acquisition of an object which does not yet belong to any individual. Second, it is not force that counts but temporal priority: "All human beings have an original (i.e., prior to any arbitrary legal act) right to possess land; that is, they have a right to be where nature, or chance (independent of their will), placed them" (*LT*, § 13). This possession is none other than the original collective property of all men within the confines of the earth. It is irrelevant for Kant's argumentation whether the land which I occupy is fertile enough to meet my needs or whether it is a plot in the desert which makes survival difficult or even impossible. It is not the will to survive but the will to law which results in ownership.

Before the creation of government, the original distribution of property has only provisional significance. Ownership gains the security imparted by a legal deed only through a collective universal (common) will, which has the power to secure the provisional distribution of property. On the other hand, legal securement presupposes private property. Hence, the common will, or constitutional government, only guarantees property but does not establish and determine it (*LT*, § 9). The natural law for which Kant argues exerts (provisional) influence even before a government has been established. The power of the state thus diminishes. Property, contracts, marriage, family and household are legal institutions valid prior to government.

9.3 PUBLIC LAW: THE JUSTIFICATION OF CONSTITUTIONAL GOVERNMENT

Property is a legal institution which precedes government. Yet it is the government which finally determines ownership, protects it against robbery, effects restitution of things taken illegally, and frees the owner from the labor of having to defend his own property. Because, on Kant's view, property is rationally necessary for freedom and the government is necessary for property, the government represents a rationally necessary institution. It is a second order institution subordinant to first-order institutions such as ownership, contracts, marriage and the family. In the tradition of Hobbes, legal security is viewed as the reason for government. The opinion of Hobbes' opponent Richard Cumberland (*De legibus naturae*,[12] 1672) is on Kant's view untenable.

Not only the institutions of civil law proposed by Kant are required for freedom of action. Life and limb are even more elementary conditions. For their protection, too, government is indispensable. Nonetheless, Kant proceeds from civil law in his justification of government, so the objection soon arises that his philosophy of law reflects the interests of the bourgeoisie and lends the appearance of objectivity, or even rationality, to the initial stages of competitive capitalism. This objection is only partially justified. Aside from the fact that civil law deals not only with possessions but also with marriage and the family, Kant indeed does not specifically emphasize personal rights, above all the integrity of life and limb. But the reason does not so much lie in Kant's not ascribing to these rights a place in reason's natural law. These rights are already included in the universal principle of law. In contrast to ownership, life and limb are not acquired but rather innate rights. This fundamental significance does not allow Kant to make them a component of civil law but of course would not prevent him from explaining them clearly before the discussion of civil law. It is a weakness in the Kantian theory that they are mentioned only indirectly and late, under the heading "Doing Away with Violence" (§ 44).

In his justification of government, Kant follows a pattern of thought known as contract theory. It ranks among the most important argumentational forms in political philosophy. In the modern age, such influential philosophers as Grotius, Hobbes, Pufendorf, Locke and Rousseau advocate this theory. Hume criticizes it under the false supposition that the contract designates an actual historical event which establishes the state (*Essays*, II 12). At present, this theory has gained new significance primarily through John Rawls (*A Theory of Justice*, 1972). Contract theories proceed from free persons living without government in a state of nature. They show that this state is unbearable for all participants and that it can only be overcome by a contract restricting freedoms. For this reason, they derive legitimate government from the original contract between free persons.

Kant considers the ideas of his predecessors, combines them with one another, and develops them with greater clarity. From Hobbes, he takes the state of nature as the reason for the necessity of the state; from Locke, the idea of inalienable human rights; from Locke and Montesquieu, the division of powers (cf. *LT*, § 45); and from Rousseau, the thesis that only the general will (*volonté générale*) represents the supreme normative and critical principle of all actual legislation. Kant's greater clarity stems from the distinction between empirical, anthropological causes and rational (moral) arguments. On this basis, the social contract is an *a priori* idea of pure practical reason independent of all experience. It means no more than the rational idea of constitutional government. The social contract thus cannot possibly be derived from empirical assumptions about the nature and history of man, but it can be applied to such assumptions (cf. *LT*, VI 217). It does not designate the origin of government as it exists but instead the rule for determining how it ought to be (cf. *Refl.*, 7734, 7740, 7956). It does not denote an historical event like the Rütli oath or the agreement of the Pilgrim fathers after their landing in North America. It rather forms the ultimate basis for the legitimacy of all public law and the supreme standard for determining whether it is just or unjust.

The state of nature is likewise a mere idea of reason. It represents a purely rational construction of coexistence in the absence of government. It means anarchy in the literal sense of the absence of governmental rule. In the state of nature, unlimited, primitive freedom reigns. Everyone can do what seems right to him, regardless of whether it promotes only his own happiness or also that of his fellow men (*LT*, § 44). The fact that it brings fear and terror does not speak against the state of nature. That is also the case in natural disasters. The problem with it is that it is a state "of outwardly lawless freedom" (*LT*, § 42). No one is obligated to refrain from infringing upon the rights of others, and no one is secure from violent encroachments. In the state of nature, lawlessness, not injustice, reigns (*LT*, § 44). The coexistent free beings do have innate as well as legitimately acquired rights. But all rights are lacking in security. Even if everyone strives to be just, views of justice will sometimes conflict with one another, and there is no authorized judge who can make a legally binding decision. No one can gain what is justly his by legal process, so the legal nature of rights disappears. They are no longer claims which can survive independently of the wishes of others. Their recognition depends on the private mercy and discretion of others, whereas law, by definition, has the task of making private desires compatible according to universal laws. One who stands by his claims to integrity of life and limb, to property and to the fulfillment of contracts can obtain what is rightly his only by means of violence. Thus, no one is safe from violence. As Hobbes (*Leviathan*, chap. 13) saw with brilliant clarity: In the state of nature, a (latent) war of all against all reigns.

Because law is for free beings the relationship demanded by reason, and because the state of nature dispenses with law as such (the authority to use force), reason requires that we overcome this state. The state of nature consists in the rule of particular wills, and thus its disappearance means the "rule" of Rousseau's general will, as that which is not particular. Kant speaks of a public state of law. This state does not ensue with just any government but only in the case of a republic (a constitutional government, as we would say today), in which, as in Aristotle (*Politics*, chap. III 11) and in contrast to despotism, (just) laws and not human desires hold power (*LT*, VI 355).

The state of law replaces war with peace. According to Hobbes, one seeks peace for fear of death and due to the desire for happiness (*Leviathan*, chap. 13). For Kant, these are pragmatic motives which have no place in a strictly rational justification. The good of the state does not consist in happiness but in law, in the rational community of outward freedom. As a consequence, the argument that only in a public state of law can justice and injustice be determined by law instead of personal opinion is the only one that holds. It is not because peace has the beneficial effect of putting a stop to bloodshed that reason demands it. It is required because it is the sole condition under which the law demanded by reason is realized.

The state of law has two distinguishing features. First, it is not private individuals but a governmental authority which determines justice. Second, it is not just any arbitrary government but only that political system of conflict resolution which (in accordance with Kant's conception of pure practical reason) is determined by a strictly universal law. It is the general will which establishes a political order corresponding to the principle of universalization. For this reason, Kant, making use of the notion of a social contract, says that law is an order which stems from the *"original contract"* ("Commonplace," VIII 295; cf. *Peace*, VIII 348f., 354ff.). Instead of the original contract, Kant also speaks of the general (united) will of the people (ibid.; *LT*, § 46). But one should view neither the united will of the people nor the contract as empirical quantities. Such an understanding would not only be incorrect from a philosophical point of view but also politically dangerous, as it would open the door to a rule of terror on the model of Robespierre and Danton (cf. "Commonplace," VIII 302). Kant welcomes the principles of the French Revolution but condemns the Jacobin terror. The united will of the people, the identity of the rulers and the ruled (*Conf.*, VII 90f.), is nothing more than the "eternal norm" (ibid.), the criterion for justice, or the "rational principle for judging absolutely every public, legal constitution" ("Commonplace," VIII 302).

In accordance with the principle of reason, the government is required to shape its social order as the common will of all citizens would, or "in the way in which a people with mature reason would prescribe for itself" (*Conf.*, VII 91; cf. *LT*, VI 327). In modern terms: the principles to which all laws are bound must be capable of universal consensus. An actual empirical discourse cannot, however, guarantee agreement with the general will. The danger of distortion by false views of one's own best interest, errors as to matters of fact, precipitous judgments, emotional barriers, structural prejudices, ideological preconceptions, hidden pressures, and finally lies and deceit threatens every concrete attempt to reach an agreement.

Kant himself gives several examples for the normative, critical function of the social contract and of the united will of the people. He demands freedom of opinion and freedom of the arts and sciences (VIII 37ff.), and he rejects privileges for the nobility (*LT*, VI 329, 369f.), serfdom (hereditary servitude, slavery: *LT*, VI 283; *Refl.* 7886), despotism ("Commonplace," VII 290f.), colonialism (*LT*, § 15; *Peace*, 3rd Def. art.), and a mandatory, immutable state religion (XXIII 133). Generally, the social contract, as a principle of reason, provides a basis for criticizing any legal discrimination due to sex, race, or creed. The idea of a general will thus proves to be the principle and criterion for human rights insofar as they have an origin prior to government and are only guaranteed by public law.

Although Kant ascribes sovereignty to the united will of the people, he does not give all citizens the right to vote, or active citizenship. In the tradition of the three ideals of the French Revolution, Kant formulates three principles of the constitutional state: freedom, equality and (departing from the revolutionary ideal of fraternity) self-sufficiency. Kant's departure has the unpleasant consequence that in Kant's constitutional government, as in the Greek city-state, not all citizens have equal rights: "The journeyman of a merchant or craftsman; the messenger . . .; the incompetent . . .; every woman and generally everyone who is forced to preserve his existence (nourishment and protection) according to the disposition of others (except that of the government) lacks a civil personality, and his existence is like mere inherence (*LT*, § 46; cf. "Commonplace," 295).

Kant rightly distinguishes active from passive citizenship and grants to incompetents only the latter. But it is not particularly convincing when he derives the stigma of passive citizenship from economic status (journeyman, messenger . . .) or sex (woman), that is, from private or even biological circumstances. Here, Kant falls prey to the prejudices of his time. It would seem more correct to bind active citizenship to legal competence and, if legal (not economic, emotional, etc.) dependencies follow from private circumstances, to change such circumstances instead of reinforcing them.

∞∞

one

Kant also speaks of unjust (legal, but not just) rule, that is, despotism or tyranny. In the face of the French Revolution, the current political question is whether there is a right to active resistance, rebellion and revolution against a thoroughly unjust rule. From Jean Bodin (1530–96) and Johannes Althusius (1557–1638) to Grotius, Locke, Pufendorf and Mendelssohn, most modern political theorists have answered this question in the affirmative. The first declarations of human rights, in Virginia (1776) and during the French Revolution (1789), reckon the right of resistance to the rights of man. Even Edmund Burke, the critic of the French Revolution, and the "very cautious Achenwall" ("Commonplace," VIII 301) allow resistance in extreme cases. The speculative "revolutionary," however, proves politically to be a strict opponent of all rebellion. Kant does not completely commit the populace to mute passivity. As the shield of unalienable human rights, he advocates the right to public criticism, or "*freedom of the pen*" (cf. "Commonplace," VIII 304), which is supposed to help force a ruler to make reforms in the name of justice. He also allows "negative resistance," according to which the people's parliamentary representatives may balk at certain demands of the administration (*LT*, VI 322). But one should not rebel even against a "seemingly unbearable abuse of supreme power" (*LT*, VI 320ff.). Is Kant obedient to authority, in contradiction to his enthusiasm for the French Revolution?

Even if Kant's arguments[13] are not ultimately convincing, they do not rest on pragmatic considerations but on questions of principle. It is not practical intelligence which precludes active resistance. Experience may teach us that even more unjust social orders often emerge from revolutionary changes and thus that, as a rule, passive resistance and reform are better. But Kant excludes the appeal to practical intelligence and to experience from his reflection on principles

In explicit contrast to Hobbes, Kant grants "inalienable rights." In violating them, a head of state treats the citizen unjustly. But according to the "Commonplace" (VIII 303f.), these rights may not be enforced by violent means. According to the *Origins of Legal Theory*, legal authority to resistance would "disintegrate" any constitution. The constitution, as the supreme law, would contain "in it the stipulation of not being supreme" and would hence contradict itself (*LT*, VI 320). The contradiction becomes quite obvious as soon as one asks who should act as judge in the conflict between the people and their sovereign (ibid.). The right to resistance, Kant says, would give every citizen a claim to *public* validity of his own legal opinion. Equal force of personal legal opinions, however, is nothing more than the state of nature, which contradicts the state of public law demanded by reason.

Against this line of argument various objections arise. First, from the standpoint of practical politics, one wonders how the people can oppose such a measure as Wöllner's religious edict (sect. 2), which banishes "freedom of the pen," or disregard for the "negative resistance" of the parliament. Secondly, and more fundamentally, Kant's own conception of a pre-existent natural (rational) law contains a revolutionary potential irreconcilable with the absolute rejection of a right to revolt. The notion of a constitutionally guaranteed right to resistance and revolution may be self-contradictory, but on Kant's normative, critical principle of the state of law, such a right is also superfluous. The violation of inalienable human rights, as the political situation prompting resistance, is, since it obviously offends the *a priori* law of reason, profoundly illegitimate. Because the state is for Kant a second-order legal institution, it is not an end in itself but is bound to the first-order institution which it is supposed to secure. If it egregiously violates first-order law, it cannot be viewed as "holy and invulnerable," nor can all resistance be prohibited *from the start*. This argument further suggests a third, methodological objection. Kant's uncompromising rejection of the right to resistance is nourished by the erroneous identification of a critical *a priori* idea of reason (the original contract) with an empirical element (the given legal system and governmental power). The irrevocability valid for the original contract, as the critical principle of all government, can never maintain for a product of history.

☙❧

The rational principle of public law holds not only for the internal constitution of a government. In the absence of international legal agreements, nations, too, live in a warlike state of nature, governed by the "right of the stronger." The international state of nature is only abolished in favor of a peaceful legal order when the community of nations is institutionalized in a "league of nations according to the idea of an original social contract" (*LT*, § 54). Kant's essay *On Eternal Peace* thus has the form of a contract describing the legitimacy and principles of the voluntary union of all nations which reason demands.

The union, or league, of all nations should not take the form of a world government, which would lead to unfettered despotism. The league of nations has no sovereign power which would allow it to interfere in a nation's internal affairs. It should be a federation of free nations (*Peace*, VIII 354) which all have republican constitutions (ibid., 349). The league protects countries from attack and indeed restricts itself to the task of promoting peace, the highest political good, in order to finally bring to an end the "atrocious waging of war, toward which as their main aim up to now all governments without exception have directed their internal preparations" (*LT*, § 62, resolution). Such a league of nations has the methodological significance of a legal principle. It is the "rational idea of a *peaceful*, if not yet amicable, complete community of all peoples on earth" (*LT*, § 62). After the First World War, Kant's idea became godfather to the League of Nations, the predecessor of the United Nations.

9.4 THE PUNISHMENT OF CRIME

Kant's theory of the punishment of crime represents one of the few parts of his philosophy of law recognized as relevant in current discussions. But Kant has attracted interest primarily as a negative example. Ever since the Enlightenment, humanitarian philosophers have strived to make traditionally cruel penal systems more humane. In view of efforts to abolish corporal punishment and the death penalty, Kant's demand to punish sexual criminals with castration and murderers with death (*LT*, VI 333ff.) seems to be a step backwards into the "Dark

Ages." When rehabilitation is seen as the appropriate aim of punishment, when, at most, deterrence is viewed as worthy of discussion, and when retribution is considered to be a primitive vindictive instinct, Kant's avid support for a law of retribution seems to deserve no other response than: farewell to Kant.

With his theory of retribution, Kant criticizes the predominant penal doctrine of the eighteenth century. On the usual view, the punishment of crime can be justified only by its utility in deterring crime. Kant adopts exactly the opposite view. The primary legitimation of criminal punishment lies solely in justice, which must be defined in terms of pure practical reason. Its analysis should thus be purged of all considerations of utility. It is not because Kant categorically claims that punishment must be,[14] that the penal code for him has the rank of a categorical imperative (*LT*, VI 331). It is rather because justice is an unqualified command, so that "in every punishment as such there must first be justice" (*CPrR*, V 37). The deterrence theory degrades man to a mere tool of society, deprives him of his inalienable human dignity and is unjust. With this argument, Kant succeeds in turning the tide and at least temporarily forcing the utilitarian theory of deterrence to retreat. Even today, Kant's theory of criminal law is not simply obsolete—assuming that we concentrate on the basic principles. All concrete references (to castration, the death penalty, etc.) are situated below the level of the principles and, substantively, must be criticized as inhumane.

Kant's theory of punishment in the general sense begins with an element which we can only mention here: (1) the idea of practical reason, which holds both morally and legally, that the violation of a moral law is deserving of punishment (*CPrR*, V 37). To this is added (2) the authority to use force, which is analytically connected with law and is valid even before the foundation of government, and (3) the establishment of a public state of law in order to secure innate and legitimately acquired rights. Only all three elements together can answer the first question of any theory of punishment: "Why should the government punish anyone at all?" Kant's theory of criminal law in the narrow sense (*LT*, general remark, E I) addresses three additional questions. It first clarifies the notion of criminal law and says, second, who may be punished and, third, what principle determines the type and degree of punishment.

The Concept of Criminal Punishment

In remarkable brevity and clarity, Kant's definition includes five essential elements (*LT*, VI 331). Criminal law is (1) an authorization which (2) attaches to the executive branch of government (the "ruler"). Criminal law thus conforms to the division of powers. While (*a*) on the basis of legislation, (*b*) the courts determine punishment, it is (*c*) the executive which enforces the authorized penalty. Only a legally authorized power, and not the victims of a crime nor angry neighbors nor a diffuse "society," has the authority to punish, and this power cannot act arbitrarily but only according to the specifications of the court, which must itself judge according to existing legislation. Hence, criminal law is not a vindictive instinct, as is sometimes claimed.

(3) Punishment is properly applied to a "subordinate," that is, to someone subject to law. Kant claims in this context that the "chief of state" cannot be punished. He can only relinquish his power (ibid.; cf. "Commonplace," 291). Here, it would seem, Kant wrongly identifies a legal person with a natural one. In fact, governmental authority should be understood as a mandate temporarily given to natural persons. This mandate can be retracted in cases of criminal behavior. Every official remains subject to the law.

(4) A person is punished "because of his crimes." Criminal punishment is thus distinguished from taxes or quarantine: it is done due to and subsequent to an offense. Kant does not speak of just any offense, and not of misdemeanors, but only of "public crimes," the most serious form. Only the crimes which, in contrast to "civil crimes," endanger the community as a whole and not just individual persons fall for Kant under criminal law, in which he advocates the principle of retribution (ibid.). As difficult as it is to apply this criterion, Kant demands retribution only for those grave offenses which jeopardize the state of law required by reason. Moreover, the concept of crime includes the subjective element of intent. The criminal is aware of his offense. An unintentional violation is called "mere fault" (*LT*, VI 224).

(5) The ruler is given the right to inflict "pain," an ill, upon the criminal. Of course, not all ills have the nature of punishment. In contrast to natural disasters, legal punishment is a conscious, voluntary act. In contrast, say, to painful dental work, the subject does not undergo the punishment voluntarily; the penalty is "inflicted" upon the criminal. This aspect of the Kantian definition also holds for measures

toward betterment and resocialization, as advocated today. A therapy which is legally required and enforced is a form of detention, and involuntary detention is an ill. Rehabilitation does not eliminate the legal institution of punishment but instead expands the range of tasks which it must meet.

General Retribution as the Principle for Punishment

Kant's answer to the additional question of who should be punished hinges, without explicitly introducing this notion, upon retribution in a preliminary, general sense. The punishment of crime is retribution in the sense that only the criminal may be punished and only because he has committed a crime. In opposition to common practices of collective or exemplary punishment and to sanctions for the welfare of the state, Kant's requirement is important: First of all, someone must be "found to be *punishable*, before one thinks about deriving from this punishment some advantage for oneself or for one's fellow citizens" (*LT*, VI 331). Because the punishment of innocent people is a gross injustice in any case, the universal concept of retribution has absolute priority over all other aspects. Only on the assumption that someone has committed a crime may other subsidiary considerations be brought into play. Kant does not entirely exclude deterrence, betterment, and resocialization from criminal law, but he allows them to play only a subordinate role.

Special Retribution as the Principle of Punishment

Kant's answer to the last basic question of any theory of punishment is based on a special, or narrow concept of retribution. In the special sense of retribution, the offense is not only a necessary but also a sufficient condition for determining criminal punishment. Special retribution appears to lead to absurd results and has thus evoked the most criticism of all. One can of course respond to offenses against property with fines, to bodily injury with corporal punishment, and to manslaughter or murder with capital punishment. But we consider such corporal punishments as chopping off a hand to be barbarous and inhumane, and we cannot at all imagine a literal retribution ("an eye for an eye") for many offenses.

On a reasonable interpretation, retribution is a formal and not a material principle. Admittedly, in a few places Kant himself adopts a material (literal) interpretation, which is rightly criticized. On the other hand, he explicates the law of retribution with the help of the formal "principle of equality, of (in the situation of the pointer on the scale of justice) not leaning more to one side than to the other" (*LT*, VI 332). The pointer shows the balance between the left and the right side of the scale. It is independent of what lies on both sides of the balance, of where one finds the weights or the objects weighed, and of which standard of measure is chosen. Accordingly, retribution in the narrow sense does not depend on how one measures the type and gravity of the crime or how one can determine the appropriate punishment. It requires only that the punishment be neither too lenient nor too strict in relation to the offense. In fact, it is a violation of criminal justice to set, for the sake of deterrence, a more severe punishment than is deserved. Justice does not rest upon the subjective preferences of the judge or on considerations of social utility but upon the gravity of the crime. The practical legal reason of the philosopher does not extend further here than the justification of this "categorical imperative of penal justice" (*LT*, VI 336). In his explanatory remarks, Kant does not pay sufficient attention to the following fact: the philosopher cannot relieve the legislator or the judge of the difficult task of establishing a just balance between crime and punishment.

PART IV

What May I Hope?—
The Philosophy of History and Religion

Having dealt with the two questions "What can I know?" and "What ought I to do." Kant turns to the third fundamental question, "What may I hope?" (cf. *CPR*, B 832f.). Hope is directed to that which does not yet exist. The third question adds the dimension of the future, of history and of the meaning of human life. It does not represent a continuation of the analysis of time in the Transcendental Aesthetic. Dealing with time as a form of intuition, the latter discussion concentrates on (pure and applied) geometry and ignores the historical dimension of human activity. The question of the future proceeds instead from the investigation of morality. Taken together, these questions mark off the domain of human action. Kant's practical philosophy thus has a future dimension, which distinguishes it from Aristotle's ethics and politics and with which it heralds in the historical thinking of Fichte, Schelling and Hegel.

Kant asks whether what ought to be will ever be reality. Here, he is concerned with the practical task of reconciling nature ("reality") and morals ("what ought to be"). He treats the problem of their epistemological reconciliation in the *Critique of Judgment* (sect. 12).

Since human activity has two basic aspects, the practical problem of reconciliation, the question of what man may hope, breaks down into two components. The philosophy of history investigates the hope for outward freedom (law), and the philosophy of religion examines the hope for inner freedom (virtue or personal morality). The philosophy

of history and of religion thus contain complementary models of meaning—not competing ones, as is usually the case today.

The systematic position of the two components has a significant
implication: the philosophy of history and of religion do not represent a
continuation of theoretical but rather, primarily, of practical philosophy. They do not enlarge the field of knowledge. Their objects of investigation have practical rather than objective reality.

10.

History as the Progress of Law

$\approx\!\!\curvearrowleft\!\!\curvearrowleft\!\!\curvearrowleft\!\!\curvearrowleft\!\!\curvearrowleft\!\!\curvearrowright$

Kant does not subject historical experience to a systematic critique comparable to his critique of our experience of nature and of morality. In contrast to Schelling, Hegel and Marx, Kant does not ascribe as great a significance to history as to objective knowledge and to moral action. Nonetheless, although Kant's contributions to the philosophy of history are dispersed among various writings and are rather popular in character, they do indeed contain a sort of critique of historical reason. The most important writings are: "Idea for a Universal History with Cosmopolitan Intent" (1784), "Conjectural Beginning of Human History" (1786), and *The Conflict of the Faculties* (1798), the second Division of which investigates the "Conflict of the Faculty of Philosophy with That of Law" and the question of "whether the human race is in constant progression to the better" (*Conf.*, VII 79).

Fascinated with the theory of science, Neo-Kantianism sought the outlines of a methodology of the historical sciences and of the humanities as a whole in Kant's philosophy of history. Particularly Heinrich Rickert (1863–1936) studied the task, methodology and basic concepts of an historical science. It is indeed wise to distinguish the humanities from the natural sciences and to characterize them more closely in their own specific nature as sciences. But a project of this sort does not build directly upon Kant. It may close certain gaps in Kant's thinking, but in his philosophy of history, Kant does not himself develop a methodology of the historical sciences. He does not establish an historical understanding of meaning, or hermeneutics, as the "method" of the humanities but instead points to the possibility of viewing history not only from the standpoint of the theory of science but also from the perspective of practical philosophy.

Kant does not study history as a vast multitude of events. He leaves this task to "strict history, which is just *empirically* recorded" ("Idea," VIII 30). He discusses history insofar as it is of interest for man as a being endowed with practical reason. Preserving continuity with his transcendental critique of reason, Kant asks about the conditions independent of experience under which the process of history appears rational and meaningful. Practical philosophy poses the question of the meaning of history, which the empirical historical sciences cannot answer.

Kant does not deny that history presents a wretched countenance. Despite occasional bits of wisdom, one finds "everything on the whole to be weaved together out of stupidity, puerile vanity, often out of puerile malevolence and destructiveness" ("Idea," VIII 18). Above all, history appears as a succession of wars which destroy everything good and lead instead to "evil and degeneration of morals" (*Conf.*, VII 86). Although history with all its ill seems meaningless, and perhaps even absurd, Kant asks if we cannot still discover meaning in it—not in the history of individuals and groups but in the history of humanity as a whole, the history of the world. Kant thus seeks the beginning and ultimate goal of the history of the world. (The demand that not only the history of mankind but also the personal biography of each individual should have meaning belongs for Kant to the philosophy of religion rather than history.) According to Kant, the beginning and the aim of history are neither objectively known nor merely imagined. The beginning can only be constructively presumed, and the goal can only be conceived as a practical idea.

There cannot possibly be historical sources for the absolute beginning of human history. Clearly aware that he is venturing on "a mere pleasure trip," Kant constructs a "history of the first development of freedom from its original presence as a disposition belonging to the nature of man" ("Beginning," VIII 109) under the guidance of the Biblical history of the Creation (*Gen.* 2–6).

The beginning is paradise, in which, from a philosophical point of view, man exists without effort, because he simply follows his instincts and is thus a completely natural animal. In paradise, man lives in ignorance and therefore innocently. He is not yet conscious of his freedom and his reason. Paradise means happiness without freedom.

With the first attempt at free choice, man discovers "in himself a capacity to choose for himself a way of life and not to be bound to one in particular, as other animals are" ("Beginning," VIII 112). With man's liberation from instinct, an infinite number of objects of desire becomes accessible to him without his having a cultivated faculty of reason, which could guide him to making correct choices. Man's step from the "guardianship of nature into the state of freedom" ("Beginning," VIII 115) is thus "on the moral side" a fall, which entails "a lot of previously unknown evils of life" as punishment: "The history of *nature* thus begins from the good, for it is the work of *God*; the history of *freedom* begins from evil, for it is the *work of man*" (ibid.).

With this interpretation of paradise and of the Fall, Kant succeeds in harmonizing several competing assertions of Rousseau. Kant agrees with the Rousseau of the two Discourses that there is an unavoidable conflict between culture and nature and that the transition from nature to culture is a fall. But, Kant says, the descent is necessary in order for the various talents and abilities of man to develop and thus to make culture possible. Rousseau is thus wrong in demanding in the two Discourses a return to nature but right in his treatment in *Émile* and the *Social Contract* of man's difficult path to culture and to his education as a responsible citizen.

The history of mankind is his development since paradise and the Fall. History appears to have meaning if it leads from the primitive state of nature to a consummate state of freedom. Not only Hegel's philosophy of history but also Kant's views history as the progress of freedom. History is supposed to progress toward an association of outwardly free human beings, so that all strengths and talents can develop. The outwardly free association is realized in (just) constitutional government, which ends despotism and barbarism. The meaning of history lies in the establishment of constitutional governments and of a just form of coexistence among nations. History is the constant progress of law for all of humanity and culminates in the worldwide peace established by the league of nations.

Progress, the development of mankind to the better, is a basic idea of the European Enlightenment. The idea is supported by the dazzling successes of natural science and of technology. In the age of geographical, mathematical and scientific discoveries and of the invention of new instruments of measure and observation, of new techniques and of new devices (one need only consider Vasco da Gama, Columbus and Cook,

as well as Galileo, Kepler, Newton, and the biologist Linnaeus), the
Enlightenment concluded that the power of human reason has no limits, that the conditions of life constantly improve, and that man and
society also develop morally. Kant considers such exaggerated hopes to
be extravagant. He rejects an interpretation of history as a process of
salvation, which ultimately fulfills all earthly interests and desires.His-
torical progress does not lead to the consummation of personal morality nor, directly, to development in art, science and technology. Kant
does not share the naïve optimism of those who, like many today, think
that upon the dissolution of imperfect political institutions and, perhaps, of religious superstition, natural amicable instincts would return
to establish a community of brotherly love and harmony. Kant limits
progress to political justice, including both national and international
law. And law, as such, involves the authority to use force. Since history
has to do with outward events, it is not at all possible that their ultimate
meaning would lie in "inner" progress such as the development of man's
moral attitude. Progress can only be expected externally, in the establishment of laws in accordance with practical reason. The founding of
constitutional governments and their coexistence in a peaceful international community is the supreme task and ultimate goal of humanity.

There are three possibilities for the course of history: (1) constant
progress toward the better, (2) a continuous decline to the worse, until
mankind finally annihilates itself, and (3) a lack of change for better or
for worse are possible (*Conf.*, VII 81f.). Neither experience nor theoretical reason is able to decide between the three possibilities. One can
prove neither historical decline nor progress by theoretical, empirical or
speculative means. There remains only the possibility of practical *a priori* knowledge of history. The progress of legal justice has practical
rather than theoretical necessity. It is a regulative idea of legal practical
reason. The interpretation of history as the progress of law parries the
thesis of its meaninglessness. It justifies the rational belief that the
human task of living together according to rational principles is not
completely unrealizable and that, on the contrary, legal practical reason
can become real.

Kant sees legal progress as being carried out neither through an
instinct nor an agreed plan but by human nature. ("Nature" coincides
roughly with providence in pre-Kantian philosophy or the world spirit
in Hegel's philosophy of history.) Kant proceeds from the teleological
assumption that all of a creature's natural abilities are designed to

unfold completely and in accordance with their purpose ("Idea," 1st proposition). The special natural abilities of man, which aim toward the use of reason, do not reach their full development in the individual but only in the succession of generations within the species as a whole ("Idea," 2nd proposition). The natural aim of man is to be achieved through human nature itself. The progress of legal justice, as the meaning of history, occurs as if behind our backs—through our efforts but without our planning it.

According to Hobbes, the basic motivation of all action lies in egoism: according to Cumberland, Pufendorf and Locke, it lies in sociability. Kant considers both views to be correct, but not absolutely so. Anticipating Hegel's "cunning of reason," he speaks of an antagonism used by nature in order to achieve the development of all human abilities. Kant characterizes this antagonism as the *unsocial sociability* of human beings, that is, their inclination to enter into society, which inclination is combined with a constant resistance continually threatening to separate the society" ("Idea," 4th Proposition). Man inclines toward association because he can develop his natural abilities socially, but he also has a strong inclination to isolate himself because he wants to arrange everything according to his own tastes, in opposition to his neighbors. Kant thinks that such opposition awakens all human powers for culture and art, which would deteriorate without it.

As the force pushing us toward an international constitution, Kant cites the damage done by constant wars and the "*spirit of commerce*," which "cannot exist together with war" (Peace, VIII 368). This may be right for the founding of the League of Nations after the First World War and of the United Nations after the Second. But the twofold attempt to establish a peaceful world community shows that man's memory is short, that bad experiences are too easily forgotten and that each generation must make its own experiences. Moreover, war can create profit for others. Finally, Kant is right in demanding for the sake of a peaceful world community first the humanization of war, then the reduction of their frequency, and finally the complete elimination of invasions. But it is doubtful whether, in light of the "unsocial" aspect of human nature, one can ever hope for the complete elimination of war. Even for Kant, the guarantee given by unsocial sociability for the final aim of history does not consist in a certainty, which would allow us to predict the future eternal peace theoretically (ibid.). From experience, history speaks too powerfully against any sure progress

(*Rel.*, VI 19f.). Kant nonetheless adopts an optimistic attitude. He sees a current event as proof of the basic interest of man in the establishment of a rational legal system: the enthusiasm for the French Revolution in the world press, even though such enthusiasm was not at all free of risk (*Conf.*, VII 85–87). Even before de Tocqueville (1805–59), Kant thus claims that at least since the French Revolution, we live in an era in which peoples strive for just forms of government despite various impediments and thus give history meaning. But it does not appear to be the antagonism within human nature but rather the pursuit of justice and the liberating events which are responsible for legal progress. And Kant's tendency toward an optimistic answer to the question of whether the pursuit of justice will always be stronger than the egoism of particular groups or of the government is not beyond all doubt.

11.

The Religion of Practical Reason

❦❦❦❦❦❦❦❦❦

In agreement with a basic conviction of the Enlightenment, Kant develops his philosophy of religion as a continuation of his moral philosophy. After the decline of metaphysical cosmotheology, the notion of God belongs primarily to ethics, and "*religion* (viewed subjectively) is the knowledge of all of our duties as divine commandments" (Rel., VI 153). The *Critique of Pure Reason* already contrasts mere doctrinal with moral faith (B 855f.) and, after the critique of all speculative proofs of the existence of God, develops a philosophical knowledge of God based upon the concept of personal morality. This "moral theology" (B 842) or "ethico-theology" (*CJ*, § 86) makes a special sort of belief necessary. God is no longer an object of knowledge but of hope—and not of an extravagant but of a philosophically justified hope. As Kant says, God is a postulate of pure practical reason.

Wilhelm Weischedel denies that Kant's philosophical theology can claim to universal validity. It is evident only to one who has resolved to lead a moral life. Certainty of the existence of God originates in moral conviction.[1] In point of fact, though, Kant's conception of God as a postulate of pure practical reason presupposes no resolution in favor of morality. The claim is valid for all beings *capable* of morality, regardless of whether they actually behave morally or not. As a (finite) rational being, man is capable of morality.

Kant gives a more detailed account of the religion of practical reason in the Dialectic of the *Critique of Practical Reason* (cf. also the "Methodology" of the *CJ*) and in the work *Religion within the Bounds of Reason Alone*. His theory hinges on the concepts of supreme good and of evil. Neither concept plays a significant role in present philosophy. This circumstance makes it more difficult to understand Kant but is no reason to push his philosophy of religion frivolously aside. It could also be an occasion for examining whether or not contemporary ethics has sufficient awareness of certain substantive problems.

11.1 THE IMMORTALITY OF THE SOUL AND THE EXISTENCE OF GOD

Upon examining the role of religion in Kant's ethics, one tends either to accept the ethical principle of autonomy and to dismiss the belief in God or to reject the ethics of autonomy due to belief in God. Kant shows that the alternative "autonomy or belief in God" is wrong. It relies on the erroneous assumption that religion either forms the foundation of morals or is irrelevant, or even harmful, for them. In fact, says Kant, morals are based on the notion of a free being which binds itself to unconditioned laws. In order to be moral, one does not have to believe in God. Furthermore, whoever acts in agreement with the moral law only because he expects just reward or punishment in the hereafter misses autonomy right from the beginning. Moral action allows no other motivation than respect for the moral law. Nonetheless, morals lead "ineluctably to religion" (*Rel.*, VI 6). Reversing the usual view, religion does not represent the foundation but rather the result of morality. Practical reason investigates the ultimate purpose or meaning of autonomous action, conceives its meaning as the supreme good and sees the existence of God and the immortality of the soul as necessary presuppositions of the supreme good. In contrast to many of his "enlightened" contemporaries, Kant upholds not only the existence of God but also the "consoling hope" of the indestructability of the person.

Kant calls the necessary presuppositions of the supreme good *postulates* of pure practical reason. He is referring here to objects which one must necessarily assume in order to view the supreme good as possible and thus to consider practical reason's desire for meaning to be realizable. Kant's postulates claim to be true. Their acceptance is not a matter of free choice. They have the significance of insights and not of (moral) imperatives. Nonetheless, for Kant, the immortal soul and God have practical, and not theoretical, existence. It is not a possible intuition but rather the reality of the moral law which demonstrates their existence. Because man is subject to the moral law, reason compels him to believe in the immortality of the soul and in the existence of God. It would thus be wrong to view the postulates, in a pragmatic sense, as useful fictions. For Kant, immortality and God are real objects belonging, however, not to the empirical but to the moral world.

The Greeks treated ethics in connection with happiness (*eudaimonia*), or satisfaction with life, and assumed that a good and just life is fulfilling and brings true happiness. It is often overlooked that Kant sticks to happiness as a necessary element of ethics. He does not, however, see happiness as the source of morality. The highest good is not happiness but virtue in the sense of morality. Furthermore, morality and happiness do not coincide. A moral person is worthy of happiness but not necessarily happy. Because happiness does not occur in a necessary proportion to worthiness of happiness, virtue signifies only the highest, and not the perfect or supreme good.

The supreme good consists in the agreement of happiness with morality (worthiness of happiness). The virtuous man is rewarded in accordance with his virtue. Contrary to possible expectations, Kant does not foresee punishment for the unvirtuous. The supreme good does not consist in punitive justice. It is not an object of fear but only of hope. One of course has no redeemable claim to the supreme good. Proportional happiness cannot be requisitioned. Otherwise, contradicting its essential exclusion of happiness as ultimate determining cause, morality might degenerate into a mere means for reaching happiness. Kant sees consummate virtue, the complete suitability of convictions to the moral law, as the uppermost condition for the supreme good. Such suitability is "*holiness*, a perfection of which no rational being in the world of sense is at any time capable. But since it is required as practically necessary, it can be found only in an *endless progress*. . . . This infinite progress is possible, however, only under the presupposition of an *infinitely* enduring *existence* and personality of the same rational being; this is called the immortality of the soul" (*CPrR*, V 122).

It is notable that this line of argumentation changes the traditional view of a future life. For Christianity as well as Plato, the battle between duty and inclination occurs only in this world. The blissful hereafter offers no temptation to do evil. For Kant, however, the moral effort in this world continues infinitely. C. D. Broad[2] considers the argument to be contradictory, since it takes moral perfection as both possible and impossible. One cannot possibly pass through an infinite process. The weakness of the Kantian argument in fact lies less in a log-ical contradiction, since, as S. Körner (1955, 166) has pointed out, one can, in agreement with modern mathematics, view an infinite series as complete, without its having to have a last member. But it is doubtful whether an infinitely prolonged process of moralization can do what it is supposed to do. Man comes no closer to holiness in the sense of a *necessary* correspondence to morality. As a finite rational being, he will always remain subject to temptation. Holiness is only possible for pure intelligences who have no need of a process of moralization.

The second postulate, the existence of God, rests upon four pre-suppositions. According to the idea of the supreme good, the moral human being deserves first happiness. Second, morality does not guar-antee proportional happiness. Third, only faith in a power which dis-tributes an appropriate amount of happiness can relieve this difficulty. Fourth, such a power of distribution can be found only in a being that is (*a*) omniscient, so that it never errs with regard to worthiness, (*b*) omnipotent, so that it can always realize the proportional distribution of happiness, and (*c*) holy, so that it unwaveringly adheres to this distri-bution. Only God has such power: "Morality thus inevitably leads to religion, through which it expands to the idea of a powerful moral leg-islator outside of man. The final aim (of the creation of the world) in the legislator's will is that which can and should also be the final aim of man" (*Rel.*, VI 6). There seem to be no historical predecessors of this "proof of the existence of God" from the problem of the supreme good (cf. Albrecht 1978, § 17). The proof is Kant's original invention.

With his theory of postulates, Kant criticizes extravagant eschat-alogies, which, in expectation of the hereafter, neglect the concrete tasks of this world. Kant distinguishes the supreme good, for which I may justifiably hope, from the practical good, which I should realize through my actions. In addition, happiness is distributed in the here-after only in proportion to actual moral practices.

11.2 RADICAL EVIL

Religion extends beyond the postulates of pure practical reason. It talks not only about the existence of God and the immortal soul but also, in the case of Christianity, about original sin, about Jesus as Christ, and about the church. According to Kant, these notions can be justified purely philosophically, that is, without any appeal to revela-tion. He thereby assumes that we do not restrict ourselves to the principles of morality but also take experience into consideration. The experience to which Kant appeals in his essay on religion is "human nature, which is laden in part with good, in part with bad abilities" (*Rel.*, VI 11).

Kant sticks to the basic idea of the Enlightenment, that there is only one true religion and that it cannot contradict reason, for "a religion which unhesitatingly declares war on reason will not be able to hold out in the long run" (*Rel.*, VI 10). On the other hand, it cannot be excluded that religious doctrines stem "from supernaturally inspired men" (*Conf.*, VII 6). In this case, they first become known by revelation and are only afterward examined by reason. Even if, from an objective standpoint, the true religion has no need of an historical revelation and if one can be religious without believing in revelation or the creed of an extant church, the true religion can, from an historical standpoint, begin with revelation. A purely philosophical theory of religion thus remains "within the bounds of reason alone," as is stated in the title of the essay on religion. But that does not mean that all religion stems *from* reason alone (without revelation)" (*Conf.*, VII 6).

Since philosophy cannot at first contest the validity of Christian revelation, Kant proceeds from a possible unity of philosophical and Biblical theology (*Rel.*, VI 12f.). Guided by the hypothesis of agreement between revelation and reason alone, Kant is able to present a philosophically and theologically impressive interpretation of Biblical stories. The hermeneutic maxim appropriate to this novel interpretation demands that we view the basic propositions of the Bible as moral statements relating to ambivalent human nature. The Christian religion thus ultimately becomes a natural religion supported by revelation—it becomes a religion at which "men *could* and *should have arrived* on their own . . . through the mere use of their reason" (*Rel.*, VI 155).

The heading of the first part of the essay on religion states the famous thesis "Concerning the Indwelling of the Evil Principle in Addition to the Good: or, Concerning the Radical Evil in Human Nature." With this claim, Kant takes up the doctrine of original sin. Evil is not just found in this or that individual but in the entire human species. It precedes all particular actions. Nonetheless, it does not stem from a biological trait but can be attributed to human freedom.

Man is not just evil by nature but, such is the second contention, also radically evil. Kant does not mean that man is thoroughly evil but that he is evil at the root. As a variety of experience shows, obviating the need of a formal proof, man has for Kant not just natural inclinations which are in and of themselves morally indifferent. He has the basic tendency to make his natural inclinations into the ultimate determining cause of his actions. He thus places himself in contradiction to the moral law, despite his awareness of it. Such rebellion against the moral law means more than mere decrepitude and impurity. It is malevolence, namely the tendency to assume evil maxims. On the other hand, we do not have to do here with a sort of evil which makes evil to an incentive in itself. That would be diabolic, according to Kant. Because malevolence is innate, to overcome it one requires not only moral betterment, or the disciplining of natural inclinations, but indeed a revolution in attitude.

Kant's theory of radical evil is not an incidental appendage to his ethics. It is closely connected to his view of man as a finite rational being. The freedom of a being which is not by nature pure (practical) reason implies not only the capacity to do evil but also actually doing it.

The recognition of evil and of guiltless suffering is a religious problem of the first order: Why did God, whose omnipotence *could* prevent all suffering and whose benevolence *should* prevent it, allow suffering—even for innocent and just persons? The story of Job represents one of the most brilliant attempts to answer this question. In philosophy, it is above all Leibniz who, in his theodicy, or vindication of God in the face of existent evil (more generally; in the face of dysfunctionality), examines the origin of evil. Kant offers a quite original solution. It grows out of his philosophy of freedom and his philosophy of religion, with its commitment to the principle of hope. Kant rejects all answers to the question of theodicy which fail to perceive the problem of evil with sufficient clarity. Specifically, he dismisses a biological approach such as that advocated by the Epicureans, the Stoics and their successors right up to the present. He further contradicts naïve optimism, which minimizes the problem and, like all good-natured moralists from Seneca and Rousseau (cf. *Rel.*, VI 20) to Marxism, believes in the natural good of man, who only becomes bad or evil due to social circumstances. Kant's theory of radical evil contains a clear dismissal of such a utopian view. But he also rejects heroic pessimism, which asserts the addiction of man to evil. All three conceptions contradict Kant's thesis that evil originates in freedom and in the possibility given by freedom of overcoming evil.

Because of the presence in man of both good and evil, there ensues, as the title of the second part of the essay on religion states, a "Battle of the Good with the Evil Principle for the Power over Man." Here, Kant develops his "philosophical Christology." For the victory of good over evil, the personified idea of the good is a perfect example. Christ, who is the "son of God," is "*mankind* (the rational terrestrial being in general) *in his complete moral perfection*" (*Rel.*, VI 60) and provides all human beings with the example of pure morality. The evil principle is not completely eliminated, but its power is broken.

The third part, "Concerning the Victory of the Good over the Evil Principle and the Establishment of a Kingdom of God on Earth," calls upon man to depart from the ethical state of nature. Just as in the legal state of nature a war of all against all reigns, the ethical state of nature means a "state of ceaseless feud of evil against the good principle which lies in every human being" (*Rel.*, VI 97). The ethical state of nature is abolished by a community in which the laws of virtue are, in contrast to the force of law, accepted free of all compulsion. Since ethical laws are supposed to promote personal morality, an internal matter, the political legislator cannot have the task or the authority to abolish the ethical state of nature. For the same reason, the ethical legislator differs from that in the legal community. It is not the general will of the people. On the other hand, ethical laws cannot be the mere commands of some authority, because they would then not be non-compulsory laws of virtue but enforcible laws of society. Thus, according to Kant, the ethical legislator is someone for whom "all *true duties* . . . must *at the same time* be conceived as his commandments." God, understood as a moral "ruler of the world," is such a legislator. Therefore, an ethical community "can be conceived only as a nation subject to divine commandments, i.e. a *nation of God on the basis of laws of virtue*" (*Rel.*, VI 99).

Because pure virtue is something internal, and thus not an object of possible experience, the community determined solely by laws of virtue cannot occur in experience. The kingdom of God is an invisible church, consisting of the community of all "men of good will." They have, according to Kant, the same characteristics as those acknowledged by the Christian creed. This invisible church, as the nation of God, is universal since it is numerically one. It is holy because, as a community based on laws of virtue, it is determined by complete moral purity. It is apostolic, since moral legislation, its constitution, is immutable.

As an invisible church, the kingdom of God cannot possibly be realized in an historical state, "a messianic kingdom on earth" (XXIII 112). Contrary to theocracy (Greek for the rule of God: governmental power based purely on religion) and various attempts at its secularization, the kingdom of God is not a political empire which could be realized by the progress of political justice. That does not mean that the kingdom of God can be nothing more than a myth or a sign. For Kant, it is an ethical kingdom and represents the final moral goal, just as eternal peace in a worldwide legal community signifies the ultimate legal goal.

Although the community based upon laws of virtue means an invisible church, Kant does not reject all visible organization. He ascribes an educational task to the visible church. Its justification consists in the perceivable representation of the moral idea of the kingdom of God. But Kant warns against taking the perceivable representation for the thing itself. Pure moral legislation forms the primary cause of all true religion. Through it, "the will of God is originally written into our hearts" (*Rel.*, VI 104). Consequently, it is for Kant not the magnificence of a visible church but the transformation of church belief into pure rational belief, or belief in a moral religion, that heralds the approach of the kingdom of God. "Pure *moral* legislation" is "not just the unavoidable condition of absolutely all true religion, but it is also that which in fact itself constitutes the latter" (ibid.).

In the fourth part, "Concerning Services and Rites under the Rule of the Good Principle, or Concerning Religion and Priestcraft," Kant, like Rousseau before him (*Social Contract*, IV 8), distinguishes the moral religion of goodness from all religions which woo favor (cults of statutes and observances). Any opportunistic intention which, deviating from moral conviction, speculates upon the grace of God, contradicts the principle of autonomy and must thus be rejected morally.

PART V

The Philosophical Aesthetics and the Philosophy of the Organic

❧❧❧❧❧❧❧❧❧❧❧

12.

The Critique of Judgment

ᘒᘒᘒᘒᘒᘒᘒᘒᘒ

12.1 THE DUAL TASK: SUBSTANTIVE ANALYSIS AND SYSTEMATIC FUNCTION

Ever since Aristotle, teleology, the orientation toward purposes (Greek: *tele*), has strongly influenced Western thought. In the modern age, however, it has been displaced by causal ("mechanistic") views. Bacon ridicules teleology as the "holy virgin whose womb is barren." In Kant's time, thought in terms of cause and effect had already won important victories—in the philosophy of Hobbes and of the French Enlightenment, in the physics of Galileo and Newton, and in biology. The doctor and philosopher J. O. de La Mettrie with his provocative work *L'homme machine*[1] (1748) ranks as one of the most radical proponents of a mechanistic view. Nonetheless, Kant ascribes an important function to teleology. It is thus wrong to think that Kant belongs to the modern anti-Aristotelian tradition, which disallows all attribution of purpose in philosophy and science.

The teleological elements are not pre-Critical residues, which show that Kant cannot, despite his intellectual revolution, completely free himself from traditional philosophy. On the contrary, the attribution of purpose forms an integral part of the transcendental critique of reason. For one thing, Kant emphasizes the subjective nature of teleological judgments. For another, such judgments are found in all of his major works. In the *Critique of Pure Reason*, the theory of regulative ideas relies upon reason's aim of complete knowledge. The teleological idea of the unity of happiness and worthiness thereof underlies the theory of postulates in the *Critique of Practical Reason*. In the philosophy of law and of history, Kant sees eternal peace as the ultimate goal ("meaning") of history. Yet Kant's thought reaches its teleological culmination only in the *Critique of Judgment*.

The third *Critique* is connected in many ways with the whole of the critique of reason. For Kant, philosophy is divided into two main parts: theoretical and practical philosophy (including the philosophy of law, history and religion). While theoretical philosophy investigates the laws given by the natural concepts of the pure understanding, practical philosophy treats the laws given by pure reason's concept of freedom. Only in the sphere of law and morals does reason make the laws itself. But the two spheres—nature and freedom, or the sensible (phenomenal) and the moral (intelligible) world—are interrelated. Freedom must present itself in the sensible world. To close the gap between the natural and the moral world, one must explain their connection with one another. Kant thinks that he has found this connection in (reflecting) judgment (for the mediating task of history and religion, 10–11). Kant views judgment as the intermediary between understanding and reason. In the third *Critique*, he investigates its *a priori* conditions.

The *Critique of Judgment* is a difficult work, which has, in part for this reason, long been neglected. It also receives less attention than other works because the significance of its subject-matter has decreased. The investigation of aesthetics has become rare in philosophy, and in the natural sciences, teleological modes of thought have virtually disappeared.

The inner difficulties begin with the complexity of the work. It has both a systematic and a substantive task, and both tasks are interwoven with one another. For one thing, we find the problem of the unity of the disparate, which acquires central importance in German Idealism. The divergent ("alienated") spheres of nature and freedom, of sensibility and spontaneity, of knowledge and action, are to be reconciled. As outlined in the two introductions and realized in the subsequent argument, the work is intended to close the system. Second the systematic function is due to a subjective faculty which, like reason and the understanding, makes laws *a priori*. The transcendental investigation of the products of judgment free from experience represents the critical foundation of a new field. The systematic problems can impede access to this field.

The faculty which is supposed to establish the connection between theoretical and practical philosophy takes on—this is a further difficulty—two quite different forms: aesthetic judgment and teleological judgment in the restrictive sense. The third *Critique* fulfills not only the systematic function of completing the critique of reason by unifying nature and morals. It also establishes the transcendental basis for two such disparate spheres as, on the one hand, the world of the beautiful and the sublime, of art and genius, and, on the other hand, the world of the organic and the systematic unity of nature as a whole.

Kant defines the concept of judgment as "the capacity to conceive the particular as contained under the universal" (*CJ*, V 179). Judgment has two forms. As "determining judgment," it subsumes the particular under a given universal—a rule, principle, or law. As reflecting judgment, it is supposed to find the universal for a given particular. Kant then investigates how pure reflecting judgment can bring something given in sensibility under a determination which is valid universally and independent of experience. With judgment, Kant makes the connection of two fundamentally distinct elements (sensibility and spontaneity) the object of a transcendental critique. For this reason, the critique of aesthetic and teleological judgment points toward further perspectives. It reveals not only the conditions of beauty and of organic nature but also the possibility of a connection between nature and morals. The substantive analysis and the systematic function do not represent two disparate interests but prove to be interrelated.

The concept which denotes the specific role of reflecting judgment and its mediation between nature and freedom is functionality. Wherever something is described as functional, one refers to certain phenomena in their entirety and attributes a purpose to the whole. While the phenomena can be empirically determined (they form the given particular), the assumption of a functional whole does not stem from experience. The functional whole is the ungiven universal which is spontaneously discovered by judgment. Thus, in judgments of functionality, nature, which is given sensibly, and spontaneous creation, or freedom, constitute an original unity.

The original unity can take on various forms. In accordance with the two pairs of concepts of reflection "formal-material" and "subjective-objective," Kant distinguishes a total of four forms. Two of them are not further examined:

Kant designates as objective, yet merely formal functionality the fact that mathematicians find in geometrical figures a connected whole without ascribing a purpose to them. This functionality resides not in the geometrical figures themselves but rather in mathematical thought. It exists only in the intellect. Kant discusses it only as a contrast to objective and material functionality (*CJ*, § 62). Kant can skip over the material and subjective functionality of human actions because they raise no problems beyond those treated in ethics.

(1) The formal (not related to existing things) and subjective functionality of aesthetic judgments, and (2) the objective (independent of the emotions and wishes of the subject) and material (relating to actually existing things) functionality of organisms and of life, as their mode of existence, remain. Kant examines them in the first and in the second part of the *Critique of Judgment*.

In addition, he treats the principle of the formal functionality of nature in the "First Introduction" (*CJ*, V 181ff.) as a transcendental principle of judgment. In so doing, Kant places the idea of the universal functionality of nature in the context of the critique of reason. Aristotle, Thomas Aquinas and their tradition, which continues far into the modern age, are thus right in viewing all of nature and not just organic life as functional. But they are wrong insofar as they think that nature itself is functional. First, formal functionality, which Kant considers to be universally valid, means no more than the regularity which every scientist expects to find in nature. The scientist looks in the vast manifold of natural events for similarities in the form of empirical laws and comprehensive theories. Second functionality, in the reduced sense of regularity, has no objective but only a subjective, albeit transcendental cause. The universal functionality of nature is nothing but the *a priori* expectation of judgment that it will find nature structured rather than chaotic. Such an expectation is not due to experience but forms the *a priori* subjective prerequisite of all experience of nature. It is independent of whether experience is guided by the principle of causality alone or by objective representations of functionality as well.

We are justified in the expectation of finding regularities and systematic connections in nature—thus runs Kant's extremely terse sketch of a transcendental deduction—because we can seek objective knowledge only under this presupposition. The formal functionality of nature is an expectation recognized by all study of nature right from the start, and hence *a priori*. This expectation originates in pure reflecting judgment and manifests itself in the methodological principles which guide scientists. For example: "Nature takes the shortest path"; "its large manifold in empirical laws is nonetheless unity under few principles" (*CJ*, V 182).

12.2 THE CRITICAL JUSTIFICATION OF AESTHETICS

The Beautiful

In the first part, the "Critique of Aesthetic Judgment," Kant examines the validity of aesthetic judgments. Such judgments claim of their objects that they are beautiful or sublime. One who does not slavishly follow the fashion of the time but is able to make his own judgments about beauty has good taste. Aesthetic judgments of beauty are thus also called judgments of taste. (On the Transcendental Aesthetic as the science of the principles of sensibility, 4.)

One cannot argue about taste, as the saying goes. It means that taste is purely subjective (cf. *CJ*, § 56). In the second edition of the *Critique of Pure Reason*, Kant still, in opposition to Baumgarten, accepts this opinion (B 35f., note). He is thus surprised when he later discovers an *a priori* condition—not just a universal characteristic but independence from experience as the strictest form of universality—even for judgments of taste. Kant does not thus claim that judgments of taste are synthetic and *a priori*. They only become possible through an *a priori* moment, but they are, as concrete judgments about a landscape or a work of art, empirical in nature.

A philosopher who "on all appearances had little receptiveness to beauty and who in addition probably never had an opportunity to see a significant work of art" (Schopenhauer, *The World as Will and Representation*, Appendix) makes, after having arrived at astonishing insights in theoretical and practical philosophy, the epoch-making discovery of the aesthetic *a priori*. This discovery justifies the independence of aesthetics in relationship to scientific knowledge and moral activity. Aesthetics has its own laws. Aesthetics and art have on the main retained their autonomy up to the present day, although the distance between Kant and the present is obvious.

The "Critique of Aesthetic Judgment," a critique of taste and art with transcendental intent, arises from the discovery of the aesthetic *a priori*. It represents a second-order critique and examines not aesthetic judgments but rather the justification of critical judgment in the domain of aesthetics. The *a priori* asserted by Kant here is of a different kind from that of the first and the second *Critique*. The aesthetic attitude toward an object, to beauty in nature, to beauty in art and to the sublime differs from the theoretical and the practical attitude. The aesthetic relationship to the world has its own form of rationality. It cannot be derived from objective knowledge or morality or both.

In his critical analysis of aesthetics, too, Kant combines a cautious and subtle treatment of the phenomena with remarkable logical consistency. With the *a priori* element, Kant justifies the possibility of making a binding claim even in the aesthetic sphere (cf. *CJ*, § 38). Because the aesthetic *a priori* does not coincide with the principles of knowledge and action, aesthetic questions cannot be adequately decided by argumentation and demonstration nor by moral zeal. Nonetheless, it is not individual preference and subjective whim which decide. Aesthetic judgments, as Kant maintains, contain a special sort of tension. They are not provable but claim to be understandable and binding for everyone. In contrast to scientific and moral statements, Kant does not ascribe objective, but only subjective universality to aesthetic judgments. The subjective experience of the self in aesthetic contexts contains, according to Kant, a universal feeling for the world and for life in general. The problem of aesthetics boils down to the question of how subjectivity can be combined with the claim of universality and necessity.

Because of Kant's specification of the aesthetic as subjective universality, Hans-Georg Gadamer, inspired by Hegel, accuses him of "subjectivizing aesthetics." Kant's "autonomous foundation of aesthetics, which is liberated from the standard of the concept," no longer asks "the question of truth in the sphere of art.[2] But Gadamer pushes the subjective aspect of Kant's "subjective universality" in the direction of "private opinion" and underestimates the universal aspect. Particularly if one follows Gadamer in making claims of truth for art, for the cultural tradition and for the humanities, such claims must be clearly distinguished from those of the mathematical sciences. Otherwise, art and the humanities appear merely as knowledge of an inferior sort. In order that they not be denigrated as a little, possibly illegitimate sister of the natural sciences, one must acknowledge their special character and speak of truth in a sense analogous to that of theoretical knowledge. Kant's notion of subjective universality could provide the basis for this project. This notion draws our attention both to what is common (uni-

versality) and to what is distinctive (a subjectivity differing from mathematical and scientific objectivity). Kant's critique of aesthetic judgment thus avoids precisely the danger that Gadamer[3] wishes to ban:
that "the self-determination of the humanities" is forced "to draw on
the methodology of the natural sciences."

There was a controversial discussion among the philosophers of
the Enlightenment concerning the essence of aesthetic judgments. The
attempt to reduce aesthetic judgments to other, more familiar phenomena is common to the three main positions. Instead of degrading aesthetic experience to an undeveloped form, a deterioration, or an
appendage of theoretical or practical knowledge, Kant sticks to the
independence of the laws of beauty. The aesthetic is an independent
way of approaching reality. Kant rejects the rationalistic aesthetic of A.
G. Baumgarten, who views judgments of taste as a (low) form of knowing. He criticizes the sensualist aesthetics (which presents a wealth of
observational material) of E. Burke, who traces judgments of taste to a
mere feeling. Finally, he dismisses empiricist aesthetics, according to
which aesthetic judgments arise from mere habit and agreement. This
view neglects the nature of taste as something which can assert its own
specific freedom and superiority over convention and fashion. According to Kant, objects are evaluated in aesthetic judgments on the basis of
a rule. Aesthetic evaluation thus adheres to something universal but is
not determined by scientific concepts or moral principles.

Because aesthetic judgment is subjective yet reflecting, the universal is not predetermined for it. In contrast to any aesthetic which
views the work of art as the bearer of a sensibly perceived objective
truth, aesthetic enjoyment results according to Kant not from a thing's
perfection, or objective functionality. It is not the object itself in its
appearance or its form which is beautiful. "Beautiful" is not an objective
but rather a relative predicate. And the aesthetic relation proceeds from
the subject. The relation is due to the creative act of aesthetically representing the object in the subject.

With the idea of subjective universality, Kant departs from any
sort of regulatory aesthetic, which prescribes fixed rules for a beautiful
picture, drama, or piece of music. Such rules, glorified as "classical,"
place unnecessary constraints on aesthetic creativity. In Kant, an aesthetics of genius takes the place of regulatory aesthetics: "*Beautiful art is
the art of a genius*" (*CJ*, § 46). The rules, which are not given up to art in
advance, are due to the genius, whom nature has favored and who

stands out due to his exemplary originality. Kant thus not only investigates the relationship of the observer, who judges beautiful objects with
the aid of good taste, to art. He also examines the artist; so, Nietzsche's
accusation that Kant "thought about art and beauty solely from the
standpoint of the 'observer'" (*On the Genealogy of Morals*, 3rd treatise,
sect. 6) does not hold.

The Romantic view of art picks up on Kant's aesthetic of the
genius no less than on the autonomy of aesthetics. But his restriction of
the notion of genius to the artist (§ 47) does not prevail. On the contrary, in the course of the nineteenth century, the notion of the genius is
amplified to a universal value and experiences, together with creativity,
whose force flows from the unconscious, a veritable deification. The
genius becomes the "hero" of the age.

Guided by the familiar "titles" quality, quantity, relation and
modality from the *Critique of Pure Reason*, Kant carries out the "Analytic of Beauty." He thus gains a fourfold specification of beauty. With
respect to *quality*, it is disinterested, and thus free, enjoyment (for ugli-
ness: displeasure). We consider objects to be beautiful if they are pleasing in and of themselves—regardless of objective concepts or sensations
of pleasure or goodness (*CJ*, §§ 2–5). It does not follow, though, as
Nietzsche assumes ibid.), that "a lot of strong personal experiences,
desires, surprises, raptures" can play no role in the consideration of
works of art. But the *pure* judgment of taste, the question of whether a
work is beautiful, cannot involve any admixture of interest in the existence of the object. In order to be binding, an aesthetic judgment must
be completely unpartisan. But to one who judges on the criteria of
ownership and use, the object is not important for its own sake but for
the sake of certain desires. His judgment is bound up with interests and
no longer purely aesthetic.

Because beauty pleases disinterestedly, Kant applies aesthetic
judgments not only to artistic representations but also to the beauty of
nature and even to the purely decorative. It is not artistic beauty but
natural beauty which proves to be superior, for only natural beauty
allows man to unintentionally find himself in reality. In German Idealism, the interest in the beauty of nature recedes behind man's encounter
with himself in works of art. Hegel, for example, sees the essence of all
art in bringing before man that which he is (*Lectures on Aesthetics*,[4] 57).

In art, man encounters himself, and the human mind encounters the human mind.

Although our evaluation of something as beautiful or ugly does not make use of objective concepts, it can still be universally valid with respect to *quantity*. A judgment of taste always appeals to the subjective sensation of enjoyment but expects others to follow the judgment (*CJ*, § 8). This expectation is possible because, independent of all individual interests, a free play of the two cognitive faculties imagination (fantasy) and understanding underlies aesthetic judgments. As soon as the cognitive powers reach a state of harmony, a special sort of pleasure is produced. It consists neither in the satisfaction of a sensual desire (since all interests are excluded) nor in the purely rational respect for the moral law (since every aesthetic judgment refers to something given in the sensible world). The enjoyment arising from beautiful objects lies conceptually between a sensible and a rational pleasure. Its intermediary position shows that the aesthetic has a mediating function for nature and freedom, for sensibility and pure (practical) reason.

Because in aesthetic experience imagination does not act alone but in concert with the understanding, such experience does not consist in mere private fantasies but in controlled and communicable thoughts. In contrast to extreme subjectivism and skepticism, aesthetic experience has a communicative dimension as well. Because, on the other hand, works of art activate not only the understanding but also imagination, they are necessarily inexhaustible. As every serious attempt at interpretation shows, no work of literature, music, or the visual arts can be completely grasped through a particular concept or made completely comprehensible by any language (*CJ*, § 49).

With respect to *relation*, aesthetic judgments are concerned with the form of functionality. Something is beautiful, if every particular fits "functionally" into the whole without the whole having any further purpose. Purposeless functionality is beautiful.

Finally, with respect to *modality*, judgments of taste can only be made under the assumption that there is a common taste (CJ, § 20). Common taste makes universal judging possible. It manifests itself in the feeling for quality: *"Beautiful* is what is recognized without a concept as the object of *necessary* enjoyment" (*CJ*, § 22). Following Rousseau, Kant does not conclude from the refinement of taste that moral sentiment has risen, too. Civilization does not mean moralization. The development of common taste has only an aesthetic significance and not a moral one.

The Sublime

A second aesthetic phenomenon examined by Kant has roots in antiquity. In Enlightenment philosophy, it acquires special significance, which it sustains with Herder, Schiller and Schelling, but begins to lose with Hegel's historicizing. This phenomenon is the sublime. It has perhaps not completely disappeared from our present life. But due to the post-Idealist critique of metaphysics and religion as well as the changed social and cultural situation, it plays no notable role in philosophy or in literary criticism.

In Greek, the sublime (*hypsos*) means an emotional raising of the soul. It is a self-elevation of man prompted by an enthusiastic poetic presentation and culminating in the catharsis (purification) of fear and sympathy. In Enlightenment philosophy, the sublime represents only a higher level of beauty and means greatness or dignity. Later, it is explicitly contrasted with beauty. According to Kant, it is true for beauty and the sublime "that both are pleasing for their own sake" (*CJ*, § 23). But Kant also points out "significant differences": "The beauty of nature relates to the form of an object, which consists in its limitation. The sublime, however, can also be found in a formless object, insofar as *unlimitedness* is represented in or due to the object." The enjoyment of the sublime is "not play but instead a serious occupation of the imagination." It does not stimulate positive pleasure "but rather wonder or respect," which Kant calls negative pleasure (ibid.).

It is not certain objects or events of nature which are sublime. These only prompt the sublime "mood." In its astonishing grandeur or awe-inspiring power, nature provokes a certain experience of the self. It awakens the feeling of having pure independent reason as a supersensible faculty.

Kant distinguishes two forms of the sublime. The mathematically sublime makes nature appear grand beyond all measure (*CJ*, V 248). In light of the sensible world, nature is then experienced as a "supersensible substratum" (V 255) the universal, the divine and the whole. In the case of the dynamically sublime, nature appears as a fearsome power, which still has no power over us (V 260): "Hurricanes with the destruction they leave behind, the boundless ocean in a state of uproar . . . make our ability to resist an insignificant trifle in comparison to their power. But their countenance becomes all the more attractive the more terrible it is, if we are in safety. And we like to call these objects sublime because they raise the strength of the soul above its usual mediocrity and allow us to discover in ourselves a quite different sort of capacity to resist, which encourages us to be able to compete with the apparent omnipotence of nature" (*CJ*, V 261). Here, man experiences himself as superior to outward nature. He feels like a moral being who can compare itself with omnipotent nature and is indeed superior to it.

12.3 THE CRITICAL TELEOLOGY

Between Universal Teleology and Universal Mechanism

Functionality is for Kant not only a transcendental principle of all knowledge of nature and the basis for all aesthetic judgments. As objective functionality, it also plays a specific role in the knowledge of natural objects. But it does not play this role for all natural objects. Kant thus rejects both the universal teleology of Aristotelianism, according to which the whole of nature is functionally organized, and universal mechanism, according to which living things can be completely grasped through causal statements. According to Kant, we need teleological propositions. They have their place in the domain which provided Aristotle with the paradigm for teleological thought: the organic realm. Objective functionality is—in its regulative, not its constitutive meaning—a principle of research in which biology excels physics. Whereas teleological assumptions have no place in physics, a mechanistic conception does not suffice for the investigation of living things. Through such a conception, we come to know only how but not with what purpose organic processes occur. Kant's philosophy of the organic prepares the way for Romanticism no less than his aesthetics.

It is the task of critical philosophy to investigate the concept of functionality specific to biology, the manner of its legitimate application, and its relationship to causal thinking. Kant takes on this task in the second main part of the *Critique of Judgment*, with which he extensively expands his theory of the knowledge of nature. It is thus wrong to look for Kant's theory of experience only in the *Critique of Pure Reason* and the *Metaphysical Origins of Science*.

In the first division, the "Analytic of Teleological Judgment," Kant develops the concept of functionality specific to the organic. In the second division, the "Dialectic," he investigates the reciprocity between teleological and causal propositions in the domain of living things and thus makes a contribution to the logic of biological research. According to the third part, the "Methodology," the final purpose of nature as a teleological system is characterized as the "*Final Aim of the Existence of a World, i.e. of the Creation*" (§ 84). As a result of a "causality from ideas," which set the goals for the "art of nature," a world is constructed, in which nature, as reason's means, steers toward an ultimate moral state. The "Critique of Teleological Judgment" thus contains more than a critical philosophy of the organic. It, too, deals with the systematic task of judgment outlined in the two introductions and mediates between nature and freedom, between theoretical and practical philosophy. With the idea of the world as a creation, freedom and happiness converge within the framework of a moral culture.

In biology, teleology has long been a loaded concept, which is usually rejected or at most accepted with grave qualifications. One fears that teleological considerations might import transcendent explanations, which are from a scientific standpoint nothing more than pseudo-explanations, into the system of scientific knowledge. Above all, genetics, together with system theory and cybernetics, have proved that organic processes can be explained physically and chemically. Consequently, the recourse to teleological factors in biology seems superfluous. On the other hand, many biologists and physicians concede that organisms represent a causal network of numerous interconnected regulatory processes, whose parts can be causally explained with the aid of physical and chemical laws but can, in their entirety, still be characterized as functional. The parts and processes promote, for example, the survival and the reproduction of the system as well as its suitability for changed environmental conditions. The biologist C. S. Pittendrigh has thus coined the term "teleonomy." With this alternative expression, biological states of affairs are to be described as functional or as serving a purpose, without making transcendent hypotheses about the origin of such functionality. The use of teleological or teleonomic concepts in the study of organisms does still remain a difficult epistemological question. Kant certainly did not answer it adequately. But his critical approach promises greater success than any naïve, realistic notion of teleology.

According to Kant, the problem of teleology breaks down into at least three components: (1) the concept of functionality specific to the organic, (2) the difference in the theoretical status of causal and teleo-logical propositions and (3) their relationship to one another.

The Functionality of Organisms

The evaluation of organic processes as functional is objective, and not subjective (*CJ*, § 61), real, and not just intellectual (§ 62), and finally internal to the object, and not external (§ 63).

Functionality is objective because it belongs to the organism itself. Teleological judgments say something about the object and not, like aesthetic judgments, about its relation to the subject. Functionality is real or material because it actually attributes a natural purpose, such as survival, to organic processes. It represents more than the formal or intellectual functionality which the mathematician discovers in con-nection with geometrical figures without ascribing a purpose to them. Finally, biological functionality is an inner state of an object and is not based on its utility for something else. It is a "property" of the thing itself and differs from the outer, relative functionality through which something is useful to man or beneficial to animals and plants. (According to the chapter on teleology in Hegel's *Science of Logic*, this is one of Kant's great insights.) As statements about an objective, real, and inner functionality, teleological judgments in biology do not repre-sent transcendent explanations. They do not, like the so-called vitalists from Louis Dumas (1765–1813) to H. Driesch (1867–1941), intro-duce an immaterial factor in the form of a vital force which is not ana-lyzable physically and chemically but has an effect upon matter. With his concept of biological functionality, Kant, no less than present biol-ogy, rejects such pseudo-explanations (he speaks of "hyperphysics," *CJ*, V 423).

Under what conditions are teleological judgments about objec-tive, real and internal functionality justified? They are legitimate if cer-tain natural processes cannot be adequately understood through mere causal explanations because they are "*cause and effect . . . of themselves*" (*CJ*, V 370). A linear conception of causality is too limited to explain such processes, which according to Kant occur in the organic sphere. Organisms are organized wholes, whose organization is not the effect of an external cause. They instead organize themselves.

Kant cites the tree as an example for the reciprocity of cause and effect, which manifests itself in self-organization. By reproduction, the tree gives rise to another tree of the same species, so that the tree as a species is at the same time cause and effect. Reciprocity can also be seen in growth, in which the tree forms the substances which it takes in "into a specifically peculiar quality." It thus gives rise to and sustains itself as an individual. Finally, the reciprocity of cause and effect manifests itself in self-help in cases of wounds and mutilation (*CJ*, § 64). Critics of teleology will no doubt attempt to explain Kant's examples purely causally and to present inorganic examples of the purportedly specific functions of reproduction, growth and self-help. They can also object that Kant does not sufficiently explain the concept of a self involved in the notion of self-organization. It is a self which does not involve consciousness.

With the notions of self-organization and of the reciprocity of cause and effect, Kant wants to draw a sharp distinction between an organism and a clock, the classic example of purely mechanical processes. The clock is an organized whole, since one part exists for the sake of another. But the part is not there *through* the other. One cog of the clock cannot create another, nor can one clock give rise to another or repair itself (*CJ*, V 374).

Due to the amazing advances in engineering since Kant's time, the absolute superiority of an organism over a machine has been seriously called into question. But insofar as one acknowledges reproduction, growth and self-repair as characteristics of self-organization, they seem still to be specific to organisms, even though there are now machines which produce or repair others. The productive machine does not propagate but "produces" machines of a different sort. And in cases where the productive machine by means of regulative mechanisms is in part able to guide itself, or even to repair itself, errors in the programming or the guidance system are repaired "from outside." For this reason, organic beings are not, as is often assumed, analogous to the products of human artifice (engineering). They require an engineer, a rational being outside of the product, whereas the organization of organisms comes "from within," from the objects themselves.

The Regulative Function of Teleology

According to the *Critique of Pure Reason*, the objects of nature are constituted through measurability, substantiality and causality. Does the Critique of Teleological Judgment contradict this conception of science? Does it restrict the conception of the first *Critique* to physics and develop for biology a new, teleological science? Kant does see the problem. In the Dialectic of Teleological Judgment, he specifies it as the antinomy that either all "production of material things is possible according to mechanical laws only" or that some "production of them is not possible according to mechanical laws only" (*CJ*, V 387). But the antinomy is on Kant's view resolved as soon as one discovers, on the basis of the transcendental critique of reason, that the basic concepts of mechanistic and teleological explanations have a different origin. Causality is a pure concept of the understanding, a category, and thus constitutive for every natural object. Inner functionality, however, stems not from the understanding but from teleological judgment. Since the natural object is already completely formed by the interaction of intuition and understanding, inner functionality can have only regulative, not constitutive, significance even for biology (*CJ*, §§ 67, 75, 77 and passim). Scientific explanations are purely mechanistic, that is, physical or chemical, in nature. The objective inner functionality of living things cannot be empirically observed. It is a conceptual addition made with the help of reflecting judgment (cf. *CJ*, V 399). The conceptual addition does not, however, arise from a subjective inspiration. It is, according to Kant, universal and necessary, for only through this addition is the organism understood as an organism, that is, as a product of nature in which "*everything is an end and also reciprocally a means*," so that nothing is "for nought, purposeless, or ascribable to a blind mechanism of nature" (*CJ*, § 66).

The idea of objective functionality provides an orientation for practical science. It is a heuristic principle for the causal research of biologists, who, in their study of the structure and behavior of plants and animals, attribute as much as possible to inner functionality and consider as little as possible to be for nought and without purpose (ibid.).

Since Kant considers teleological propositions only to be regulative and not constitutive, the "rehabilitation of teleology"[5] tends to think that Kant in his critical justification grossly underestimates the significance of teleological modes of thought for biology. If its object, the organism or life as such, can only be understood teleologically, then teleology is no longer just a regulative principle. The heuristic idea of functionality can doubtless inspire causal research. But with the completion of causal research, the living organism is resolved into physical and chemical processes. As a result, it gives up its "essence" as a self-organized whole.

Such criticism of Kant makes a mistake similar to that of vitalism. It views the functionality of living things as empirically observable, although in functional propositions, observable natural events are judged from the standpoint of an end, which is an unobservable universal. In addition, this criticism is only logical under the assumption that causal research can someday resolve life completely into physical and chemical processes. According to Kant, though, causal research can never achieve such resolution, for it refers to all natural processes as a temporal sequence of events, that is, as the effect of a cause. But as self-organized wholes, organisms are not characterized by the succession but instead by the simultaneity of cause and effect. Kant thus views it as "inappropriate" to hope that "someday a Newton could arise, who would make even the production of a blade of grass comprehensible according to natural laws, not ordered with any intent" (*CJ*, V 400).

Kant does not attempt to break the causal continuity of nature. On the contrary, his critical teleology is intended as a supplementary orientation for it. The necessary, yet only regulative character of teleological thought allows us to look for a merely causal explanation of all natural processes and also to demand higher principles of judgment, based on the idea of an objective, real, and inner functionality, for the organic realm (cf. *CJ*, § 80). In biology, causal and teleological thought are not mutually exclusive but rather complementary. This basic idea of the Methodology of Teleological Judgment seems to have a certain degree of validity for biological method right up to the present. It makes it understandable why modern biology, despite unanticipated advances in the causal explanation of organic processes, does not wish to do without such teleological concepts as survival or teleonomy. A biological state of affairs is only considered to be completely understood scientifically if, in addition to the analysis of physical and chemical causes, two further questions have been answered: the questions of evolutionary origin and of biological significance. The biological significance of a state of affairs is understood as its function within the framework of life processes: the development of the organism and the survival of the species. The question of biological significance is thus teleological.

The second part of the *Critique of Judgment* goes beyond a critical contribution to the logic of biological research. Since Kant considers teleological thought to be "vindicated" as the "guide" to the study of nature, he wishes to "at least try the supposed maxim of judgment on the whole of nature" (*CJ*, V 398). He thereby discovers the "only proof valid both for common sense and for the philosopher that" the whole world "depends on and originates from a being existing outside the world and . . . having understanding" (*CJ*, V 398f.). Teleological thought thus finds none but a theological completion (*CJ*, V 399).

The connection between teleological and theological thought is familiar to us from philosophers such as Aristotle and Thomas Aquinas. It seems strange, however, to find such a connection in critical philosophy, too, whose great achievement lies precisely in the destruction of all proofs of the existence of God. Does Kant in the end give up his critical thought and return to the womb of metaphysical theology?

Such a supposition overlooks the methodological place of critical teleology. The concept of objective and inner functionality is neither an empirical generalization nor a pure concept of the understanding. It stems from reflecting judgment, which has only a regulative significance for the study of nature. Thus, "even the most complete teleology" cannot prove the existence of a reasonable being to which the world as a whole is due (*CJ*, V 399). Kant by no means rehabilitates traditional metaphysical teleology. He clearly denies the status of objective knowledge to the theological completion of teleology.

PART VI
Kant's Influence

13.

Reception, Further Development, and Criticism of Kant's Ideas

࿇࿇࿇࿇࿇࿇࿇

13.1 INITIAL CIRCULATION AND CRITICISM

If we consider epistemology and metaphysics, the theory of mathematics and natural science, ethics, the philosophy of religion or the philosophy of art, we observe a singular phenomenon in all cases: Kant places central problems of modern thought, which have previously been treated by schools in part ignorant of, in part at war with one another, onto a higher level of clarity and reflection. He seeks to solve such problems on the basis of common principles. Kant's critical, transcendental treatment has transformed the philosophical discussion in various fields and influenced intellectual developments right up to the present. His "successors" are by no means in agreement as to his exact achievements and limitations nor as to the direction in which his philosophy should be further developed or changed. Starting with German Idealism, a strict Kantian will read most of the history of Kant's influence as a history of creative misunderstandings in the sense of a modified passage from *Faust*: "It is the gentlemen's own spirit in which Kant's works are reflected."

Although the dissertation from 1770 already contains several main ideas of critical transcendental philosophy, its influence begins only with the appearance of the first *Critique*. Only M. Herz in his *Observations from Speculative Worldly Wisdom*[1] recognizes as early as 1771 the significance of the dissertation. But after 1781, Kant experiences rapid recognition. First in Germany, and soon in neighboring countries as well, the number of advocates of the new mode of thought grows. Some enthusiastically promote the critique of reason without even sufficiently understanding it . The *Jenaer Allgemeine Literaturzeituna*, a journal founded in 1785, becomes a forum for Kantianism under the editorship of C. G. Schütz and G. Hufeland. Kant himself writes a review here of Herder's *Ideas for a Philosophy of the History of Mankind*[2] (1785) . Important explanatory pieces appear within only a few years after the first edition of the *Critique*. Although they seek to mollify the difficulties, they also show how quickly Kant has gained a prominent position in the philosophical discussion: K. C. E. Schmid' s *Critique of Pure Reason in Outline for Lectures along with a Dictionary for Easier Use of Kantian Philosophy*[3] (1786) intends to make Kant's philosophy better known. With his *Explanatory Notes on Prof. Kant's Critique of Pure Reason*[4] (1784), Johann Schultz promotes the propagation and better understanding of Kant. Particularly important are the "Letters on Kantian Philosophy" (1786–87), which Karl Leonhard Reinhold publishes in the *Deutscher Merkur* and which Kant himself praises highly in a letter to the author (*Letters*, 292/177). Later, J. S. Beck's *Explanatory Excerpt from the Critical Writings of Prof. Kant, on Kant's Advice*[5] (1793-96) and a six-volume *Encyclopedic Dictionary of Critical Philosophy*[6] (1797–1804) by G. S. A. Mellin appear.

The criticism of Kant begins no less quickly than praise. The writer and bookseller Friedrich Nicolai of Berlin steps forward with various satirical polemics. And such influential Enlightenment philosophers as J. J. Engel, J. G. H. Feder, C. Garve, C. Meiners, M. Mendelssohn and E. Platner, who in part have entertained friendly relations with Kant prior to 1781, strongly oppose the "revolution in the manner of thinking." Garve writes a bitter criticism (sect. 2). In his *Morning Hours, or On the Existence of God*[7] (1785), Mendelssohn defends the ontological proof against Kant, the "pulverizer of metaphysics." To oppose Kantian thought, Johann August Eberhard (1738–1809) founds the journal *Philosophisches Magazin*[8] (1789–92). Kant answers its attacks with the work *Concerning a Discovery by Which Every New Critique of Pure Reason is Supposed to Be Rendered Unnecessary by an Older One*[9], (1790).

Such conflicts mark the retreat of Leibnizian and Wolffian metaphysics. Of greater philosophical significance is the criticism by Johann Georg Hamann, a declared opponent of the rationalist Enlightenment. Rejecting Kant's division of the faculty of knowledge into the two stems of sensibility and understanding/reason, Hamann asserts the "genealogical priority of *language*" (*Metacritique on the Purism of Reason*,[10] 1784). Although Johann Gottfried Herder has attended Kant's lectures (during Kant's pre-Critical period; sect. 1), he takes up Hamann's criticism. Language, with which reason is awoken, in his opinion reveals the abstract nature of any theory separating sensibility from the understanding/reason (*Understanding and Experience Reason and Language. A Metacritique of the Critique of Pure Reason*,[11] 1799)

Kant's critical transcendental philosophy is thus by no means uncontroversial. But despite all philosophical criticism and often bitter opposition from political and religious groups (of note is the two-volume *Anti-Kant* by the Jesuit B. Stattler; 1788), the new thinking takes hold in many German universities: at first in Protestant north and central Germany, but soon also in the Catholic south and in Austria. In addition to the aforementioned Schmid, Schultz, Reinhold, Beck and Mellin, J. H. Tieftrunk in Halle, J. G. K. C. Kiesewetter in Berlin, K. H. Heydenreich in Magdeburg, (with modifications) F. Bouterwek in Göttingen, W. T. Krug (originally in Wittenberg) and G. B. Jäsche (the editor of Kant's Logic) in Dorpat are followers of Kant. Not only his followers but also his critics bear witness to the outstanding role of his thought in the philosophical discussions of the time.

13.2 GERMAN IDEALISM

While the Kantians are still propounding Kant's views in lecture halls, the avant-garde among German writers and philosophers begin to discuss Kant more creatively. This discussion ultimately leads them to "overcome Kant." At first, enthusiasm predominates—not only for the *Critique of Pure Reason* but also for Kant's ethics. Jean Paul writes to a friend: "Buy two books for heaven's sake: Kant's Groundwork for a Metaphysic of Morals and Kant's Critique of Practical Reason, 1788 Kant is not a light for the world but a whole shining solar system" (13 July 1788). Hölderlin, the great inspirer of Schelling and Hegel from their time together in the "Tübinger Stift," calls Kant the "Moses of our nation" (letter of 1 January 1799). Both Kant's philosophy of freedom and the "Critique of Aesthetic Judgment" exercise a strong influence on Friedrich Schiller, for instance, on his letters *On the Aesthetic Education of Man*[12] (1795). But Schiller also seeks to go beyond Kant and, in particular, to eliminate the dichotomy between duty and inclination by introducing the ideal of the "beautiful soul.[13] Insofar as Goethe is interested in philosophy, he considers Kant to be the best of the more recent philosophers and recommends the *Critique of Judgment* (*Conversations with Eckermann*, 11 April 1827). In his *Prince Friedrich von Homburg* (1810, published in 1821), Heinrich Kleist dramatizes basic ideas from Kant's philosophy of law.

But the most significant discussion of Kant does not revolve around the later writings but concerns the first major work of critical philosophy, in particular its distinction between appearance and thing in itself. According to Friedrich Heinrich Jacobi (1743–1819), one cannot enter into the critique of reason without the assumption of things in themselves, and with it, one cannot stay there. Reinhold still hopes to solve the difficulties with an "elementary philosophy."[14] Like Hamann and Herder, he has trouble with sensibility and understanding as the dual stems of knowledge, but, closer to Kant, he seeks their unity not in language but in representation: *New Theory of the Human Faculty of Representation*[15] (1789). Salomon Maimon (*Essay on Transcendental Philosophy . . .,*[16] 1790) and the skeptic G. E. Schulze (*Aenesidemus . . .,* 1792), however, object to this solution.

In the new climate of criticism and modification of Kant, the first person who wants neither to defend nor to reject but instead to consummate Kant's theory by thinking through its ultimate consequences is Johann Gottlieb Fichte (1762–1814). Although he likes, especially at first, to claim that he has only discovered the spirit behind the letter of Kantian philosophy, Fichte in reality does much more. With him begins, during Kant's lifetime, the rapid succession of speculative theories known as German Idealism. This movement proceeds from the Copernican turn of the first *Critique*, the principle of freedom of the Second, and the systematic interest of the third *Critique*. It adds to these components a (more Cartesian or Spinozistic) claim to ultimate justification, which significantly transforms Kant's critical transcendental philosophy and perhaps gives rise to a frequent misinterpretation of it. The speculative idealism of Fichte, Wilhelm Joseph Schelling (1775–1854) and Georg Wilhelm Friedrich Hegel (1770–1831) seeks to overcome Kantian dichotomies and distinctions and to develop all fields of knowledge (nature and mind, theory and practice) from a common root.

Fichte's first work, his *Essay toward a Critique of all Revelation*[17] (1793), gains Kant's recognition and makes the young philosopher famous overnight. But Kant distances himself publicly from Fichte's basic philosophy, the Science of Knowledge (7 August 1799). Fichte writes to Schelling thereupon, on 20 September of the same year, that "Kantian philosophy, if it is not supposed to be taken as we take it, is utter nonsense." The development of German Idealism thus brings a devaluation of Kant as well as a new philosophical tone, which quickly ascribes "complete and total falsity" to other views (Fichte, *F. Nicolai's Life* . . ., chap. 9). Schelling, too, sees in Kant only the "dawn of philosophy" and not its fulfillment, which he attempts to realize in competition with Fichte, and later with Hegel.

Starting with Fichte, the Idealists accuse Kant of not really justifying transcendental apperception in theoretical philosophy and personal morality in practical philosophy. In a radicalization of critique so as to question even the most basic assumptions and in the attempt to explain the connection of theoretical and practical knowledge from one common principle, Fichte seeks the supreme principle of unity for knowledge in general. In each new draft of his "Science of Knowledge" he transcends the limits of critical thought delineated by Kant. He transforms the transcendental illumination of the *a priori* deep structure of human knowledge and moral action into a "forcing" derivation from a single principle. To avoid an endless regress, Fichte does not appeal to an existing *fact*. The basic unifying principle of his philosophy is the free act of the ego. He designates transcendental productivity as the ultimate foundation. Fichte thus promotes autonomy, which Kant limits to practical reason, to the rank of a universal principle.

Because Schelling thinks that nature comes away too poorly in Fichte's thought, he views its philosophical justification as the decisive task. Schelling's brilliant early writings raise the infinite activity of nature to the same rank as the mind. Both are developed from the same source. Both in his early and, even more clearly, in his later philosophy, Schelling, the leading philosopher of Romanticism, devotes broad theoretical attention to the unconscious, which receives no systematic treatment by Kant.

With his theory of regulative ideas, Kant has cautiously mediated between the empirical standpoint of scientific knowledge and the need of reason to conceive the unconditioned. In speculative Idealism, so it seems, such caution is abandoned. A new assessment of the Dialectic forms the methodical basis for this change. Whereas Kant views dialectic as a "Logic of Illusion," it acquires a positive and constructive significance for Fichte, Schelling and particularly Hegel. According to a fundamental tenet of German Idealism, the conception of the absolute together with its notions of totality does not automatically lead to irresolvable contradictions (antinomies). Reflection on the part of the understanding fails to grasp the absolute, but speculative dialectics does not. With its help, natural theology is also rehabilitated. Kant's momentous turn in philosophical theology thus is not accepted for long. While Fichte, Schelling and Hegel wish to raise speculative theology to new heights despite Kant's destruction of it, Feuerbach, Marx and Nietzsche later do not even give credence to a moral "justification" of God.

Despite many common features, German Idealism is not a completely unified movement. In his early treatise *Belief and Knowledge*[18] (1802/03), Hegel rejects not only Kant's position but also that of Fichte and indeed of any philosophy of reflection. It is supposed to give way to a philosophy of the spirit which no longer adheres to the critical principle that "the hidden essence of the universe has no force which could offer resistance to courageous cognition" (inaugural lecture in Berlin, 22 October 1818). Hegel associates the notion of the absolute spirit with that of history. Hegel's, as well as Schelling's, attempts to take into account the historical nature of philosophy contribute to the increased importance of history in nineteenth century European thought. Following Hegel and Schelling, the historical dimension gains central importance.

Whereas Kant does not derive the categories in their inner determinations, Hegel's *Logic* presents the fundamental determinations of thought, including more than just Kant's categories, as a systematic whole justified by the "movement of the concept." Through the self-movement of the logical, every concept flows automatically into its opposite, and both the concept and its opposite move toward their speculative sublation in synthesis. Hegel is also critical of Kant's philosophy of personal morality, which he rejects as an abstract ought removed from practical political life. He views the separation of practical reason from the historical circumstances in which people exist as an expression of alienated life.

Hegel provides the most influential realization of the universal Idealist project of completing classical philosophy. His school gives rise to the cliché of a development from Kant to Hegel which follows an inner, objective and logical necessity. In it, Kant is no more than a beginning which is further developed by Fichte and Schelling and then brought to final completion by Hegel. While Kant sinks to the rank of a mere precursor of Hegel, the latter is viewed as the consummation of Idealism. After Hegel's death, people are soon speaking of the collapse of Idealism. The creative philosophical impulses come from David Friedrich Strauss, Ludwig Feuerbach and particularly Karl Marx, all explicit opponents of Idealism. But Hegel remains for them the dominant point of reference. They essentially adopt his critique of Kant as well as his assessment of critical transcendental philosophy as a revolutionary watershed in the history of western philosophy. Materialistic speculation no longer relates directly to matter and its laws, as it did before Kant. It is guided by anthropological questions and in this way pays tribute to Kant's emphasis on the subject.

On the other hand, one should not forget the contemporaries of Fichte, Schelling and Hegel who stand outside of the Idealist mainstream and, despite their independent ideas, refer directly to Kant. In the very title of his most important philosophical work, the *New Critique of Reason* (1807), Jakob Friedrich Fries (1773–1843) expresses his obligation to Kant. But an empirical, psychological investigation of inner experience takes the place here of transcendental critique. The influential educator and psychologist Johann Friedrich Herbart (1776–1841) studies under Fichte but turns away from speculative Idealism. Drawing from Wolff and Leibniz, he seeks to give a realistic bent to transcendental philosophy. Of greater philosophical significance is Arthur Schopenhauer (1788–1860). Although his philosophy differs considerably from Kant "in its results," it arises from the continued study of Kant's works: "For 27 years, Kant's theory never stopped being a central object of my studies and thoughts." (to Rosenkranz and Schubert, 24 August 1837). In particular, both the renunciation of epistemological realism adopted in Kant's "Copernican turn" and the priority of practical reason, as distinguished from theoretical, provide the foundation of Schopenhauer's main ideas in *The World as Will and Representation* (1818). Finally, we should remember the late Idealists who, like Fichte's son Immanuel Hermann (1796–1879), have a more positive attitude toward Kant due to their opposition to Hegel.

13.3 KANT'S INTERNATIONAL INFLUENCE

Without significant resistance, but somewhat more slowly, critical transcendental philosophy (later, in conjunction with Idealist thought) attracts attention in surrounding European countries.

Because a number of future pastors from the German speaking population of the Baltic States as well as Lithuanians, Latvians, Poles, and Russians attend Kant's lectures, his initial reception in Eastern Europe constitutes an exception. The lasting respect for Kant can be seen in the fact that later such outstanding figures as Dostoyevsky and Tolstoy consider themselves to share his views. In the Netherlands, P. van Hemert publishes in 1796–98 a four-volume outline of Kant's philosophy. In 1798, together with others, he founds a "Magazine for Critical Philosophy" and a Critical Society to promote Kantianism. In Denmark, a circle of admirers of Kant forms for several years around the poet Jens Baggesen. Kant's ideas reach Sweden through D. Boëtius (1751–1810). In Italy, F. Soave writes the first book on Kant (1803). A follower of Kant in Freiburg, Switzerland, is J. M. Bussard.

The first work to be translated into French is *On Eternal Peace* (1795). Three years later, the Institut National in Paris organizes a special colloquium on Kant. A figure of such importance as Wilhelm von Humboldt, whom Friedrich Schiller had won over to Kant's ideas, presents the new philosophy. Important French intermediaries are Charles de Villers,[19] then Antoine Destutt de Tracy[20] and Joseph Hoene-Wronski.[21] But presumably no work influenced the understanding of Kant's philosophy and of German thought in general as much as the book *On Germany*[22] by Madame de Staël (-Holstein). Here, Kant is interpreted as a reaction of emotion against rationalism and as the beginning of Romanticism. In 1820, Victor Cousin holds his influential lectures on Kant's philosophy, which are printed in 1842. In the fifties, with Charles Renouvier (1815–1903) and then J. Lachelier (1832–1918), a movement opposing the predominance of positivism (A. Comte) begins, and in it, reflection on Kant's critical philosophy plays a significant role. In the theoretical domain, Renouvier develops a dialectical theory of categories (1854); in the practical domain, an ethical personalism (1903), which retains its influence up to the time after the Second World War (E. Mounier, J. Maritain). Kant remains important not only for Renouvier's student Octave Hamelin (1856–1907) but also for such idealists as Émile Meyerson (1859-1933) and Léon Brunschvicg (1869–1944) as well as E. Le Roy, R. Le Senne and L. Lavelle.

In Great Britain, the first publications on Kant by F. A. Nitsch (1796) and A. F. M. Willich (1798) attract little attention. With the author and philosopher S. T. Coleridge (1722–1834), however, Kant, together with Schelling and German Romanticism and in opposition to the predominance of empiricism, gains sustained influence upon British intellectual life. Of the academic philosophers, W. Hamilton (1788–1856), W. Whewell (1794–1866) and T. H. Green (1836–1883) take up Kant's ideas, while Green's friend Edward Caird (1835–1908), under the influence of Hegel, wishes to go beyond Kant. But only with F. H, Bradley (1846–1924), who is influenced by Green, do Kant's thought and, to an even greater extent, Hegel's speculative idealism gain a significance comparable to their influence in France around 1870. Up to Moore, Russell and Wittgenstein in the twentieth century, Bradley, together with other idealists such as B. Bosanquet (1848–1923), dominate the British philosophical scene. Even Moore, despite his criticism of Bradley's idealism, agrees with Kant as to the possibility of synthetic *a priori* judgments.

Even more than the theological and philosophical movement of transcendentalism (Ralph Waldo Emerson et al.), pragmatism, the most important philosophical development in the United States, arises under the auspices of an intensive examination of Kant. In contrast to tendencies in Great Britain, Kant's critique of knowledge and metaphysics receives more attention than his association with idealist metaphysics. For three years, C. S. Peirce (1839–1914) devotes two hours every day to the study of the *Critique of Pure Reason*. In the end, he rejects the argumentation of the "Analytic" but esteems the "Dialectic" highly. With the description of his theory of meaning as "pragmatic," Peirce reminds us of Kant's definition of pragmatic belief as a "contingent belief, which yet underlies the actual employment of means to certain actions" (B 852).

Kant's philosophy reaches Italy at a time when French thought—due in part to the French Revolution—predominates. Even such philosophers as Gallupi (1770–1846), who are open to Kant's ideas, take them up hesitatingly. A more intensive reception of Kant begins only with A. Testa (1784–1860), O. Colecchi (1773–1847) and above all B. Spaventa (1817–83). Neo-Kantianism, which in the late nineteenth century begins to flourish in Italy, too, strives for a more detailed explanation of the relationship between philosophy and psychology. Later, V. Mathieu examines modern physics under aspects provided by Kant's *opus postumum*.

In Japan, the study of Kant begins soon after the first consideration of European philosophy around 1860. It is indicative that here, as in France, a translation of the work *On Eternal Peace* initiates the examination of Kant. Important Kantians are Genyoku Kuwaki (1874–1943), Peiyu Amano (1884–1979) and Masaaki Kosaka (1900–1969). Two Japanese editions of the complete works of Kant and a number of translations of important Kant scholars have now been published; there has been a Japanese Kant Society since the mid-1970s.

13.4 NEO-KANTIANISM

The "collapse of idealism" in Germany favors not only materialist thought. It also encourages positive research and a philosophy committed to it. The new climate of faith in science and experience gives rise to a form of reflection upon Kant's thinking which, in conscious opposition to idealistic and materialistic speculation, emphasizes Kant's critical perspective and its significance for the empirical sciences. But Neo-Kantianism, which dominates academic philosophy in Germany for at least half a century (1870–1920), does not simply wish to recite Kant's doctrines. As a rule, its adherents are convinced that "understanding Kant means going beyond him" (Windelband). Neo-Kantianism centers around philosophy as epistemology and as the foundation for science: first for the mathematical sciences, then for the cultural sciences (humanities), and, in the case of Cassirer, finally for the non-scientific world as well.

Eduard Zeller already pleas in his lecture *On the Significance and Task of Epistemology*[23] (published in 1862) for a return to epistemology, specifically to Kant. In 1860 Kuno Fischer publishes his monumental work *Kant's Life and the Foundations of his Teachings*[24] But the cry for a return to Kant rings most clearly in the programmatic piece *Kant and the Epigones* (1865) by the young Otto Liebmann, who rejects all post-Kantian philosophy from Fichte, Schelling and Hegel to Herbart, Fries and Schopenhauer. No less important are Friedrich Albert Lange's *History of Materialism* (1866) and Alois Riehl's *Philosophical Criticism*[25] (3 vols., 1876–87). And Hermann von Helmholtz, the most important scientist in Germany, presents himself as an advocate of Kant.

Among the Neo-Kantians, we find not only an astonishing number of original philosophers but also significant historians of philosophy, whose philological, biographical and interpretative research provides a new foundation for the understanding of Kant and of German philosophy. Of particular note is the two-volume *Commentary to Kant's Critique of Pure Reason*[26] by Hans Vaihinger (1881 and 1892), which treats no more than the Transcendental Aesthetic. It is also Vaihinger who, 100 years after Kant's death, founds the Kant Society[27] in 1904. The *Kant-Studien* have appeared since 1897.

Because of the anti-idealistic impulse, one of Kant's main intentions, the critical justification of a new metaphysics on the basis of practical reason, recedes into the background during his rediscovery. Kant is understood primarily on the basis of the *Critique of Pure Reason*, particularly from the perspective of the "Analytic," while the "more speculative" viewpoint of the "Dialectic" is displaced by questions of epistemology and the theory of science. That science has *a priori* foundations and that the conditions of the possibility of objective experience can be demonstrated from the fact of science—this approach, originating with Hermann Cohen, certainly does not contradict Kant's critique of reason. But it is a metaphysical interest which leads Kant to ask about the legitimacy of viewing the *a priori* concepts of the understanding as objectively valid, and in his answer, he does not restrict himself to the justification of existing sciences.

Hermann Cohen (1842–1918), a student and junior colleague of Lange in Marburg, examines in three works Kant's three *Critiques* and then presents, in a corresponding threefold division, his own elaboration of Kantian ideas, in which he rejects the duality of the stems of knowledge and the idea of a thing in itself. Cohen's student Paul Natorp (1854–1924) becomes famous due to his work on Plato and his critical foundation for the natural sciences, psychology and education. Ernst Cassirer (1874–1945), the last great representative of the Marburg School, examines not only the theory of relativity and quantum theory in recent physics. In addition to his work in the history of philosophy, he develops the notion of a relative *a priori* and expands Kant's "static" critique of reason into a philosophy of symbolic forms, which analyses the different manners of constituting the world in mythical thought, in everyday language and in science.

In addition to Wilhelm Windelband (1848–1915), the great scholar of the history of philosophy, Emil Lask (1875–1915), the author of an important theory of categories and judgments, as well as B. Bauch, J. Cohn and above all Heinrich Rickert (1863–1936) belong to the second, Heidelberg School of Neo-Kantianism (sometimes called the "School of Southwest Germany" or "School of Baden"). Following up on ideas of Windelband and his teacher H. Lotze, Rickert elaborates the methodological difference between the cultural (humanities) and natural sciences and draws attention to the constitutive significance of values. The theory of values, which has no counterpart in Kant's philosophy, has since experienced many further developments. It ranks as one of the most influential theories of Neo-Kantianism.

Although strictly speaking, Wilhelm Dilthey (1833–1911) does not belong to the Neo-Kantians, he is still heavily influenced by Kant. With his "critique of historical reason," he wants to achieve for the humanities something similar to what Kant's *Critique of Pure Reason* did for the mathematical sciences. The philosopher and sociologist Georg Simmel (1858–1918) is also influenced by Kant.

Whereas Rickert bases methodology on epistemology, Max Weber (1864–1920) dissolves this connection and creates an autonomous methodology for the social sciences. In it, the decisive distinction is that between objective statements of fact and merely subjective value-judgments. The Neo-Kantian distinction between knowledge and value thus finds its consummation. It seems to stand in the tradition of Kant's distinction between theoretical and practical reason but, with Weber, relinquishes the emphatic notion of reason in the (legal and moral) domain of values.

Kant's influence is by no means limited to philosophy and science. After the July revolution in 1830 in France and in the revolution of 1848, German liberals and democrats appeal to the authority of Kant. After the Gotha Program (1875), a controversy arises among the social democrats regarding their philosophical foundations. The conflict is understood in terms of the slogans "Kant versus Hegel" or "Kant versus Marx." From the field of philosophy, important Neo-Kantians (Cohen, M. Adler, K. Vorländer) participate. The "Meißen formula," in which the German youth movement proclaims its self-conception in 1913, shows the extent to which Kant's views effect a broad spectrum of culture. The programmatic statement that "free German youth wishes to shape its life according to its own determination, on its own responsibility, and in inner honesty" is demonstrably inspired by Kantian ethics.

13.5 PHENOMENOLOGY, EXISTENTIALISM AND OTHER MOVEMENTS

In the development of German, then of French, and most recently of American thought, phenomenology plays a decisive role. Although many perceive it soon after the turn of the century as a deliverance from "sterile" Neo-Kantianism, no philosopher and no contemporary philosophical movement influences the education of a number of its representatives as much as Kant and Neo-Kantianism. Edmund Husserl (1859–1938), the central figure of the phenomenological movement, inherits from his teacher F. Brentano a hearty antipathy toward Kant, but under the influence of Natorp, he later speaks of phenomenology as "transcendental" (*Ideas for a Pure Phenomenology . . .,*[28] I, 1913), considers it to be the "attempt . . . to realize the most profound sense of Kantian philosophizing" (*"Kant and the Idea of Transcendental Philosophy,"*[29] 1924), and takes it to be the third and final step in a development beginning with Descartes and including Kant (*The Crisis of the European Sciences . . .,*[30] 1936). Husserl values Kant as the first explicitly transcendental philosopher but criticizes him for overestimating the cognitive role of the natural sciences. He neglects (Husserl reminds us of Cassirer here) the constitutive role of pre-scientific experience for all scientific knowledge. Husserl thus considers himself to have adopted a more profound and a broader form of critical transcendental reflection than Kant. With the notion of a "life-world,"[31] the phenomenology of time and of cultural life, or with the analysis of intersubjectivity, he does indeed open new areas of thought. On the other hand, Husserl undertakes an uncompromising quest for ultimate justification from undisputable evidence. Such a quest is less Kantian than Cartesian or idealistic.

In contrast to Husserl, the phenomenologists Max Scheler (1874–1928) and Nicolai Hartmann (1882–1950) are influenced by Kant right from the start. Like Husserl, though, they view not only the formal conditions of all (theoretical and moral) experience but also substantive claims about essence as *a priori*. On the basis of this assumption, they criticize Kant's ethics as being merely formal, and they offer a "material ethic of values" as an alternative.

In Neo-Kantianism, Kant is intentionally interpreted in an antimetaphysical manner. It is thus not surprising that both original thinkers who criticize Idealism as well as Neo-Kantianism take up Kant under the auspices of metaphysics. Karl Jaspers (1883–1969) and Martin Heidegger (1889–1976) both seek a rejuvenation of metaphysics, and both refer to Kant—in very different ways. Jaspers' existentialism presents Kant's justification of metaphysics from practical reason in a new form. Heidegger, by way of contrast, does not take Kant's practical philosophy into consideration but, after his residence in Marburg, sees the *Critique of Pure Reason* as the true rediscovery of metaphysics. A Kantian theme underlies Jaspers' talk of the necessity in human existence of crossing borders as well as the step into transcendence and deciphering of its signs. In conscious opposition to Husserl's idea of ultimate justification in the transcendental ego, Heidegger takes up Kant's theory of sensibility and understanding as the two stems of knowledge, attributes fundamental significance to receptive sensibility, and, consequently, gives the Aesthetic of the first *Critique* priority over the Analytic. Like Fichte before him, Heidegger characterizes transcendental imagination as the hidden unity behind the two stems of knowledge. Heidegger, and perhaps Jaspers, has presented the last German Kant interpretation in the grand style, and also with creative originality. With his own idea of a phenomenological recovery of an ontological philosophy (cf. *Being and Time*, 1927), Heidegger sheds a new light on Kant's theoretical philosophy. Even in his later philosophy, in which critical, transcendental thought recedes into the background, he continues to grapple with Kant's ideas.

Like the interpretations of Jaspers and Heidegger, Georg Lukács' Marxist interpretation of Kant goes beyond a mere exegesis of Kant's epistemology and theory of science. Kant's philosophy is seen, in conjunction with German Idealism, as a speculative anticipation of the proletarian rebellion. According to Lukács, in "classical German philosophy," a "peculiar point of transition" in the development of bourgeois thinking, all problems of class society come to light, but they enter "into consciousness only conceptually" (*Reification and the Consciousness of the Proletariat*,[32] 1923, 133f.).

In opposition to rationalist philosophy and theology, Catholic thought in the nineteenth century undertook a restoration of Thomistic philosophy. Ever since D. J. Mercier (1851–1926) and J. Maréchal (1879–1944), so-called Neo-Scholasticism has devoted much attention to Kant's transcendental philosophy and to German Idealism, particularly Hegel (cf. also K. Rahner, J. B. Lotz and C. Nink). Catholic philosophy and theology thus takes up the critique of reason and the philosophy of freedom and terminates its narrow commitment to the metaphysical epistemology and practical philosophy of St. Thomas Aquinas.

The critical rationalism of K. R. Popper (1902–   ) also is beholden to Kant's thinking—less to his results or to his method than to the basic idea of critique in order to eliminate illusions and errors. He does not, however, as Kant does, apply this intention to metaphysics as the foundation of philosophy but to the sciences and then to politics. Ever since, even the natural sciences are considered to be fundamentally fallible. The community of scientists seeks for the truth without ever being sure of it. In the form of fallibilism, which is speculatively somewhat shallow in the absence of an attempt toward a critique of reason, criticism has become a basic element in the modern theory of science.

13.6 AFTER THE SECOND WORLD WAR

The philosophers striving in this century for a genuine understanding of Kant are legion. Even as an exemplary sample, we can only name a few of the older scholars: in the German-speaking world after the war G. Martin, F. Kaulbach, G. Funke and H. Wagner in addition to M. Wundt, H. Heimsoeth, J. Ebbinghaus, G. Lehmann and H. Reich; in the English-speaking world after N. Kemp Smith, H. J. Paton, W. H. Walsh and L. W. Beck; in the French after V. Delbos and H. J. de Vleeschauwer, A. Kojève, J. Vuillemin and A. Philonenko; G. Tonelli has set new standards for the study of Kant's development.

In contemporary analytic philosophy, we find a systematically motivated discussion of Kant. P. F. Strawson develops in *Individuals* (1959) a descriptive metaphysics which wishes to reveal the categories underlying our everyday language and thought. In contrast to behaviorism and skepticism, Strawson claims that there is an *a priori* conceptual scheme for the spatio-temporal structure of the individuals in the world. *The Bounds of Sense* (1966) bears the subtitle "An Essay on Kant's Critique of Pure Reason." But the work goes beyond analysis and reconstruction of Kantian theories. It contains the beginnings of a transcendental philosophy which, in place of Kant's transcendental idealism, illuminates the basic structure of all experience with the aid of analytic modes of argumentation.

Strawson initiates a renaissance of transcendental philosophy among analytic philosophers. This renaissance brings forth a number of incisive interpretations of central passages of the Aesthetic, Analytic and Dialectic of the first *Critique* (e.g., J. Bennett) as well as systematic consideration of the structure and possibility of transcendental arguments. In comparison to Fichte, Schelling and Hegel, Kant's speculative claims are much more modest, but they still seem somewhat extravagant to analytic philosophers. It is not clear, the objections begin, what is to be understood under transcendental arguments.

According to Quine, the distinction between analytic and synthetic propositions cannot be maintained; according to S. Körner, transcendental deductions are fundamentally impossible. The most radical criticism of Kant is contained in R. Rorty's claim that the development of analytic philosophy from Wittgenstein's *Tractatus* to the *Philosophical Investigations* and from the early Russell to Sellars and Davidson is nothing more than a progressive de-transcendentalization. The original search for necessary and sufficient non-empirical conditions for the world and our experience of it increasingly gives way to a more modest project which finally dispenses completely with constitutive elements free of experience. Skepticism of *a priori* truths is of course by no means new. Nietzsche rejected all purported *a priori* truths with no less vehemence than analytic philosophy and radicalized the finitude of human thought: we are hoaxed and know it, but we do not have the power to keep ourselves from being hoaxed. On the other hand, analytic criticism of Kant has not remained uncontested. J. Hintikka, for example, undertakes to reconstruct transcendental arguments by a combination of means from the theory of speech acts and from first-order logic. Moreover, the very fact that Kant finds such important opponents shows how highly he is regarded even today.

While analytic philosophy is beginning to take up ideas from the discussion in Germany, analytic thinking is widely read in the German-speaking world. Thus, in part due to the discussion of Kant, but also due to a turn toward language in a manner critical of Kant, two philosophical traditions which have long been separated from or opposed to one another appear to be converging: the empirical, analytic thought predominant in the English-speaking world and the tradition of hermeneutics and transcendental philosophy. An explicit interest in mediation, as well as the attempt to overcome Popper's skepticism as to justifiability, underlies the philosophy of K.-O. Apel. Apel wants to transform Kant so as to arrive at a critique of meaning, in the spirit of Peirce, and at a philosophy of language, in the sense of the late Wittgenstein. He sees the ultimate foundation for the objective validity of (scientific) argumentation not in transcendental self-consciousness but in a "transcendental language game." The supreme point of unity is not the (purportedly) solipsistic "I think" but rather communicative society, which constitutes the transcendental presupposition of the social sciences and the supreme principle of ethics.

Attention is paid to Kant not only in theoretical but also in practical philosophy. The rehabilitation of Kant's ethics and legal philosophy is due more to his substantive views than to his critique of reason. This is true for the principle of universalization, which, in the sense of the categorical imperative, is taken as the supreme criterion of morality (Hare, Singer). It is also true for John Rawls' theory of justice, which appeals to Kant's notion of autonomy, for the constructivist ethics of the Erlangen School (P. Lorenzen, O. Schwemmer et al.) and for J. Habermas' ethics of discourse, but not for work from the circle around H. Krings. The political philosophy of F. A. von Hayek also exhibits Kantian features. Even the theory of moral judgment developed by L. K. Kohlberg in continuation of J. Piaget's work defines the highest level of moral consciousness in terms of Kant's notions of autonomy and universalization.

☙❧

These fragmentary references on Kant's influence can only suggest his extraordinary importance. Whether the philosopher has been improved upon, creatively developed, or misunderstood—in any case, the history of philosophy since Kant is to a great extent the history of his influence: interpretation and further development, transformation, critique and reassessment of Kantian ideas. Critical transcendental philosophy seems to contain a potential which is not quickly dissipated and the measure of which is perhaps still unknown.

NOTES

PART I. LIFE AND PHILOSOPHICAL DEVELOPMENT

1. Wissenschaft.
2. E. Cassirer, *Kants Leben und Lehre*, 2nd ed. (Berlin, 1921), 4.
3. *Gedanken von der wahren Schätzung der lebendigen Kräfte.*
4. *Allgemeine Naturgeschichte und Theorie des Himmels.*
5. "A Brief Sketch of Certain Meditations about Fire."
6. The habilitation is in Germany the highest university degree and presupposes the Ph.D.
7. "New Elucidation of the First Principles of Metaphysical Knowledge."
8. "Physical Monadology."
9. *Neue Anmerkungen zur Erläuterung der Theorie der winde.*
10. *Vernunftlehre.*
11. Borowski in: Groß, F. (ed.) *Immanuel Kant. Sein Leben in Darstellungen von Zietgenossen. Die Biographien von L. E. Borowski, R. B. Jachmann und A. Ch. Wasianski* (Darmstadt, 1968 [1st ed. Berlin, 1912]), 86.
12. Jachmann, in ibid., 135f.
13. *Abhandlung über den Ursprung der Sprache.*
14. Rektor.
15. *Letters*, 24.
16. K. W. Böttiger (ed.), *K. A. Böttiger, Literarische Zustände und Zeitgenossen, 2 Bde. in einem* (Frankfurt a.M., 1972 [1st ed. Leipzig, 1838]).
17. K. Stavenhagen, *Kant und Königsberg* (Göttingen, 1949), 21.
18. Ibid., 19.
19. Ibid., 75.
20. *Der einzig mögliche Beweisgrund zu einer Demonstration des Daseins Gottes.*
21. *Untersuchung über die Deutlichkeit der Grundsätze der natürlichen Theologie und der Moral.*
22. *Versuch den Begriff der negativen Größen in die Weltweisheit einzuführen.*

23. *Träume eines Geistersehers, erläutert durch Träume der Metaphysik.*
24. "On the Form and Principles of the Sensible and Intelligible World."
25. "General Phenomenology."
26. *Die Grenzen der Sinnlichkeit und der Vernunft.*
27. Cf. G. Tonelli, "Das Wiederaufleben der deutsch-aristotelischen Terminologie bei Kant während der Entstehung der 'Kritik der reinen Vernunft'," *Archiv für Begriffsgeschichte* 9 (1964): 233–42.
28. A. Hübscher (ed.), *Gesammelte Briefe*, 157.
29. *Erläuterungen über des Herrn Professor Kant Critik der reinen Vernunft.*
30. K. Vorländer, *Immanuel Kant. Der Mann und das Werk* (Hamburg, 1977 [1st ed., 2 vols., Leipzig, 1924]), I, 286.
31. *Idee zu einer allgemeinen Geschichte in weltbürgerlicher Absicht.*
32. *Beantwortung der Frage: Was ist Aufklärung?*
33. *Metaphysische Anfangsgründe der Naturwissenschaft.*
34. *Die Religion innerhalb der Grenzen der bloßen Vernunft.*
35. *Das Ende aller Dinge.*
36. *Anthropologie in pragmatischer Hinsicht.*
37. Wasianski, in: F. Groß (ed.), ibid., 306.
38. *Über Pädagogik.*
39. *Über die philosophische Religionslehre.*
40. *Menschenkunde oder philosophische Anthropologie.*

PART II. WHAT CAN I KNOW?

1. Cf. R. Bubner, K. Cramer and R. Wiehl (eds.), *Zur Zukunft der Transzendentalphilosophie* (= *Neue hefte für philosophie* 14) (Göttingen, 1978) as well as P. Bieri, R. P. Horstmann and L. Krüger (eds.), *Transcendental Arguments and Science: Essays in Epistemology*, (Dordrecht: Reidel, 1979).
2. *Zur modernen Physik.*
3. *Schein.*
4. Phädon oder Über die Unsterblichkeit der Seele.
5. *Die Erziehung des Menschengeschlechts.*
6. "New Essays Concerning Human Understanding."

PART III. WHAT OUGHT I TO DO?

1. *Pädagogik.*
2. "Collected Political Writings.."
3. William Klaas Frankena, *Ethics* (Englewood Cliffs, N.J., ²1973), 32.
4. N. Hoerster, "Kants kategorischer Imperativ als Test unserer sittlichen Pflichten," in: M. Riedel (ed.), *Rehabilitierung der praktischen Philosophie*, vol. II (Freiburg i.Br., 1974), 455–75.
5. *Über ein vermeintes Recht aus Menschenliebe zu lügen.*

6. *Vorarbeiten zur Rechtslehre.*
7. "Authority, not truth, makes the law."
8. "Foundations of the Laws of Nature and of Peoples."
9. "What is Property?"
10. According to Bernd Ludwig, this passage should be placed after § 6. Cf. "Der Platz des rechtlichen Postulats der praktischen Vernunft innerhalb der Paragraphen 1–6 der kantischen Rechtslehre," in: R. Brandt (ed.), *Rechtsphilosophie der Aufklärung* (Berlin/New York, 1982), 219–32.
11. "On the Laws of War and Peace."
12. "On the Laws of Nature."
13. On the early discussion of Kant (F. Gentz, A. W. Rehberg), cf. Dieter Henrich (ed.), *Kant, Gentz, Rehberg. Über Theorie und Praxis* (Frankfurt a.M., 1967).
14. Maximilian Forschner, "Kant versus Bentham. Vom vermeintlich kategorischen Imperativ des Strafgesetzes," in: R. Brandt (ed.), *Rechtsphilosophie der Aufklärung* (Berlin/New York, 1982), 386.

PART IV. WHAT MAY I HOPE?

1. *Der Gott der Philosophen*, 1979, I 212f.
2. *Five Types of Ethical Theory* (London/New York, ⁹1971 [¹1930]), 140.

PART V. THE PHILOSOPHICAL AESTHETICS

1. "Man machine."
2. *Wahrheit und Methode* (Tübingen) ²1965), 56.
3. Ibid., 38.
4. Vorlesungen über die Ästhetik (ed. by G. Lasson).
5. E.g., Robert Spaemann.

PART VI. KANT'S INFLUENCE

1. *Betrachtungen aus der speculativen Weltweisheit.*
2. *Ideen zur Philosophie der Geschichte der Menschheit.*
3. *Critik der reinen Vernunft im Grundrisse zu Vorlesungen nebst Wörterbuch zum leichten Gebrauch der Kantischen Philosophie.*
4. *Erläuterungen über des Herrn Professor Kant Critik der reinen Vernunft.*
5. *Erläuternder Auszug aus den kritischen Schriften des Herrn Prof. Kant, auf Anrathen desselben.*
6. *Enzyklopädisches Wörterbuch der kritischen Philosophie.*
7. *Morgenstunden oder über das Daseyn Gottes.*
8. "Philosophical Magazine."

9. *Über eine Entdeckung, nach der alle neue Kritik der reinen Vernunft durch eine ältere entbehrlich gemacht werden soll.*

10. *Metakritik über den Purismum der Vernunft.*

11. *Verstand und Erfahrung, Vernunft und Sprache. Eine Metakritik zur Kritik der reinen Vernunft.*

12. *Über die ästhetische Erziehung des Menschen.*

13. "Schöne Seele."

14. "Elementarphilosophie."

15. *Neue Theorie des menschlichen Vorstellungsvermögens.*

16. *Versuch über die Transcendentalphilosophie . . .*

17. *Versuch einer Kritik aller Offenbarung.*

18. *Glauben und Wissen.*

19. *Philosophie de Kant,* 2 vols., 1801.

20. *De la métaphysique de Kant,* 1802.

21. *Philosophie critique découverte par Kant,* 1803.

22. "De l'Allemagne."

23. *Über Bedeutung und Aufgabe der Erkenntnistheorie.*

24. *Kants Leben und die Grundlagen seiner Lehre.*

25. *Der philosophische Kritizismus.*

26. *Commentar zu Kants Kritik der reinen Vernunft.*

27. Kant-Gesellschaft.

28. *Ideen zu einer reinen Phänomenologie . . .*

29. "Kant und die Idee der Transzendentalphilosophie" (lecture, *Husserliana* VII 287).

30. *Die Krisis der europäischen Wissenschaften . . .*

31. "Lebenswelt."

32. *Die Verdinglichung und das Bewußtsein des Proletariats.*

CHRONOLOGY

<table>
<tr><td>1724</td><td>April 22: Immanuel Kant born in Königsberg</td></tr>
<tr><td>1730–32</td><td>Vorstädter Hospitalschule (elementary school)</td></tr>
<tr><td>1732–40</td><td>Attended the pietistic Friedrichskollegium (further schooling)</td></tr>
<tr><td>1737</td><td>Death of Kant's mother</td></tr>
<tr><td>1740–46</td><td>Study of philosophy, mathematics, natural sciences and theology at the University of Königsberg</td></tr>
<tr><td>1746</td><td>Death of Kant's father—Thoughts on the True Estimation of Living Forces presented to the department of philosophy, appears: 1749</td></tr>
<tr><td>1747–54</td><td>Private tutor for three families in the vicinity of Königsberg</td></tr>
<tr><td>1755</td><td>Universal Natural History and Theory of the Heavens—doctoral degree in Königsberg with the dissertation De igne—Habilitation with the Nova dilucidatio</td></tr>
<tr><td>1756</td><td>Three treatises on the earthquake in Lisbon—Monadologia Physica—New Notes Explaining the Theory of the Winds—Unsuccessful application for a professorship in logic and metaphysics, again at the end of 1758</td></tr>
<tr><td>1762</td><td>"The False Distinction of the Four Syllogistic Figures Proved" ("Die falsche Spitzfindigkeit der vier syllogistischen Figuren erwiesen")—Herder attends Kant's lectures (until 1764)—The only Possible Basis for a Demonstration of the Existence of God (date of publication given as 1763)</td></tr>
</table>

1763   *Attempt to Introduce the Concept of Negative Quantities into the Wisdom of the World*

1764   Rejection of a professorship for literature—*Observations on the Feeling of the Beautiful and the Sublime*—*Enquiry Concerning the Clarity of the Principles of Natural Theology and Morals* (completed in 1762)

1766   Assistant librarian in the palace library—*Dreams of a Sorcerer*

1769   Rejection of a professorship in Erlangen

1770   Rejection of a professorship in Jena—Full professorship for logic and metaphysics at the University of Königsberg—*De mundi sensibilis atque intelligibilis forma et principiis*

1781   *Critique of Pure Reason*

1783   *Prolegomena to Any Future Metaphysics*—Kant buys a house

1784   "Idea for a Universal History with Cosmopolitan Intent"—"Answer to the Question: What is Enlightenment?"

1785   *Groundwork of the Metaphysic of Morals*

1786   *Metaphysical Origins of Science*—"Conjectural Beginning of Human History"—Summer term: president (Rektor) of the university—Non-resident member of the Academy of Sciences in Berlin

1787   Second edition of the *Critique of Pure Reason*

1788   Critique of Practical Reason—Summer term: second term as university president

1790   *Critique of Judgment*

1793   *Religion within the Bounds of Reason Alone*—"On the Commonplace: That may be right in theory but is not valid in practice"

1794   Election to the Academy of Sciences in St. Petersburg—Conflict with the Prussian censor

1795   *On Eternal Peace*

1796   July: Kant's last lecture

1797   *The Metaphysic of Morals*

1798   Election to the Academy of Sciences in Siena—*The Conflict of the Faculties—Anthropology from a Pragmatic Point of View*

1803   October: Kant's first serious illness

1804   February 12: Kant dies—February 28: Kant's funeral

BIBLIOGRAPHY

KANT'S WORKS

Gesammelte Schriften, begonnen von der Königlich Preußischen Akademie der Wissenschaften (Academy Edition, abbreviated as Acad. Ed. or as AA). 1st Division (vol. I–IX): Works. 2nd Division (vol. X–XIII): Correspondence. 3rd Division (vol. XIV–XXIII): posthumous works. Berlin, 1900–55. 4th Division (vol. XXIV–XXIX): Lectures. Berlin 1966– . 5th Division (vol. XXXff.): Index, not yet in print.

Werke. Akademie Textausgabe, vol. I–IX. Berlin 1968. Notes, 2 vols. Berlin/New York, 1977.

Sämtliche Werke, ed. by K. Vorländer together with O. Buek et al. 10 vols. Leipzig, 1904–14.

Werke, ed. by E. Cassirer together with H. Cohen et al. 11 vols. Berlin, 1912–22.

Werke in sechs Bänden, ed. by W. Weischedel. Wiesbaden 1956–64 (reprint: Darmstadt 1963–64; 12 vol. paperback edition with identical pagination: Frankfurt a.M. 1968; Index: Frankfurt a.M., no year given).

Critical editions in Meiner's "Philosophische Bibliothek" (Hamburg), various editions also by Reclam (Stuttgart) and Suhrkamp (Frankfurt a.M.).

Politische Schriften, ed. by O. H. v.d. Gablentz. Cologne/ Opladen, 1965.

Schöndörffer, O. (ed.). *Immanuel Kant. Briefwechsel*, selection and notes by Otto Schöndörffer, introduction by Rudolf Malter and Joachim Kopper. Hamburg: Meiner, ²1972.

ENGLISH TRANSLATIONS

Paul Guyer and Allen W. Wood are at present preparing a new edition of Kant's works in English translation, which will supersede many of the following translations.

Abbott, Thomas Kingsmill. *Kant's Critique of Practical Reason and Other Works on the Theory of Ethics.* London: Longmans, Green, ⁶1909 (reprinted 1954.

———. *Kant's Critique of Practical Reason and other Writings in Moral Philosophy.* Chicago: University of Chicago Press, 1949.

———. *Prolegomena to Any Future Metaphysics.* New York: Liberal Arts Press, 1951.

Beck, Lewis White. *Critique of Practical Reason.* Indianapolis: Bobbs–Merrill, 1956.

———. *Perpetual Peace.* New York: Liberal Arts Press, 1957.

Bernard, J. H. *Critique of Judgment.* New York: Hafner, 1951.

Carus, Paul and James W. Ellington. *Prolegomena to any future Metaphysics That Will Be Able to Come Forward as Science.* Indianapolis: Hackett Publishing Co., 1977.

Ellington, James W. *Metaphysical Foundations of Natural Science.* Indianapolis, 1970.

England, F. E. *Kant's Conception of God*, App., pp. 213–52 (trans. of *Principiorum primorum cognitionis metaphysicae nova dilucidatio*). London: Allen & Unwin, 1929.

Greene, Theodore M. and Hoyt H. Hudson. *Religion within the Limits of Reason Alone.* Chicago: Open Court, 1934.

Handyside, John. *Kant's Inaugural Dissertation and Early Writings on Space.* Chicago and London: Open Court, 1929.

Infield, Louis. *Lectures on Ethics.* New York: Century Co., 1930.

Kemp Smith, Norman. *Critique of Pure Reason.* London and New York: Macmillan Co. 1929.

Kerferd, G. B. and D. E. Walford. *Kant: Selected Pre-Critical Writings and Correspondence with Beck.* Manchester: Manchester University Press, 1968.

Lucas, P. G. *Prolegomena to any Future Metaphysic that will be able to present itself as a Science.* Manchester, 1953.

Meredith, J. C. *Critique of Judgment.* Oxford, 1952.

Paton, H. J. *Groundwork of the Metaphysic of Morals.* New York: Harper & Row, 1964 (orig. pub. as *The Moral Law*, London: Hutchinson & Co., Ltd., 1948).

STUDY AIDS

Adickes, E., *German Kantian Bibliography.* 2 vols. Boston/New York: B. Franklin, 1895–96 (reprint: Würzburg, no year given).

Eisler, R. *Kant-Lexikon, Nachschlagewerk zu Kants sämtlichen Schriften, Briefen und handschriftlichem Nachlaß.* Berlin, 1930: reprint: Hildesheim, 1961 (paperback 1972).

Hinske, N. "Kant." In *Neue Dt. Biographie*, vol. XI. Berlin, 1977, pp. 110–25.

Hinske, N. and W. Weischedel. *Kant-Seitenkonkordanz.* Darmstadt, 1970.

The *Kant-Studien* provide as of vol. 60 (1969) a running bibliography (by R. Malter) of works on Kant (including all titles since 1952).

Lehmann, K. H. and H. Horst. "Dissertationen zur Kantischen Philosophie." *Kant-Studien* 51 (1959/60): 228–57.

Martin, G. *Sachindex zu Kants Kritik der reinen Vernunft.* Berlin, 1967.

Mellin, G. S. A. *Encyklopädisches Wörterbuch der kritischen Philosophie.* 6 vols. 1797–1804; reprint: Aalen, 1970–71.

Ratke, H. *Systematisches Handlexikon zu Kants Kritik der reinen Vernunft.* Leipzig, 1929; Hamburg, ^{2}1965.

Schmid, C. C. E. *Wörterbuch zum leichtern Gebrauch der Kantischen Schriften.* ^{4}1798; newly ed. by N. Hinske, Darmstadt, ^{2}Jena, 1980.

LITERATURE

General Works

Akten des Vierten Internationalen Kant-Kongresses 1974. Part I: *Kant-Studien, Sonderheft*, Symposia. Part II: Section Lectures, 2 vols. Part III: Lectures. Berlin/New York: de Gruyter, 1974–75.

Akten des 5. Internationalen Kant-Kongresses Mainz 4.–8. April 1981, ed. by Gerhard Funke. Part I,1: Sections I–VII. Part I,2: Sections VIII–XIV. Part II: Lectures. Bonn: Bouvier, 1981–82.

Beck, L. W. *Studies in the Philosophy of Kant*. New York: Bobbs-Merrill, 1965.

———— (ed.). *Kant Studies Today*. La Salle, Ill.: Open Court, 1969.

Böhme, H. & G. *Das andere der Vernunft. Zur Entwicklung von Rationalitätsstrukturen am Beispiel Kants*. Frankfurt a.M., 1983.

Boutroux, E. *La Philosophie de Kant*. Paris: Presses Universitaires de France, 1926.

Broad, C. D. *Kant: An Introduction*. Cambridge: Cambridge University Press, 1978.

Delekat, F. *Immanuel Kant. Historisch-kritische Interpretation der Hauptschriften*. Heidelberg, [3]1969.

Fischer, K. *Immanuel Kant und seine Lehre*. 2 vols. Heidelberg, [6]1928 (reprint of vol. 2: 1957).

Förster, E. (ed.). *Kant's Transcendental Deductions: The "Critiques" and the "Opus Postumum."* Stanford: Stanford University Press, 1989.

Gerhard, V. and F. Kaulbach. *Kant* (= *Erträge der Forschung*, vol. 105). Darmstadt, 1979.

Goetschel, W. *Kant als Schriftsteller*. Vienna, 1990.

Gram, M.S. (ed.). *Kant: Disputed Questions*. Chicago: Quadran Books, 1967.

Grondin, J. *Kant et le problème de la philosophie. L'a priori*. Paris: J. Vrin, 1989.

————, *Emmanuel Kant. Avant/après*. Paris: Criterion, 1991.

Guyer, P. (ed.). *The Cambridge Companion to Kant.* Cambridge: Cambridge University Press, 1992.

Heimsoeth, H. *Studien zur Philosophie Immanuel Kants.* Vol. 1: Bonn, ²1971. Vol. 2: Bonn, 1970.

Hinske, N. *Kant als Herausforderung an die Gegenwart.* Freiburg/Munich, 1980.

Jaspers, K. *Kant.* In *Die großen Philosophen*, vol. 1. Munich/Zurich, 1981, pp. 397–616. Also as *Kant. Leben, Werk, Wirkung.* Munich/Zurich, ²1983.

Kaulbach, F. *Immanuel Kant.* Berlin, 1969.

Kojève, A. *Kant.* Paris: Gallimard, 1973.

Körner, S. *Kant.* Harmondsworth: Penguin, 1955.

Laberge, P., F. Duchesneau, and B. E. Morrisey (eds.). *Proceeding of the Ottawa Congress on Kant in the Anglo-American and Continental Traditions Held October 10–14, 1974.* Ottawa: The University of Ottawa Press, 1976.

Marcucci, S. (ed.). *Studi Kantiani.* Pisa: Giardini Editori e Stampatori, 1988– .

Philonenko, A. *L'oeuvre de Kant. La philosophie critique.* 2 vols. Paris: J. Vrin, 1969.

Prauss, G. (ed.). *Kant. Zur Deutung seiner Theorie von Erkennen und Handeln.* Cologne, 1973.

Proceedings of the IVth International Colloquium in Biel. In: *Dialectica* 35, nos. 1–2 (1981).

Scruton, R. *Kant.* Oxford: Oxford University Press, 1982.

Walker, R. *Kant: The Arguments of the Philosophers.* London: Routledge & Kegan Paul, 1978.

——— (ed.). *Kant on Pure Reason.* Oxford: Oxford University Press, 1982.

Wood, A. W. (ed.). *Self and Nature in Kant's Philosophy.* Ithaca, N.Y.: Cornell University Press, 1980.

Wolff, R. P. (ed.). *Kant: A Collection of Critical Essays.* London/Melbourne: Macmillan, 1968.

1 and 2. Life and Philosophical Development

Adickes, E. *Kants Opus Postumum.* Berlin, 1920; reprint: Vaduz, 1978.

Beck, L. W. *Early German Philosophy: Kant and His Predecessors.* Cambridge, Mass.: The Belknap Press of Harvard University Press, 1969.

Böttiger, K. W. (ed.). *K. A. Böttiger, Literarische Zustände und Zeitgenossen.* 2 vols. in one. Frankfurt a.M., 1972 (orig. Leipzig, 1838).

Cassirer, E. *Kants Leben und Lehre.* Darmstadt, 1977 (orig. Berlin, ²1921).

Groß, F. (ed.). *Immanuel Kant. Sein Leben in Darstellungen von Zeitgenossen. Die Biographien von L. W. Borowski, R. B. Jachmann und A. Ch. Wasianski.* Darmstadt, 1968 (orig. Berlin, 1912).

Gulyga, A. *Immanuel Kant.* Frankfurt a.M., 1981 (Russian: Moscow, 1977).

Heine, H. *Zur Geschichte der Religion und Philosophie in Deutschland.* In: Heine, *Beiträge zur deutschen Ideologie.* Frankfurt a.M., 1971, pp. 1–111.

Heimsoeth, H., D. Henrich and G. Tonelli (eds.). *Studien zu Kants philosophischer Entwicklung.* Hildesheim, 1967.

Hinske, N. "Die historischen Vorlagen der Kantischen Transzendentalphilosophie." *Archiv für Begriffsgeschichte* 12 (1968): 86–113.

———, *Kants Weg zur Transzendentalphilosophie. Der dreißigjährige Kant.* Stuttgart, 1970.

Kreimendahl, L. *Kant. Der Durchbruch von 1769.* Cologne, 1990.

Laberge, P. *La Théologie kantienne précritique.* Ottawa: Editions de l'Université, 1973.

Mathieu, V. *La filosofia transcendentale e l'Opus postumum di Kant.* Turin, 1958.

Ritzel, W. *Immanuel Kant. Zur Person*. Bonn, 1975.

Schilpp, P. A. *Kant's Precritical Ethics*. Evanston, Ill./Chicago: Garland, 1938.

Schmucker, J. *Die Ursprünge der Ethik Kants in seinen vorkritischen Schriften und Reflexionen*. Meisenheim a.Gl., 1961.

————, *Die Ontotheologie des vorkritischen Kant*. Berlin/New York, 1980.

Schultz, U. *Immanuel Kant in Selbstzeugnissen und Bilddokumenten*. Reinbeck, 1965.

Stavenhaben, K. *Kant und Königsberg*. Göttingen, 1949.

Tonelli, G. *Kant dall'estetica metafisica all'estetica psicoempirica. Studi sulla genesi del criticismo, 1754–1771, e sulle sue fonti*. In *Memorie dell'Accademia delle Scienze di Torino*. Turin, 1955, vol. III, 2, pp. 77–420.

————, *Elementi metodologici e metafisici in Kant dal 1745 al 1768*. Turin: Edizione di Filosofia, 1959.

————, "Das Wiederaufleben der deutsch-aristotelischen Terminologie bei Kant während der Entstehung der 'Kritik der reinen Vernunft'," *Archiv für Begriffsgeschichte* 9 (1964): 233–42.

Verneaux, R. *Le Vocabulaire de Kant*. Vol. I: *Doctrines et Méthodes*. Paris, 1967. Vol. II: *Les Pouvoirs de l'esprit*. Paris: Presses Universitaires de France, 1973.

Vorländer, K. *Immanuel Kant. Der Mann und das Werk*. Hamburg, ²1977 (orig. 2 vols.: Leipzig, 1924).

3. Critique of Pure Reason

Allison, H. E. *Kant's Transcendental Idealism: An Interpretation and Defense*. New Haven, Conn.: Yale University Press, 1983.

Ameriks, K. *Kant's Theory of Mind: An Analysis of the Paralogisms of Pure Reason*. Oxford: Clarendon Press, 1982.

Baumgartner, H. M. *Kants Kritik der reinen Vernunft. Anleitung zur Lektüre*. Freiburg/Munich, 1985.

Beck, L. W. (ed.). *Kant's Theory of Knowledge*. Dordrecht: Reidel, 1974.

Bennett, J. *Kant's Analytic*. London/New York: Cambridge University Press, 1966.

Bird, G. *Kant's Theory of Knowledge: An Outline of One Central Argument in the Critique of Pure Reason*. New York/London: Routledge & Kegan Paul, 1962, ²1965.

Brittan, G. G., Jr. *Kant's Theory of Science*. Princeton: Princeton University Press, 1978.

Bröcker, W. *Kant über Metaphysik und Erfahrung*. Frankfurt a.M., 1970.

Brunschvicg, L. *Écrits philosophiques*. Vol. I: *L'humanisme de l'Occident. Descartes-Spinoza-Kant*. Paris: Presses Universitaires de France, 1951.

Cassirer, H. W. *Kant's First Critique: An Appraisal of the Permanent Significance of Kant's "Critique of Pure Reason."* London, 1968.

Clavel, M. *Critique de Kant*. Paris: Flammarion, 1988.

Cohen, H. *Kants Theorie der Erfahrung*. Berlin, ⁴1924 (¹1871).

Cramer, K. *Nicht-reine synthetische Urteile a priori. Ein Problem der Transzendentalphilosophie Immanuel Kants*. Heidelberg, 1985.

Daval, R. *La métaphysique de Kant*. Paris: Presses Universitaires de France, 1951.

Gram, M. S. *Kant: Ontology and the A Priori*. Evanston, Ill.: Northwestern University Press, 1968.

Guyer, P. *Kant and the Claims of Knowledge*. Cambridge: Cambridge University Press, 1987.

Heidegger, M. *Kant und das Problem der Metaphysik*. Frankfurt a.M., ⁴1973 (¹1929).

———, *Kants These über das Sein*. Frankfurt a.M., 1963.

———, *Phänomenologische Interpretation von Kants Kritik der reinen Vernunft*. Ed. by I. Görland. Frankfurt a.M., 1977.

Hintikka, J. *Knowledge and the Known.* Dordrecht: Reidel, 1974.

————, *Logic, Language Games and Information.* Oxford: Oxford University Press, 1975.

Holzhey, H. *Kants Erfahrungsbegriff. Quellengeschichtliche und bedeutungsanalytische Untersuchungen.* Basel/Stuttgart, 1970.

Kaulbach, F. *Philosophie als Wissenschaft. Eine Anleitung zum Studium. Kants Kritik der reinen Vernunft in Vorlesungen.* Hildesheim, 1981.

Kemp Smith, N. *A Commentary to Kant's "Critique of Pure Reason."* London: Macmillan, 1923; reprinted London: Macmillan, 1979.

Kopper, J. and R. Malter (eds.). *Materialien zu Kants "Kritik der reinen Vernunft."* Frankfurt a.M., 1975.

Kopper, J. and W. Marx (eds.). *200 Jahre Kritik der reinen Vernunft.* Hildesheim, 1981.

Lachièze-Rey, P. *L'idéalisme kantien.* Paris: J. Vrin, ²1950.

Lauener, H. *Hume und Kant. Eine systematische Gegenüberstellung einiger Hauptstücke ihrer Lehren.* Bern/Munich, 1969.

Macann, C. E. *Kant and the Foundations of Metaphysics: An Interpretative Transformation of Kant's Critical Philosophy.* Heidelberg, 1981.

Malherbe, M. *Kant ou Hume. Ou la raison et le sensible.* Paris: J. Vrin, 1980.

Marquard, O. *Skeptische Methode im Blick auf Kant.* Freiburg/Munich, 1958, ²1978.

Martin, G. *Immanuel Kant. Ontologie und Wissenschaftstheorie.* Berlin, ²1968.

Marty, F. *La naissance de la métaphysique chez Kant. Une étude sur la notion kantienne d'analogie.* Paris: Beauchesne, 1980.

Meyer, M. *Science et métaphysique chez Kant,* Paris: Presses Universitaires de France, 1988.

Mohr, G. *Das sinnliche Ich. Innerer Sinn und Bewußtsein bei Kant.* Würzburg, 1991.

Paton, H. J. *Kant's Metaphysic of Experience: A Commentary on the First Half of the "Kritik der reinen Vernunft."* 2 vols. London: Humanities Press, 1936 ('1965).

Philonenko, A. *Études kantiennes.* Paris: J. Vrin, 1982.

Prauss, G. *Erscheinung bei Kant. Ein Problem der "Kritik der reinen Vernunft."* Berlin, 1971.

————, *Kant und das Problem der Dinge an sich.* Bonn, 1974.

Prichard, H. A. *Kant's Theory of Knowledge.* Oxford: Clarendon Press, 1909.

Riedel, M. "Kritik der reinen Vernunft und Sprache. Zum Kategorienproblem bei Kant." *Allgemeine Zeitschrift für Philosophie* 7 (1982): 1–15.

Rohs, P. *Transzendentale Logik.* Meisenheim a.Gl., 1976.

Schaper, E. and W. Vossenkuhl (eds.). *Reading Kant. New Perspectives on Transcendental Arguments and Critical Philosophy.* Oxford/New York: Basil Blackwell, 1989.

Schwyzer, H. *The Unity of Understanding: A Study in Kantian Problems.* Oxford: Clarendon Press, 1990.

Secrétan, Ph. *Méditations kantiennes. En deça de Dieu, audelà de tout.* Lausanne: L'Âge d'Homme, 1982.

Sellars, W. *Science and Metaphysics: Variations on Kantian Themes.* London: Routledge & Kegan Paul, 1968.

Stegmüller, W. "Gedanken über eine mögliche rationale Rekonstruktion von Kants Metaphysik der Erfahrung." *Ratio* 9 (1967): 1–30; 10 (1968): 1–31.

Strawson, P. F. *The Bounds of Sense: An Essay on Kant's "Critique of Pure Reason."* London: Methuen, 1973.

Tuschling, B. (ed.). *Probleme der "Kritik der reinen Vernunft". Kant-Tagung Marburg 1981.* Berlin/New York 1984.

Vaihinger, H. *Kommentar zur Kritik der reinen Vernunft.* 2 vols. New York/London, 1976 (Aalen, 1970; orig. Stuttgart, vol. I: 1881, vol. II: 1892).

Verneau, R. *Critique de la raison pure de Kant.* Paris: Aubier-Montaigne, 1972.

Vuillemin, J. *Physique et métaphysique kantienne.* Paris: Presses Universitaires de France, 1955.

Walker, R. C. S. *The Coherence Theory of Truth: Realism, Anti-Realism, Idealism.* London/New York: Routledge, 1989.

Walsh, W. H. *Reason and Experience.* Oxford: Clarendon Press, 1947.

Wilkerson, T. E. *Kant's Critique of Pure Reason.* Oxford: Clarendon Press, 1960; reprinted 1976.

Wolff, R. P. *Kant's Theory of Mental Activity.* Cambridge, Mass.: Harvard University Press 1963; reprinted Gloucester, Mass.: Smith, 1973.

4. Transcendental Aesthetic; Kant's Theory of Mathematics

Beth, E. W. "Über Lockes 'allgemeines Dreieck'," *Kant-Studien* 48 (1956–57): 361–80.

Körner, S. "Zur Kantischen Begründung der Mathematik und der mathematischen Naturwissenschaften." *Kant-Studien* 56 (1965): 463–73.

Rohs, P. *Transzendentale Ästhetik.* Meisenheim a.Gl., 1973.

5. Transcendental Analytic of Concepts

Baum, M. *Die transzendentale Deduktion in Kants Kritiken.* Cologne, 1975.

Bieri, P., R. P. Horstmann and L. Krüger (ed.). *Transcendental Arguments and Science: Essays in Epistemology.* Dordrecht: Reidel, 1979.

Brouillet R. "Dieter Henrich et 'The Proof-Structure of Kant's Transcendental Deduction'. Réflexions critique." *Dialogue* 14 (1975): 639–48.

Bubner, R. *Selbstbezüglichkeit als Struktur transzendentaler Argumente.* In: W. Kuhlmann and D. Böhler (eds.), *Kommunikation und Reflexion.* Frankfurt a.M., 1982, pp. 304–32.

Bubner, R., K. Cramer and R. Wiehl. *Zur Zukunft der Transzendentalphilosophie* (= *Neue hefte für philosophie* 14). Göttingen, 1978.

Carl, W. *Der schweigende Kant. Die Entwürfe zu einer Deduktion der Kategorien vor 1781.* Göttingen, 1989.

————, *Die transzendentale Deduktion der Kategorien in der 1. Auflage der Kritik der reinen Vernunft. Ein Kommentar.* Frankfurt a.M., 1992.

Henrich, D. "The Proof-Structure of Kant's Transcendental Deduction." *The Review of Metaphysics* 22 (1969): 640–59.

————, *Identität und Objektivität. Eine Untersuchung über Kants transzendentale Deduktion.* Heidelberg, 1976.

Maier, A. *Kants Qualitätskategorien.* Berlin, 1930.

Reich, K. *Die Vollständigkeit der kantischen Urteilstafel.* Berlin, 1932, [2]1948.

Wagner, H. "Der Argumentationsgang in Kants Deduktion der Kategorien." *Kant-Studien* 71 (1980): 352–66.

6. *Transcendental Analytic of Principles; Kant's Theory of Natural Science*

Allison, H. E. "Transcendental Idealism and Descriptive Metaphysics." *Kant-Studien* 60 (1969): 216–33.

Beck, L. W. "Die Zweite Analogie und das Prinzip der Unbestimmtheit." In: G. Prauss (ed.), *Kant.* Cologne, 1973, pp. 167–74.

Gloy, K. *Die Kantische Theorie der Naturwissenschaft. Eine Strukturanalyse ihrer Möglichkeiten, ihres Umfangs und ihrer Grenzen.* Berlin/New York, 1976.

Heidegger, M. *Die Frage nach dem Ding. Zu Kants Lehre von den transzendentalen Grundsätzen.* Tübingen, [2]1975 ([1]1962).

Heidemann, J. *Spontaneität und Zeitlichkeit* (= *Kantstudien Ergänzungshefte*, no. 75). Cologne, 1975.

Melnick, A. *Kant's Analogies of Experience.* Chicago/London: University of Chicago Press, 1973.

Philonenko A. "Lecture du schématisme transcendental." In: J. Kopper and W. Marx (eds.), *200 Jahre "Kritik der reinen Vernunft,"* Hildesheim, 1981, pp. 291–312.

Plaas, P. *Kants Theorie der Naturwissenschaft.* Göttingen, 1965.

Schäfer, L. *Kants Metaphysik der Natur.* Berlin, 1966.

Scheffel, D. *Kants Theorie der Substantialität. Untersuchung ihrer Entwicklungsgeschichte.* Cologne/Vienna, 1979.

Schüßler, I. *Philosophie und Wissenschaftspositivismus. Die mathematischen Grundsätze in Kants Kritik der reinen Vernunft und die Verselbständigung der Wissenschaften.* Frankfurt a.M., 1979.

Vleeschauwer, H. J. de. *La déduction transcendentale dans l'oeuvre de Kant.* 3 vols. Antwerp/Paris/The Hague: de Sikkel, 1934–37 (abridged version: *The Development of Kantian Thought*, London: Routledge & Kegan Paul, 1962).

Warnock, J. J. "Concepts and Schematism." *Analysis* 9 (1949): 77–82.

Walsh, W. H. "Schematism." *Kant-Studien* 49 (1957): 95–106.

von Weizsäcker, C. F. "Kants 'Erste Analogie der Erfahrung' und die Erhaltungssätze der Physik." In: G. Prauss (ed.), *Kant.* Cologne, 1973, pp. 151–66.

7. Transcendental Dialectic

Al-Azm, S. *The Origins of Kant's Arguments in the Antinomies.* Oxford: Clarendon Press, 1972.

Bittner, R. *"Über die Bedeutung der Dialektik Immanuel Kants,"* Diss., University of Heidelberg, 1970.

Heimsoeth, H. *Transzendentale Dialektik. Ein Kommentar zu Kants Kritik der reinen Vernunft.* 4 parts. Berlin, 1966–71.

8. Ethics

Acton, H. B. *Kant's Moral Philosophy.* London: Macmillan, 1970.

Allison, H. E. *Kant's Theory of Freedom.* Cambridge: Cambridge University Press, 1990.

Alquié, F. *Introduction à la lecture du critique de la raison pratique.* Paris: Presses Universitaires de France, 1966.

———, *La morale de Kant.* Paris: Presses Universitaires de France, 1974.

Aune, B. *Kant's Theory of Morals.* Princeton: Princeton University Press, 1979.

Beck, L. W. *A Commentary on Kant's Critique of Practical Reason.* London/Chicago: University of Chicago Press, [2]1966.

Benton, R. J. *Kant's Second Critique and the Problem of Transcendental Arguments.* The Hague: Nijhof, 1977.

Bittner, R. and K. Cramer (eds.). *Materialien zu Kants "Kritik der praktischen Vernunft."* Frankfurt a.M., 1975.

Broad, C. D. *Five Types of Ethical Theory.* London/New York: Rutledge & Kegan Paul, [9]1971 ([1]1930), chap. V: Kant.

Carnois, B. *La cohérence de la doctrine kantienne de la liberté.* Paris: Seuil, 1973.

Cohen, H. *Kants Begründung der Ethik nebst ihren Anwendungen auf Recht, Religion und Geschichte.* Berlin, [2]1910 ([1]1877).

Delbos, V. *La philosophie pratique de Kant.* Paris: Presses Universitaires de France, [3]1969.

Duncan, A. R. C. *Practical Reason and Morality: A Study of Immanuel Kant's Foundations for the Metaphysics of Morals* London: T. Nelson, 1957.

Ebbinghaus, J. *Gesammelte Aufsätze, Vorträge und Reden.* Darmstadt 1968, pp. 80–96, 140–60.

Forschner, M. *Gesetz und Freiheit. Zum Problem der Autonomie bei I. Kant.* Munich/Salzburg, 1974.

———, "Der Begriff der sittlichen Einsicht und Kants Lehre vom Faktum der Vernunft." In: G. Prauss (ed.), *Kant.* Cologne, 1973, pp. 223–54.

Henrich, D. "Die Deduktion des Sittengesetzes." *Denken im Schatten des Nihilismus, Festschrift W. Weischedel.* Darmstadt, 1975, pp. 55–112.

————, *Selbstverhältnisse.* Stuttgart, 1982, pp. 6–56: Ethics of Autonomy.

Höffe, O. *Ethik und Politik. Grundmodelle und -probleme der praktischen Philosophie.* Frankfurt a.M., ³1987, pp. 84–119.

————, *Introduction à la philosophie pratique de Kant.* Albeuve (Switzerland): Castella, 1985, part I.

———— (ed.). *Grundlegung zur Metaphysik der Sitten. Ein kooperativer Kommentar.* Frankfurt a.M., 1989, ²1992.

Hoerster, N. "Kants kategorischer Imperativ als Test unserer sittlichen Pflichten." In: M. Riedel (ed.), *Rehabilitierung der praktischen Philosophie*, vol. II. Freiburg i.Br., 1974, pp. 455–75.

Ilting, K. H. "Der naturalistische Fehlschluß bei Kent." In: M. Riedel (ed.), *Rehabilitierung der praktischen Philosophie*, vol. I. Frieburg i.Br., 1972, pp. 113–30.

Kaulbach, F. *Immanuel Kants "Grundlegung zur Metaphysik der Sitten."* Darmstadt, 1988.

Kemp, J. "Kant's Examples of the Categorical Imperative." In: R. P. Wolff (ed.), *Kant.* London/Melbourne: Macmillan, 1968, pp. 246–58.

Krüger, G. *Philosophie und Moral in der kantischen Kritik.* Tübingen 1931, ²1969.

Moritz, M. *Kants Einteilung der Imperativ.* Lund/Copenhagen: Berlingska Boktrykkeriet, 1960.

Neue hefte für philosophie, no. 22: *"Kants Ethik heute."* Göttingen, 1983.

Nisters, T. *Kants Kategorischer Imperativ als Leitfaden humaner Praxis.* Freiburg/Munich, 1989.

O'Neill, O. *Acting on Principle: An Essay in Kantian Ethics.* New York: Columbia University Press, 1975.

————, *Constructions of Reason: Explorations of Kantian Practical Philosophy.* Cambridge: Cambridge University Press, 1989.

Oelmüller, W. (ed.). *Transzendentalphilosophische Normenbegründungen.* Paderborn, 1978.

Ortwein, B. *Kants problematische Freiheitslehre.* Bonn, 1983.

Paton, H. J. *The Categorical Imperative: A Study in Kant's Moral Philosophy.* London: Hutchinson, 1947 (paperback 1971).

Patzig, G. "Die logischen Formen praktischer Sätze in Kants Ethik." In: Patzig, *Ethik ohne Metaphysik.* Göttingen, 1971, pp. 101–26.

Prauss, G. *Kant über Freiheit als Autonomie.* Frankfurt a.M., 1983.

Ross, W. D. *Kant's Ethical Theory: A Commentary on the "Grundlegung zur Metaphysik der Sitten."* Oxford: University Press, 1954.

Rossvaer, V. *Kant's Moral Philosophy: An Interpretation of the Categorical Imperative.* Oslo/Bergen: Universitätsverlag, 1979.

Scheler, M. *Der Formalismus in der Ethik und die materiale Wertethik.* Bern/Munich, ⁵1966.

Singer, M. G. *Generalisation in Ethics: An Essay in the Logic of Ethics, with the Rudiments of a System of Moral Philosophy.* London: Eyre & Spottiswoode, 1963.

Sullivan, R. J. *Immanuel Kant's Moral Theory.* Cambridge: Cambridge University Press, 1989.

Vialatoux, J. *La morale de Kant.* Paris: Presses Universitaires de France, ⁵1968.

Williams, T. D. *The Concept of the Categorical Imperative: A Study of the Place of the Categorical Imperative in Kant's Ethical Theory.* Oxford: University Press, 1968.

Wolff, R. P. *The Autonomy of Reason: A Commentary on Kant's "Groundwork of the Metaphysics of Morals."* New York: Harper & Row, 1973.

Yovel, Y. *Kant's Practical Philosophy Reconsidered: Papers Presented at the Seventh Jerusalem Philosophic Encounter, December 1986.* Dordrecht/Boston: Kluwer, 1989.

9. *Philosophy of Law and Government*

Altmann, A. *Freiheit im Spiegel des rationalen Gesetzes bei Kant.* Berlin, 1982.

Batscha, Z. (ed.). *Materialien zu Kants Rechtsphilosophie.* Frankfurt a.M., 1976.

Berkemann, J. *Studien über Kants Haltung zum Widerstandsrecht.* Karlsruhe, 1974.

Brandt, R. (ed.). *Rechtsphilosophie der Aufklärung.* Berlin/New York, 1982.

Burg, P. *Kant und die französische Revolution.* Berlin, 1974.

Busch, W. *Die Entstehung der kritischen Rechtsphilosophie Kants: 1762–1780.* Berlin/New York, 1979.

Cattaneo, M. A. *Dignità umana e pena nella filosofia di Kant.* Milan: Giuffrè Editore, 1981.

Cohen, H. *Kants Begründung der Ethik nebst ihren Anwendungen auf Recht, Religion und Geschichte.* Berlin [2]1910 ([1]1877).

Deggau, H.-G. *Die Aporien der Rechtslehre Kants.* Stuttgart/Bad Cannstatt, 1983.

Delbos, V. *La Philosophie pratique de Kant.* Paris: Presses Universitaires de France, [3]1969, part 2, chap. VIII.

Ebbinghaus, J. *Gesammelte Aufsätze, Vorträge und Reden.* Darmstadt, 1968, pp. 24–57, 161–93.

Goyard-Fabre, S. *Kant et le problème du droit.* Paris: J. Vrin, 1975.

Haensel, W. *Kants Lehre vom Widerstandsrecht.* Berlin, 1926.

Henrich, D. (ed.). *Kant, Gentz, Rehberg. Über Theorie und Praxis.* Frankfurt a.M., 1967.

Höffe, O. *Introduction à la philosophie pratique de Kant.* Albeuve (Switzerland), 1985.

———, *Kategorische Rechtsprinzipien. Ein Kontrapunkt der Moderne.* Frankfurt a.M., 1990.

Institut international de philosophie politique (ed.). *La philosophie politique de Kant* (*Annales de philosophie politique* 4). Paris: Presses Universitaires de France, 1962.

Kaulbach, F. *Studien zur späten Rechtsphilosophie Kants und ihrer transzendentalen Methode*. Würzburg, 1982.

Kersting, W. *Wohlgeordnete Freiheit. Immanuel Kants Rechtsund Staatsphilosophie*. Berlin/New York, 1984.

Losurdo, D. *Autocensura e Compromesso nel Pensiero Politico di Kant*. Naples: Bibliopolis, 1983 (German: *Freiheit, Recht und Revolution*, Cologne, 1987).

Mulholland, L. A. *Kant's System of Rights*. New York/Oxford: Columbia University Press, 1990.

Philonenko, A. *Théorie et praxis dans la pensée morale et politique de Kant et Fichte an 1793*. Paris: J. Vrin, 1976.

Reich, K. *Rousseau und Kant*. Tübingen, 1936.

Ritter, C. *Der Rechtsgedanke Kants nach den frühen Quellen*. Frankfurt a.M., 1971.

Saage, R. *Eigentum, Staat und Gesellschaft bei Kant*. Stuttgart, 1973.

Saner, H. *Kants Weg vom Krieg zum Frieden. Bd. I: Widerstreit und Einheit. Wege zu Kants politischem Denken*. Munich, 1967.

Vlachos, G. *La pensée politique de Kant. Métaphysique de l'ordre et dialectique du progrès*. Paris: Presses Universitaires de France, 1962.

Ward, K. *The Development of Kant's View of Ethics*. Oxford: Basil Blackwell, 1972.

———. (ed.). *Kant's Political Philosophy*. Cardiff: University of Wales Press, 1992.

Williams, H. S. *Kant's Political Philosophy*. Oxford: Basil Blackwell, 1983.

10. Philosophy of History

Castillo, M. *Kant et l'avenir de la culture*. Paris: Presses Universitaires de France, 1990.

Galston, W. A. *Kant and the Problem of History*. Chicago/London: University of Chicago Press, 1975.

Linden, H. van der. *Kantian Ethics and Socialism*. Indianapolis/Cambridge: Hackett Publishing Company, 1988.

Weiand K. *Kants Geschichtsphilosophie*. Cologne, 1964.

Weil, E. *Problèmes kantiens*. Paris: J. Vrin, ^{2}1970, pp. 109–41: Histoire et politique.

Yovel, Y. *Kant and the Philosophy of History*. Princeton: Princeton University Press, 1980.

11. Philosophy of Religion

Albrecht, M. *Kants Antinomie der praktischen Vernunft*. Hildesheim/New York, 1978.

Bohatec, J. *Die Religionsphilosophie Kants in "Die Religion innerhalb der Grenzen der bloßen Vernunft."* Hamburg, 1938 (reprint: Hildesheim, 1966).

Bruch, J.-L. *La philosophie religieuse de Kant*. Paris: Aubier-Montaigne, 1969.

England, T. E. *Kant's Conception of God*. London: T. Nelson, 1929.

Greene, T. M. *The Historical Context and Religious Significance of Kant's Religion: Introductory Essay to "Religion with the Limits of Reason Alone."* New York, 1960.

Oelmüller, W. *Die unbefriedigte Aufklärung. Beiträge zu einer Theorie der Moderne von Lessing, Kant und Hegel*. Frankfurt a.M., ^{2}1979.

Reboul, O. *Kant et le problème du mal*. Montreal: Presses Universitaires, 1971.

Schweitzer, A. *Die Religionsphilosophie Kants vor der "Kritik der reinen Vernunft" bis zur "Religion innerhalb der Grenzen der bloßen Vernunft."* Freiburg, 1899 (reprint: Hildesheim/New York, 1974).

Webb, C. C. J. *Kant's Philosophy of Religion*. Oxford: Clarendon Press, 1926 (reprint: New York, 1970).

Weil, E. *Problèmes kantiens*. Paris: J. Vrin, ^{2}1970, pp. 143–74.

Wood, A. W. *Kant's Moral Religion*. Ithaca/London: Cornell University Press, 1970.

——, *Kant's Rational Theology*. Ithaca/London: Cornell University Press, 1978.

12. *Critique of Judgment*

Baeumler, A. *Kritik der Urteilskraft. Ihre Geschichte und ihre Systematik.* Halle, 1923 (reprinted as *Das Irrationalitätsproblem in der Ästhetik und Logik des 18. Jahrhunderts bis zur Kritik der Urteilskraft*, Darmstadt, 1981).

Bartuschat, W. *Zum systematischen Ort von Kants Kritik der Urteilskraft.* Frankfurt a.M., 1972.

Basch, V. *Essai critique sur l'esthétique de Kant.* Paris: Alcan, ²1927.

Cohen, T. and P. Guyer (ed.). *Essays in Kant's Aesthetics.* Chicago/London: University of Chicago Press, 1982.

Crowther, P. *The Kantian Sublime: From Morality to Art.* Oxford: Clarendon Press, 1989.

Düsing, K. *Die Teleologie in Kants Weltbegriff.* Bonn, 1968.

Gadamer, H.-G. *Wahrheit und Methode.* Tübingen, ²1965, pp. 27–96.

Guyer, P. *Kant and the Claims of Taste.* Cambridge, Mass./London: Harvard University Press, 1979.

Kohler, G. *Geschmacksurteil und ästhetische Erfahrung. Beiträge zur Auslegung von Kants "Kritik der ästhetischen Urteilskraft."* Berlin/New York, 1980.

Kulenkampff, J. *Kants Logik des ästhetischen Urteils.* Frankfurt a.M., 1978.

—— (ed.). *Materialien zu Kants "Kritik der Urteilskraft."* Frankfurt a.M., 1974.

Kuypers, K. *Kants Kunsttheorie und die Einheit der Kritik der Urteilskraft.* Amsterdam/London: North-Holland Publishing Comp., 1972.

Lebrun, G. *Kant et la fin de la métaphysique. Essai sur la "Critique de la faculté de juger."* Paris: A. Colin, 1970.

Löw, R. *Philosophie des Lebendigen. Der Begriff des Organischen bei Kant, sein Grund und seine Aktualität.* Frankfurt a.M., 1980.

Macfarland, J. D. *Kant's Concept of Teleology.* Edinburg: Edinburgh University Press 1970.

Marc-Wogau, K. *Vier Studien zu Kants Kritik der Urteilskraft.* Uppsala/Leipzig: Lundequist, 1938.

Schaper, E. *Studies in Kant's Aesthetics.* Edinburgh: Edinburgh University Press 1979.

Zumbach, C. *The Transcendent Science: Kant's Conception of Biological Methodology.* The Hague: M. Nijhoff, 1984.

13. On Kant's Influence

Aetas Kantiana, up to 1982: 369 vols. Brussels: Editions Cultures et Civilisation.

Baumgartner, H. M. (ed.). *Prinzip Freiheit. Eine Auseinandersetzung um Chancen und Grenzen transzendentalphilosophischen Denkens.* Freiburg/Munich, 1979.

Delbos, V. *De Kant aux postkantiens.* Paris: Aubier-Montaigne, 1940.

Erdmann, J. E. *Die Entwicklung der deutschen Spekulation seit Kant.* 2 vols. Leipzig, 1848–53 (reprint: 3 vols., Stuttgart, 1931).

Flach, W. and H. Holzhey (eds.). *Erkenntnistheorie und Logik im Neukantianismus.* Hildesheim, 1980.

Kröner, R. *Von Kant bis Hegel.* 2 vols. Tübingen, 1921–24, ³1977.

Laberge, P. *"Kant dans les traditions anglo-américaines et continentales."* In: *Actes du Congrès d'Ottawa sur Kant dans les traditions anglo-américaines et continentales* (1974). Ottawa: Éditions de l'Université, 1976.

Lehmann, G. *Geschichte der nachkantischen Philosophie. Kritizismus und kritisches Motiv in den philosophischen Systemen des 19. und 20. Jahrhunderts.* Berlin, 1931.

————, *Beiträge zur Geschichte und Interpretation der Philosophie Kants.* Berlin, 1969.

Malter, R. and E. Staffa (eds.). *Kant in Königsberg seit 1945. Eine Dokumentation.* Wiesbaden, 1983.

Marcucci, S. *Kant in Europa.* Lucca, 1986.

Sauer, W. *Österreichische Philosophie zwischen Aufklärung und Restauration. Beitraäge zur Geschichte des Frühkantianismus in der Donaumonarchie.* Würzburg/Amsterdam: Rodopi, 1982.

Vallois, M. *La formation de l'influence kantienne en France.* Paris, 1925.

Wellek, R. *Immanuel Kant in England: 1793–1838.* Oxford, 1931.

Zambelloni, F. *Le origini del kantismo in Italia.* Milan, 1971.

INDEX OF NAMES

Nietzsche, F. 8, 22, 47, 105, 136, 218,
  236, 246
Nink, C. 244
Nitsch, A. F. 238

Paley, W. 122
Parmenides 106
Parsons, C. 45
Pascal, B. 7
Paton, H. J. 86, 245
Paul, St. 121
Peirce, C. S. 239, 246
Philonenko, A. 245
Piaget, J. 247
Pittendrigh, C. S. 222
Platner, E. 232
Plato 7, 39, 60, 67, 75, 106, 111, 114,
  120, 122, 129, 203, 241
Poincaré, H. 44
Popper, K. R. 93, 244, 246
Prichard, H. A. 86f.
Proudhon, J. P. 176
Pufendorf, S. 169, 179, 181, 185, 199

Quine, W. V. O. 39f., 246

Rahner, K. 244
Rawls, J. 135, 181, 247
Rehberg, A. W. 185
Reich, H. 71, 245
Reichenbach, H. 42
Reinhold, K. L. 232ff.
Renouvier, C. 238
Rickert, H. 195, 241f.
Riehl, A. 240
Riemann, B. 60
Rink, F.T. 8
Ritter, C. 167
Robespierre, M. 183
Rorty, R. 246
Rosenkranz, K. 237
Rousseau, J. J. 2, 17, 157, 160, 167, 169,
  175, 181ff., 197, 206, 208, 219
Russell, B. 22, 44, 46, 239, 246

Saage, R. 167
Scheler, M. 136, 144, 243
Schelling, F. W. J. 7f., 55, 96, 193, 195,
  220, 233ff., 240, 245
Schiller, F. 136, 160, 220, 233, 238
Schlick, M. 42
Schmid, K. C. E. 232f.
Schopenhauer, A. 8, 86, 167, 175, 237,
  240
Schubert, H. 237
Schuhmann, K. 5
Schultz, F. A. 9
Schultz, J. 22, 232f.
Schulze, G. E. 234
Schütz, C. G. 232f.
Schwemmer, O. 247
Sellars, W. 246
Seneca 206
Shaftesbury, A. 160
Simmel, G. 242
Singer, M. G. 135, 153, 247
Smith, A. 168
Soave, F. 238
Socrates 67
Spaemann, R. 225
Spaventa, B. 239
Spinoza, B. 32, 63, 125, 234
Staël (-Holstein), A.-L. G. de 238
Stattler, B. 233
Stavenhagen, K. 15
Stegmüller, W. 93, 103
Stein, K. Freiherr v. 168
Strauss, D. F. 237
Strawson, P. F. 60, 71, 79, 245
Svarez, C. G. 171
Swedenborg, E. 19

Testa, A. 239
Thomasius, C. 11, 169, 174
Tieftrunk, J. H. 233
Tillich, P. 122
Tocqueville, A. de 200
Tolstoy, L. 238
Tonelli, G. 21, 245
Tracy, D de 238

Vaihinger, H. 47f., 53, 240
Villers, C. de 238
Vlachos, G. 175

INDEX OF TOPICS